LOCKED UP
and
PUT AWAY

To Elissi

Thank you for the support.

Enjoy,

Booker Garz

LOCKED UP
and
PUT AWAY

My 10 Years as a Juvenile Counselor

BOOKER GEEZ

urlink
PRINT & MEDIA

Locked Up and Put Away

Copyright © 2019 by Booker Geez. All rights reserved.

The opinions expressed by the author are not necessarily those of URLink Print and Media.

1603 Capitol Ave., Suite 310 Cheyenne, Wyoming USA 82001
1-888-980-6523 | admin@urlinkpublishing.com

URLink Print and Media is committed to excellence in the publishing industry.

Published in the United States of America
ISBN 978-1-64367-197-0 (Paperback)
ISBN 978-1-64367-198-7 (Hardcover)
ISBN 978-1-64367-196-3 (Digital)

1. Non-Fiction
2. Memoir
08.01.19

DEDICATION

This book is dedicated to the life of Maurice Caple a.k.a. DJ SugKat, my homeboy and road dog. You were the Cochise to my Preacher, and my inspiration for writing this book. You taught me to never be afraid to take chances and to never settle for mediocrity. My man 50 grand, I miss you, I love you, and I thank you. See you on the other side…

CONTENTS

ACKNOWLEDGEMENT

‹ ♦ ♦ ♦ ♦ ♦ ›

ALL PRAISES GO OUT TO the Most-High for giving me the strength and fortitude to persevere during my most turbulent times and helping me stay positive.

To my ancestors, who have made the sacrifices that put me in a position to be able to function in a free state and pursue my dreams.

To Parker, for being a friend from the beginning. You helped guide me and protected me at times when nobody else would. The union is in good hands with you involved.

To Lawrie, for showing me the right way to maneuver in this environment and for being like a big brother, I'm forever grateful.

To Evan, thank you, my brother, for blessing my book with your artistry and for being the artistic inspiration for my book cover. Love you, man.

To my boy Chris, you are my true BFF. You always dropped your shit to pick up mine. My homie for life. Love you, bro.

To my mother, for standing by me when all the chips were down. I couldn't get this far without your help. You always believed in me and never turned your back. You were always there to pick the kids and me up, and you showed my brother and me what it takes to be good parents. I owe you everything. Love you dearly.

To Ana, for putting up with my shit; you are my true ride-or-die. You rode this rollercoaster ride with me and I love you for it. You are my earth, my queen, and my everything.

To my four children, I love you all more than anything. You all make me proud to be your father.

To my Skyview family a.k.a. the View Crew, we were fortunate to have parents who worked hard to provide us with a childhood that most kids could only dream of having. We were all Cosby kids before the Cosby Show. I cherish our friendship and love you all dearly.

To Cheryl Bradley, for being my day one from day one and for being the big sister I never had. I love you for always being there.

To Esco, you were the best partner and friend I ever had in the building. If you would have stayed, things would have been better for me. I love you for always having my back.

To Pastrana and Campbell, you guys were the rock on the PM tour. Even though I'm older than both of you guys, you were my big brothers in the building. Love you for holding me down.

To Mrs. Roberts, I always looked forward to the smell of your perfume when you came in the building. I hated how they treated you because you were like a beacon of light and the most beautiful person that worked there. They always wiped the smile off your face, and I can't wait until you retire so I can see you smile every day. Almost there, Ma. Love you.

To all the male JCs who were on the basketball team, because you guys were the true role models to all the male residents. You guys were the All-Stars of the building. They looked up to you and you always delivered. I looked up to you, guys, to help me create my own style, and I can't thank you enough for showing me the way. I guess God has other plans for me. Keep doing what you do.

To all the women in the building, especially those female JCs who sat at that back table during roll call on the PM tour. Without you, ladies, everybody would have killed each other. Your motherly instincts were always the right remedy for every situation. You all protected me like your brother. Anytime one of you got assaulted, I will take it personal, like it was my sister or mother. I love you all.

To my DSU family, for providing me with a great college experience. I will never forget the time we, the student body, protested by standing on the stoop of the college president's home when we felt that our rights were being violated. That day, we shut down the school and made change. That was epic.

To the 1984 Kennedy Knights and Coach Jerry Horowitz, for laying the foundation of the greatest New York City public school football team ever. Red Rage for life.

To Pasols, I can't thank you enough for how much you helped me keep my head up during such a difficult time in my life. If anybody knows about keeping their head up, it's you, because you have stayed solid through your whole ordeal, and, unlike me, you were just doing your job. I hope my book sheds light on your situation. Like you told me, "This too shall pass," stay up, bro. Love you.

To the ACS staff, for making me feel like a person again and showing me that true professionalism starts with a smile.

To my forefathers of hip-hop, your music is the seams to the fabric of my story. Over twenty years ago, hip-hop represented black pride, love of self, and community awareness. Where did that go? Hopefully, my book will bring that back.

To all the JCs still on their grind, may God protect you in that hellhole. You will always be my family, stay up. Someone had to speak up for us.

To all the young men whose lives I've crossed, always remember your life is important. Live it and make choices that make the people who love you be proud of you. Word!

PROLOGUE

◆◆◆◆◆◆

A s I BEGAN MY JOURNEY into the field of juvenile counseling, I quickly realized that the entire system was stuck in a catch-22. I approached my position as someone who could make a difference in the lives of so many lost souls. New York City is a place with the haves and the have-nots. I dealt with the have-nots or, maybe when dealing with the Bureau of Child Welfare (let's call them by their real name), the haves.

I say that because when I started on this job, we were structured more along the lines of corrections. We were assiduous in how we enforced punishment where room confinement was enforced and all the juveniles in detention had consequences for their actions. Since 2011, under the umbrella of BCW (Bureau of Child Welfare), the staff has consequences for their actions. You see, if you know the history of BCW, they have been under scrutiny for several neglectful acts involving children in the past; the last thing we needed was to be working with them.

Thank you, Mr. Mayor. You really fucked this system up. It feels like KFC merged with PETA—it was a conflict of interest. BCW sees these criminals as victims; crazy but true. I've seen kids beat up staff and still be involved in their daily routine; kids get away with smoking and still live in the hall. If any kid stole something like a pen, a snack, or a laptop, the staff would get in trouble for them having it.

I was trained to put pain to volatile children in order to bring them to justice; but if I hurt them, I could be brought up on charges. We were like human pillows paid to make sure these precious commodities weren't damaged. To assault a bus driver is a felony and seven years in prison; but I ask the question: why was our safety any less important? Some of us were getting assaulted more than three times a day. We were city workers, too; it just didn't seem to matter. The occupational hazards were like raindrops that never stopped falling, and nobody ever felt safe entering the building because it could be the day you got hurt, fired, or arrested. Pins and needles were our mentality, and low morale was the sentiment that resonated with all of us; but the administration saw this as a myth.

Every day was like a crime scene; it was inevitable that something crazy would happen. And when the shit went down, and we asked what could be done, we were reminded that we were lucky to have a job, and that if we didn't like it, we should make sure the door didn't hit us on the way out. You hear something enough times you start to believe it. It was incredulous that those in charge were above the fray of ridicule and discipline, but it was their blueprint to retirement; the rest of us weren't that lucky.

What bothered me the most is that the programs in the facility don't help prepare them for life after detention. The agency provides them with video games, yoga, movie nights, and popcorn machines. Who pays for this stuff? You, me, and everybody who pays taxes. I'm not a hater, I understand they're kids; but what's up with teaching them about finances (banking) or how to fill out a résumé? These kids need to learn etiquette and how to conduct themselves in a job interview. These are the things that make positive contributors in society, not movie night. It's too much fun, they enjoy this experience when they should hate it and learn something from it. It's okay to have fun, but that should come with the balance of life skills; we were sending the wrong message.

God doesn't like ugly, and Lord knows it's ugly what goes on in there. I'm not on a crusade for the justice of these young people because they lived swell; it's the injustice of the staff that had far greater ramifications on these children than anyone could imagine. In this environment, we were treated like second-class citizens. When you look at the economic breakdown, these kids were more valuable than we were. We were movable objects that could always be replaced given the circumstance or situation. But if you asked these kids, they would beg to differ because to most of them, we were like family. It was hard to disassociate; we were all human. My innocuous approach to this job left me totally vulnerable to this agency's bulling ways; to be nice was to get shitted on.

The labor law violations were endless, but nobody cared that a supervisor hurt your feelings or that you were talked to in a way that was less than human. To have thick skin was the only way to survive in this environment, but to have thick skin was usually a push-back effect that led to discipline or termination. Until this agency moves pass its inertia, which came from the back wash and residue that was left from Spofford, they will never rehabilitate the children who enter these facilities. I say this because twenty years ago, Spofford Detention Center, located in the Bronx, was a hellhole; but even though it's now closed, most of the old practices still exist today.

The longer I worked in this toxic environment, I realized that BCW had no clue who they were getting in bed with. These were dirty dogs, and the only way for us to survive was to get dirty with them. Working in this environment, I was never afraid of the kids; I was afraid of losing my job. However, the longer I worked there, I realized it was because of the kids that I could lose my job. And don't let me get started on Justice Central, what a joke. They're supposed to be fair, but they are just a lynch mob out to destroy the lives of the juvenile counselors one after another.

But who are they? It's not Batman, Superman, and Wonder Woman. No, that's the Justice League. Really, who are they? All I know is that they hide behind this shield of superiority where their job security is probably mandated. Justice Central has ruined more families than they have saved. If there is an allegation that leads to a lawsuit, any counselor who was involved is roadkill and loses their job to cover the cost of that lawsuit. It's almost like they say to the parent suing the agency, "Hey, back off. We got rid of the counselor that touched your child. Now we're even."

Why even have juvenile counselors, seriously? Just make robots or, better yet, clones to watch these kids. This way, if a child gets hurt, instead of ruining an entire family (because we have families too) they can get rid of the robot or the clone and just throw them away with no remorse, which is how they treat us now. Our livelihood and families came secondary to the families they serve. The way the system is structured works for them; there is no incentive for them to change.

It's so racially disproportionate against the juvenile counselors, who are predominantly African-American, that it's surprising any of us apply for this job at all. What did we know? We thought we would be treated fairly but *au contraire, mon frère,* not in this place. Then they put these Uncle Toms in these high positions just to cover their ass as to say, "Look, my husband is black, so I like black people and I care about their children." Whatever, man. The whole thing is a modern-day plantation real talk. Blood, sweat, and tears aren't enough, they want our pensions. Don't let my language distract you, call it what it is, it's straight up discrimination, hands down.

I'm trying to make sense of my life right now. My current situation is that I have been reassigned and relocated to the main office in lower Manhattan, but for what? It's the equivalent of being in the rubber room like a teacher or modified duty like a cop. What the fuck did I do? They won't tell me no funny shit; I'm in complete limbo. I'm scheduled to meet the investigator tomorrow, and I guess I will find out what this is about. If this is what I think it is, I'm in deep shit. To say this is a nightmare of a scenario would be an understatement. Now I walk around zombied out, not knowing what's going to happen next.

In my time down here, I took advantage of it and put together my memoirs from when I started down this road. You will be fascinated to hear my story. Most of the names were changed to protect the innocent and the guilty.

I wrote this to appeal to the youth of today. Written as storytelling, you will find all of the stories to be true. If you find yourself in trouble, go to a responsible adult who will hold you down.

In the history of juvenile detentions, nobody has ever told the truth about the activities and events that transpire on the inside from a counselor's perspective. This will be a first. I invite you to enjoy. Feel free to laugh, cringe, or cry, but never forget that you are bearing witness to the fuckery that goes on in secure detention.

CHAPTER ONE

◆ ◆ ◆ ◆ ◆

I might be old enough to be your dad
but I will beat you when I'm mad
call ACS tell them hold this
I don't control this, I don't claim too
I'm not the nigga that puts his name to just anything

—Sadat X
"Turn It Up"

MY PURSUIT OF HAPPINESS STARTS off like a sad Ghostface song, lots of bass and a tearjerker. In 2005, at the age of thirty-seven, my life was at a crossroads. With two kids, a failing marriage, and no job, what the hell am I going to do? I was going through a rough patch in my life with a failing business while raising two very young children. I owned a women's boutique in Harlem on 116th Street; it was the wave, but traffic was very slow.

I just quit a part-time job that I worked in Chelsea as a night manager at Murray House, a nonprofit organization that provided affordable housing for people with AIDS. Quitting that position was a mistake, because how was I going to pay rent, buy food, and get back and forth to the shop? But the dumb-ass that I was at the time, I put all my chips into the store even though I had no real assets. There were times we had to go to my mother's house just to feed the kids, it was depressing.

But I kept my head up because I had these fire-ass designs that I printed on T-shirts, which were photos that my father took. My father was a photographer in the sixties, he died before my fourth birthday in a car accident from a drunk driver. We saved all his prints and I used some for the designs on my T-shirts.

Now, your next question might be, how did a guy from the Bronx get into designing women's clothes? Simple. My grandmother was a sewing teacher at IS 183, a school in the South Bronx; and out of four of her grandchildren, I was the one who gravitated to sewing and making clothes. I started out making pillow cases, and then in high school, I was charging people to put permanent creases on jeans. I was on a mission to become the Dapper Dan of the Bronx.

But unlike Dapper Dan, I was just focused on women's wear. First, I was making outfits for strippers and for women who went to music-industry parties. Then after becoming a father, I toned it down and created a women's T-shirt collection. It was a clothing line that I created after working for a clothing company in California called Gold Sport. The money I made from that experience was enough to develop a website which was an online women's clothing company consisting of T-shirts and accessories (hats, bags, and jewelry).

My boy Darryl, a friend from college, was working for Nappy Jeans and attended a clothing tradeshow and met this woman who was looking for a designer. Her name was Susan Arnold, a red-headed white woman in her midforties. Knowing Darryl, he was trying to hit it, but then realized it would be a great opportunity for me and put me on.

I met up with Darryl and Susan at the Bad Boy office in midtown Manhattan. Darryl was down with the Hit Squad which was Puffy's production team. Susan was impressed with my portfolio and wanted to send my designs to California to show the jean manufacturer who produced several lines, along with Gold Sport. The manufacturer's name was Mr. Lee, an Asian guy who wanted to work with me on producing my collection. This was it, I was about to get it on and poppin'.

See, I was having the hardest time in the fashion industry as an up-and-coming designer. Nobody was trying to help a heterosexual black man make it as a designer in this town, that's like being a gay football player. I never really got a chance to shine in New York. Let me take that back, that's not necessarily true. Around this same time,

I met up with the staff at Phat Farms prior to their development of Baby Phat. When I heard that Russell Simmons was going to produce a women's line to compliment Phat Farms, I would go to the store in Soho every day, hoping to see him. The sales staff got tired of seeing me coming in there with my portfolio. They probably told him that he had a stalker. But then one day, he was there; and after I showed him my work, he put me in contact with his people. The staff at his office were impressed enough to schedule another meeting, but within that week of the meeting I had already committed to work with Mr. Lee in Cali.

Sometimes, I wonder how that would have turned out. Mr. Lee produced a line of shirts, jackets, and dresses that I displayed in a show at the Tunnel. In the '90s, the Tunnel was the hottest hip-hop night club in New York City, so to display my work there was a good look. The show was off the hook; it was a great send off to show my potential and cemented the beginning of my business venture with Mr. Lee.

He arranged to send me out to California and stay at a hotel for a week and then his place the second week. The plan was to put together a twenty-five-piece collection to be presented at the Magic Show in Vegas, and he was footing the bill. Susan was going to manage the line and represent us at Magic. But by doing this, she was going behind the back of her boss because she was the production manager at Gold Sport.

The owner of Gold Sport was Maylyn, a tenacious little Chinese woman with a lot of bread. She was about four feet nine inches tall; with the business acumen of a Wall Street banker, she ran her business like a drill sergeant. Maylyn started Gold Sport at the suggestion of Bob Wang who was a California businessman who did a lot of business from the US to China. He kind of hustled the idea to Maylyn that Gold Sport would be a great investment. Mr. Lee produced the denim jeans for Gold Sport and was very close to Maylyn. They were both Chinese and from the same countryside in China.

Susan underestimated the relationship between Mr. Lee and Maylyn, so when Maylyn heard about me, she wanted to meet me.

Susan was so nervous, she thought Maylyn would fire her and told Maylyn it was always her intention to introduce us. Gold Sport was in desperate need of a designer. The crazy twist is that Gold Sport was a bullshit line that Bob Wang created with Saul Sani as the designer and Maylyn's money. For those who don't know, Saul Sani was the top urban wear designer in the 90s. When Maylyn agreed to put the money up, she was made to believe that it would be Saul's good designs, but it was Saul's worst. To Saul Sani, it was easy money, and nobody knew that he was affiliated with Gold Sport. This dude gave them designs based on team colors on sweatpants and hoodies—the corniest, wackiest shit you ever saw.

When I met Maylyn, she thought the gods had sent her a gift. She told me that she would pay me $200 a design. So I got on my grind and I had Susan buy me hip-hop and skateboard magazines and scotch tape. In my hotel room, there were pages everywhere on the walls. I came up with thirty different pieces, and to her word, she cut me a check for $6000 and offered me a contract to be Gold Sport's full-time designer. I couldn't believe what was happening. When I showed up at the showroom, the entire staff treated me like royalty. I had my own office, my own production team, and the only person I answered to was Maylyn. Whenever she walked through the showroom, the entire staff was shook behind her back they called her the Dragon Lady because she cracked a verbal whip. The only time she smiled was when she saw me, she was convinced that I was the answer. She told Mr. Lee that I was signed to Gold Sport and would no longer be working with him on my collection, she even paid him back the money he put out for the hotel bill.

At the time, I couldn't turn down the money and Mr. Lee couldn't afford to keep me in the hotel, I felt bad but Maylyn was my only chance to succeed. She promised me that when I boost the sales for Gold Sport, she would back my clothing line. When Saul Sani found out, he was pissed; but nothing in their contract said that Gold Sport had to exclusively use his designs or that they couldn't promote a designer. He was just entitled to a percentage of sales. He had no wins, he never thought she would do this.

Maylyn rode me like Puffy did Biggie, she saw me as her golden goose who was going to bring Gold Sport into prominence. She flew me to Dallas, Texas, for a meeting with JC Penny. I was sent to Taiwan to source out fabrics, and after the fabric was selected, I was sent to China and stayed in Maylyn's apartment in Hong Kong. My chaperone was a man named Mr. Lynn, a well- dressed middle-age Chinese man who met me at the Taiwan airport with a sign that had my name on it. What a welcome mat; In the Bronx, we call this "the get down." At that point, nobody could tell me shit. He took me everywhere in Taiwan. We went to his friend's restaurant where we drank beers all night. After that, they took me to a place where there was karaoke being played on a huge wall in a private room and these beautifully half-dressed Taiwanese women fed us grapes. I was on cloud nine, and I said to myself, my dudes back in NYC won't believe this shit. Somehow, I made it back to my hotel room, and when I woke up, there were two women in bed with me. I thought I was dreaming; this was beyond anything I could've ever imagined.

When Mr. Lynn took me to China, we went to the same type of place; but the women looked like little girls. I told him I wasn't feeling it, and he said I would offend the owner if I didn't leave the place with one of his girls. They looked fourteen, and much to the disappointment of Mr. Lynn, I refused to accept any of the girls. I could tell he wasn't too pleased, but I told him that, "I can turn down your generosity and it shouldn't offend you." They couldn't force me to do anything, but later, Mr. Lynn respected my stance.

The next day, when we got to the production site in midland China, it was like a fortress. It looked like six hundred years ago, it was owned by the Ming Dynasty. There were giant doors at the entrance that needed two men to open. As I walked through the production site, I saw the labels of so many reputable clothing companies, and then it hit me. Maylyn was the sweat shop queen, she was responsible for the production of more than five different American clothing lines. That's when I realized how she got her pot of gold.

They treated me like a king. The only thing I would eat was seafood, so they blessed me with shrimp the size of buffalo wings along with fresh vegetables every night. When we ate, they allowed me to say the prayer even though they didn't understand me. They were very humble, and all the people who worked for Maylyn lived on the production site. It was crazy these people worked long hours with no breaks; a horn went off to tell them the day was over and when it began. I couldn't understand how someone could coexist under these conditions. It was deplorable how they worked like this for pennies. It was as if Maylyn owned them.

I called Maylyn and told her this was disgraceful, but she said they did better working for her than on the other countryside where they picked rice for half the pennies. In my country, this was a violation of labor laws, but I wasn't in my country. I had to accept my situation as just a product of my success. My presence changed their daily routine; this wasn't the highly cultivated city of Hong Kong. This was more inland where they built homes with bamboo sticks for scaffolding. I became a spectacle wherever I went. Traffic would stop and people would stare and some just wanted to touch my skin. It was weird because in their custom, black was bad luck; but I realized that they never saw a black person, and maybe not ever on TV or in books. Their lives were so primitive; I don't believe they had TVs, and in the late '90s, cell phones were rare. I even saw a man get arrested for having too many children.

These were very hardworking people, even the children worked. If you gave me a dollar for every playground or park that I saw, I would be broke because there were none. Now I understand why these people go to the United States and start businesses; it's ingrained in them from birth. The entire experience was culture shock to me. Here I was, a dude from the Bronx in the middle of China. I started to get homesick. Once all the pieces were assembled, I flew back to California to prepare for the Magic Show in Vegas. But something was different. While I was overseas, Maylyn stayed in the states and hired this white dude from Texas named Tom Dudley that worked for JC Penny and was at the meeting that I attended. He convinced her that as the president of Gold Sport, he would help her grow the company and get it in more stores. She made him president and changed everything. My power was gone, my staff was gone, and he even got rid of Susan.

I was cool with the advertising director, Miguel Gomez. He told me our days at Gold Sport were numbered with Tom running the company. Miguel was about to put a hit out on Tom or try to scare him out of town, but I told Miguel it wasn't worth it. I said Maylyn isn't going to let us go. Miguel was a second-generation Mexican-American who was boys with the rap group Cypress Hill and helped them promote their clothing line. Miguel was very important; he plugged Gold Sport with Los Angeles radio stations, the hip-hop magazine *Rap Pages*, and even got Jamie Foxx to do an ad. Without him, Gold Sport would never have gotten attention. We thought we were good.

But when I met up with Tom Dudley, something about him wasn't right. He drove me to my hotel one night, and as we were talking, and the sun was setting behind the mountains in the Pomona Valley, the glare must have obstructed his vision and he ran over a cat that was crossing the road. I thought he would pull over, but he kept on driving. He even laughed about it, I felt the evil in his heart and started to think Miguel was right.

After the collection was prepared for Magic, I had Miguel take me to the airport; but we sat at his crib and smoked cloves and drank Henny and I ended up missing my flight. So, after I set up my flight for the next day, Miguel gets off the phone and said, "This motherfucka just fired me." I was like, "Holy shit." Miguel said I was next. I called Maylyn and she assured me that my job was secure. I felt bad for Miguel, but I had to fulfill my own dreams.

When I got back to New York, Miquel told me that Cali was blackballing Gold Sport because he gave the streets and radio stations the scoop on Tom and Maylyn. He said they were trying to get paid off the culture and didn't employ minorities. I was stuck in the middle, so I focused on promoting Gold Sport in New York. I had boys like DJ Kid Capri and Sadat X of the rap group Brand Nubians to help me advertise it. I just saw it as an east coast/west coast beef; it was going on at the time anyway.

But then, Magic came and went, and nobody sent for me to be there to promote the line. I realized I was getting the shaft. A week later, Tom met me at the ESPN Zone restaurant on 42nd Street and told me that they were voiding my contract and that the collection didn't sell at Magic. I was stunned, Miguel was right. This dude was a snake in the grass. What he did was have Maylyn lean more toward Saul Sani's stuff and didn't display any of my good shit. Someone later told me that out of thirty of my pieces, they only had eight and put them behind Saul's pieces. Gold Sport did bad at Magic, Tom tried to tell me they were letting me go because my stuff didn't sell. Tom was a six-foot-two sloppy, middle-aged white guy, but I didn't care. I threw my drink in his face and walked out.

It was then that I started my own clothing line; it was an underground women's T-shirt collection. The money I made from Gold Sport I invested in creating a website which was an indie type of streetwear, featuring images focused on civil rights leaders, old-school hip-hop flavors from the early '80s, and my father's photographs. In the beginning, I was the new wave in Harlem; I had flyers in every store and an ad in the Amsterdam Newspaper. I combined the T-shirts with bags and hats made by this sister named Keli Fresh. Keli was a funky and very earthy soul sister that was a true free spirit. Her energy was perfect for the shop. We took turns working there, the vibe was great, and we were the buzz on the street, but only Keli's stuff was selling and it got tight. I had to power another move.

To generate more money for the business, I joined Project Enterprise, a nonprofit organization that helped small businesses get funding. I had to attend meetings and do shows with them for a small business loan. A week before I got the loan from the Project Enterprise, I was stuck with dilemma every loving father who is separating from their spouse is confronted with, getting custody of my children. On the 4th of July in 2005, I remember it like it was yesterday, I set up a table to work at a street fair at BAM in Brooklyn, and on that day, it was scorching. I had the kids with me, and it was borderline child abuse that I had them out in the heat that day. When they started to cry from being too hot, I said, "Fuck this," and had the girl I shared the table with sell my merchandise while I took the kids to the pool uptown. As much as I loved to create new trends, there was nothing I loved more than these two children. They were my greatest creations. I had my best friend James who is

LOCKED UP AND PUT AWAY

my daughter's godfather, help me with my dilemma. He told me to go to court and file for custody. MJ, my son, was six and Rosemary, my daughter, was two. It was stressful on them because there was so much going on with the whole custody thing. I had no wins. In court, they granted my wife custody and me visitation. It was then that I realized that I had to get a real job.

CHAPTER TWO

◆ ◆ ◆ ◆ ◆

Now life in this world can be such a bitch
And dreams are often torn and shattered and hard to
stitch Negative's
the attitude that runs the show
When the stage is the G-H-E-T-T-O

—De La Soul
"Ghetto Thang"

I'M IN SOUNDVIEW ON STORY Avenue at the park with my kids, struggling to find something to smile about. This dude Boo is there with his five kids also. Boo is this big dude married to Samantha. She always knew everybody's business in the building. He doesn't say much but when he does, it always makes sense. He always has a toothpick in his mouth, a Yankee fitted cap to the back, and all his kids with him. If I could be half the father he is, I would be doing something. He was a street dude that had a good job and promoted parties on the side.

Boo asked me if I was good, I said yeah. He said, "Nigga, you ain't good, that chick is fucking your head up."

It was no secret what I was going through, everybody in the building was talking about it. He said he worked as a recreation director for the Department of Juvenile Justice. He told me to call this woman in the personnel department and that she would help me get hired. I asked him what the job was about, and he said, "Watching badass-kids and getting paid for it." At this point, I had no choice; this would have to be my next move. I had experience working for the summer youth in Yonkers and worked off grants for programs that catered to kids at risk. Boo said I would qualify and it would help me get custody of my children.

I was all in, I had to sacrifice the shop to father my kids. It was a no-brainer. The designing thing was stressing me out and going nowhere. I had to save my children. I never worked with those type of kids before; I dabbled in the street, but I never lived it. Before my grandmother passed away, I took over her place which was in the South Bronx, but this was not where I grew up. I grew up in the Riverdale section of the Bronx which didn't make me the most streetwise person. All I did as a kid was play organized sports and go to school. Riverdale wasn't known for its thugs and gangsters, it was a suburban area of the Bronx that was multicultural with middle-class families; most of my next-door neighbors were Russian or Jewish. I was skiing and water skiing at twelve. How many kids can say that? I hung out with the Jack-and-Jill kids from New Rochelle; they lived like the Huxtables. Their families were more privileged than the average folks, so hood life was never anything I aspired to.

During high school, I dated a girl from the west side of Harlem and made lots of friends from the projects; but at the end of the day, they grew up dodging bullets while I grew up around kids that had lemonade stands and walked dogs for extra money. There were no hustlers in my hood, if I could call it that. My wife on the other hand was more street savvy than I was. I'm still buggin' on how she got me to marry her, but that's a whole other story.

Once I got hired, I went into training. In training, we learned about the population of kids we would be working with and their behavior patterns. After two days of training, half the people in the class quit; but Boo told me what to expect, so I knew what I signed up for. Most of the people hired learned about the job through an ad in the newspaper. In the newspaper, the description of a juvenile counselor sounded like you would be at a desk in an office counseling young people. The ad didn't say that you could be physically assaulted or that you would be spat on or cursed at. When the trainers said that most people didn't come back after lunch, my class went from twenty-one to eight when we finished the training.

The juvenile justice system in New York is made up of three buildings: the infamous Spofford located in the Hunts Point section of the Bronx, another detention center which is also in the Bronx called Fairvue, and Greenwood in Brooklyn.

Growing up in the Bronx, I heard about Spofford and the legendary stories of how juvenile delinquents were mistreated by the staff and how the kids would assault each other while being there. Some kids I grew up with got napped on a robbery charge and put the fear of God in me with the stories they told about Spofford. They were the older homies and were probably trying to scare us straight and it worked because I wasn't getting in trouble to be sent there for nothing.

When I went there to observe, the Spofford facility was everything I imagined it to be—barbed wire atop the fences and big metal doors that were mechanically controlled. Hunts Point is one of the worst areas in the Bronx; it's infested with pimps, prostitutes and drug addicts. So when you go to Hunts Point, it looks like hell, and a detention center located here feels like a jail in hell. Inside the walls were dark and the hallways were long and drab. Each unit had a day area with a TV bolted to the wall, a card table with chairs, and a long hallway with twenty-four rooms with doors that didn't lock. Did I just say didn't lock? So I'm thinking, "How do you keep these kids from attacking each other at night?" The night staff is responsible for patrolling the hallways like guard dogs. This looked like a cross between a psych ward and a dungeon.

The staff was nice, but I didn't feel comfortable. They even had a supervisor working there who supposedly married one of the kids who was locked up at one time. When I heard that, I thought I heard it all, isn't that a classic case of pedophilia? I was saying to myself, please, don't send me there. Their leadership was morally twisted.

The other facilities were more updated. Greenwood was the craziest of the three detention centers with regards to lack of control. If you know anything about Brooklyn, these kids aren't with anything, they will fight you in a heartbeat. During my observation, I witnessed three restraints and two fights before lunchtime.

At this point, I'm saying to myself, what did I get myself into? But the more I thought about my children, I realized I had to do this. I finally had health coverage, a pension, and a salary. I felt like Goldilocks, but the only difference is she had a choice; my fate was in the hands of the people making the decisions. I didn't want to be assigned to Brooklyn because it was out of control, and Spofford was too depressing. Once I got to observe Fairvue, I was feeling it, plus it was the location Boo worked at. I was very lucky; maybe Boo pulled some strings.

When I got the assignment to work at Fairvue, nobody was more welcoming than Deputy Director Morales. He was a short Puerto Rican man who was very hands on. He met us at the front door and welcomed us to the Fairvue family. He gave us a tour of the building and introduced us to the staff on duty. He even took us to the basement and a tour through the kitchen. The welcoming mat was out, and I really felt like a member of the team. When I met Executive Director Sanchez, she had the same warm nature as Morales; they couldn't have been nicer. It was cool because the juvenile counselors were like one big family. The AM tour was from 7 a.m. to 3 p.m., the PM tour was from 3 p.m. to 11 p.m., and then the night tour was from 11 p.m. to 7 a.m. I requested the PM tour because it worked best for me with the visitation agreement with my children.

Like most work environments, there were clicks; but overall, everybody showed each other love. The staff was predominantly African-American and African with a few Hispanic juvenile counselors. I figured because the population of kids in the building was all African-American and Hispanic, it made sense to have staff that could relate to them. Every now and then, a white or Asian kid would get locked up, but they were gone in less than a week or the next day. Most of the white kids had paid lawyers and got out fast. Even if they did something horrific, they were moved from the facility quickly. I wouldn't doubt that the judges that are mostly white cut slack to the white kids, but then again, a paid lawyer makes all the difference. It always comes down to the haves and the have-nots. The black and Hispanic kids relied on appointed lawyer, and who knows how seriously they took their wins and losses.

Early on, I realized that there was a caste system applied to the treatment of these residents. If the staff knows a kid and that kid has a reputation with the other residents (we were supposed to refer to them as residents), that kid got extra. Behavior is monitored based on a points system. If a resident was on level three, they got more privileges, and anything less than level three got limited privileges. It didn't mean anything to be on level three and be a nondescript resident amongst your peers; if a resident was well-known and had status in the building, it didn't matter what level he was, he got to live.

Some residents had their own lotion, soap, hair grease, du-rags, magazines, and some had portable headphones. If none of these things were agency issued, we were trained it was contraband and it had to be removed. The funny shit is that if we removed anything, the resident would get it back; and if he found out it was you that removed it, he would step to you. The resident would say, "The next time you search my room, put my shit back." It wasn't always worth getting into it with a kid like that because some of these residents had more power than the staff. If I searched a resident's room that had excessive items, I would remove them and tell the staff what I removed because sometimes the staff on that hall provided it for them. I've seen staff get into fights because the staff on the hall would say, "That's my shit you threw away," and if supervision got involved, everybody got in trouble. I would just do my job and deal with the consequences later.

In the beginning, I watched the interaction between the residents and the staff. Some female JCs (juvenile counselors) were extra friendly with the residents, giving them kisses and hugs, and some of the male JCs gave the residents dap and hugs. In training, we were told that this wasn't allowed, but that's the difference between practice and policy. Most of the JCs in the building conducted the job based on what they saw other JCs do; it was never right, but it would always get you through the day incident free.

I had a hard time trying to understand how kids who were murderers, thieves, and gangbangers could be treated with so much love and respect, but they were. There was so much laughing, joking, and fraternizing that it completely threw me off. The same kid who just tried to choke a staff member would be eating Chinese food in his room later that night. That's how bad kids are treated? Where was the punishment? At this time, the agency still enforced room confinement, but rarely used it. Room confinement was an effective method of punishment because it stifled their freedom and they hated it. Ten years later, it's considered child abuse, so it's been outlawed. Getting acclimated into the workflow was no easy task, I had to shake off the free-flowing lifestyle I was accustomed too. I had to change the way I dressed, I had to get meaner and tougher, and get used to taking orders. Looking mean wasn't hard but acting mad all the time wasn't my style. I had one supervisor tell me to wipe that smile off my face which took me by surprise. I didn't know how to react to that. First, I was embarrassed then I got mad, which was probably his intention all along. Talk like that was fighting words, but it was clear that the authority in the building had no shame talking down to the JCs because they ran the building. I realized fast that trying to make a point with supervision was pointless; they were never wrong. The administration conspired with the leadership about cracking the verbal whip. It was reminiscent of how Maylyn would chew the ass out of her staff. Damn, how did the script get flipped on me? A price to pay for giving up my dreams.

Within twenty days on the job, I hit the trifecta; everybody was waiting for me to pop my cherry and, boy, did I ever. Not only did I have my first restraint, I had my first incident and suspension all at once. When these things go down, you don't have time to think. This agency puts so much credence in the safety and protection of these kids. I violated that premise when my partner and I forgot one resident during a fire drill. I got the assignment to work on E-Hall because JC Digga called out, and it was my first time working with Ms. Mays. She was given a duty free by Ms. Todd, a woman in my class. I questioned that decision because we were both new, but who was I to say anything.

We were conducting showers at the time and the tone was high and got higher when Ms. Mays stepped off the hall. When we heard the fire bell, I got that skittish feeling like, what do I do? We started getting the group to line up to exit the hall, but in one room the light was off because that resident went to sleep after he showered; but Ms. Todd didn't know that. As they lined up prior to going to the gym, the residents were arguing which occupied my attention and we never got a proper count. I was overwhelmed with the responsibility of controlling fifteen residents who were looking right through me as they went at each other. Ms. Todd wasn't much help, she was a Muslim woman and she wore the Muslim garb, so her religious beliefs kept her from putting her foot in their ass; and being an older woman in her fifties, she didn't belong there in the first place.

A fire drill, fifteen out-of-control young men, and a grandmother was not a formula for success. I wanted to walk out of there, but they would have eaten Ms. Todd alive. It was so helter-skelter I had to maintain my composure. As we left en route to the gym, you could hear us yelling in the staircase; the gym was quiet until we got there. In the gym, all the other halls were there properly lined up and we got there looking like the drunk cousins. Some of the other JCs were embarrassed for us; they were probably thinking why are they working together, which was the same shit I said.

All was good until the security guard entered the gym with the resident we forgot in the room, I was never more mortified. How could we forget someone? What a car wreck! I wanted to blame Ms. Todd because she opened the doors on that side of the hall, but this was on me. I knew the count and I saw him shower, I had to eat this.

The gym was packed, and all the eyes were on me. As the supervisor walked toward me, you could hear a pin drop but, instead, you heard the clacking of her heels on the gym floor. Then she approached me and said out loud, "You know you are going to get conferenced for that." The supervisors never addressed us with the respect and discretion adults deserve. The residents on E-Hall flipped. They came to my defense. They were saying, "He's new. It's not his fault and why do you have to blow up his spot?" As low as I felt at that moment, I felt better with their support.

When we left the gym, the tone skyrocketed. All the kids that had beef with each other got in each other's face. I told them to hold it down till we get on the hall. That's exactly what they did, and as soon as we entered the hall, a riot broke out. At this point, all my logical thoughts were out the window. I was restraining two and three residents at a time; the best thing Ms. Todd could do was start screaming so that somebody could hear her. She didn't touch anybody, but she did call security. When security got there, I had three residents on the floor with their hands behind their back. I was so out of breath it's amazing I didn't get hurt. I popped my cherry big time. That night when I left the building, all the male JCs were outside clapping like I took one for the team. I finally felt like one of them, especially after being suspended for seven days.

CHAPTER THREE

Your punk ass will be grass quick
fast like my name was flash
When a nigga try and rob me for my cash
You thought you had a sweet vick nice pick
But you didn't anticipate that I might be sick

—Brand Nubian
"Punks Jump Up to Get Beat Down"

AFTER THAT INCIDENT, I WAS more vigilant in how I did things, and I felt like I was more a member of the platoon. Nobody questioned my restraining skills and it helped because the other residents gave me props too. Everywhere I worked, I was that dude who survived the riot on E-Hall.

When I returned from my suspension, everybody wanted to work with me, but with the gift came the curse and supervisors were under the pretense that I could handle anything. I was good on my feet, but my verbal skills had much to be desired. As a juvenile counselor, it's very important to establish your personality and your presentation. When you step onto a hall, the kids need to know that you're in charge or they will take over. If they don't like you, they will fuck with you, and if they don't know you, they will fuck with you more.

My first time working on D-Hall, I was nervous as shit. Because they had the reputation for violating new staff. To them I looked like fresh meat. As soon as I got there, this one resident stepped to me and put me on blast. He said, "Yo, you a cop." Now, in my head I'm saying, why would I be a cop working in a detention center?

But this wasn't the introduction I needed. Being called a cop in this environment was like screaming fire in a crowded room. I never disassociated from something so fast, but I quickly told him, "Never that. I'm just a juvenile counselor." He said, "You look like a cop." I told him that I've been told that, but that's not my thing. My own children would tell me that when I don't smile, I looked mean, maybe that's what he saw. This was just a little something in my physical toolbox I could use to keep the haters at bay. Instead of jumping in the water, I observed and watched the interaction between the staff I was working with and the residents. Around this group, all these kids are manipulators; they will ask for things they know they can't have just to see your response.

On this day, a resident asked the staff for Chinese food and the JC made it very clear that he wasn't the one to ask. He told that resident, "Nigga, please, I know you didn't just ask me for Chinese food? The next time you mention the word Chinese food, I'm dropping you to the floor and the only thing you will be eating is the dust under the desk." After that, the resident fell back and didn't say much the rest of the day, but I knew that movie was for me. He wasn't testing the other JC; he was testing me to see my reaction.

The next day, I got assigned again to D-Hall and that same resident asked me the same thing, but this time he demanded it. He told me that the next time I show up at his hall, I better bring him Chinese food. I flipped it on him.

I told him, "What do you want?"

He said, "Beef and broccoli, an egg roll, and iced tea."

I said, "That's it?"

He said, "Yeah and bring it after dinner."

I didn't know where I was going, I just played along. The more I looked at him as a child and not a man, the more confident I got with this conversation.

Then I just said, "Good luck."

He said, "Good luck with what?"

I said, "Good luck with getting your Chinese food."

The other residents started laughing, and I could tell he didn't like that.

He said, "O, you that nigga?"

I said, "What nigga?"

He said, "That nigga that I'm going to have to violate."

I told him, "Go and violate, I get paid to make examples of residents like you."

He said, "By who?"

I said, "By me, try me."

He laughed and walked away. But I knew I had to watch my back, he was a heavy hitter in the building and had an army of soldiers who would do anything he said.

The JC I was working with asked me when I want to take him down. I said, "Why?"

He said, "This shit ain't over, he is going to swing on you or one of his goons will."

There were sixteen male residents on the hall. This kid was a gang member and he recruited five other residents on the hall to his gang.

I told the other JC, "What about conflict resolution and de-escalating the situation by talking to him and squashing it."

He said, "Conflict resolution my ass. That shit won't work. The only way to earn your stripes and end this is to drop him and then we'll de-escalate."

I said to myself, what the fuck did I get myself into? I want to avoid confrontation not initiate it. Is this what I signed up for?

I started to think of all those people in my class who quit and wondered why I didn't quit with them. But then I realized who I was, and that I'm not a quitter. I never give up, plus there was no buyer's remorse with me. I bought in. There was no turning back now.

The JC said, "We can do this one or two ways—you can go over and provoke him into an incident or you can meet him in his room and shoot a fair one. If you don't do something, they will jump you. I'll take down one or two, but you got sixteen motherfuckas in here that don't know you and they will all take their shots. If you initiate the restraint, the other residents will respect that and let you handle your business. I'll control his boys."

This can't be happening. None of this was in my training manual. This kid was about five feet nine, built like Lebron, and he was brawler. I was no brawler. The last fight I had was six years ago over some chick. This was more important; this was for respect and my place in this building. I outweighed him, so I needed to use my size to my advantage. I had to do something, or it would go throughout the building that I was soft, and my life would be hell wherever I got assigned.

I took the first approach and stepped to him. I wrote something on a piece of paper and gave it to him.

He said, "What is this?"

"That's my list of what I want you to get me from the Chinese restaurant." I told him.

He said, "O, you think I'm pussy," and he got out of his seat and took two steps in my direction.

Before he could get any closer, I tackled him and knocked him over the bricks (what they refer to as seats). We both flipped to the floor and I put him in an upper torso restraint, a technique I learned in training. With everyone watching, I lost my cool and made it personal.

I said to him, "You wanna test me? You fucked with the wrong nigga today."

I could tell he was in pain and was telling me to get off him, but I was trying to hurt him, this was the only way I would get my respect. The other residents were shocked; they never saw him take an L.

My partner separated us and placed him in his room until supervision would show up. The other residents took notice and looked at me differently. It felt good, like when I played football and took down somebody hard on their sideline.

When all the residents were locked in their rooms so that we could write our incident reports, my coworker told me I did good. He said the other residents were afraid of this kid, but now he said, "They will be afraid of you."

He said, "He won't fuck with you anymore and now he's going to try to be your friend because he's not going to want to be restrained by you again."

I asked him, "Was that a restraint I did?"

He said, "Man, listen, any way you take down a resident is a restraint. That shit you learned in training doesn't always work. You have to do what you have to do, by any means necessary."

It was straight out of the Malcolm X handbook, the Martin Luther King way of doing things won't work in here. It's survival of the fittest, I had to put my foot down to earn respect in this bitch. Supervision was all for this; they wanted the resident to fear the counselors.

The next day, when the kid saw me, I apologized and told him I didn't mean to go so hard, but the kid said it was all good and admitted he deserved it for fucking with me. Now he was telling other residents to not fuck with me because if they did, I would put them on their neck. After that, supervision congratulated me on a job well done. From then on, they considered me a heavy which meant that I could hold down a hall. I didn't know if I was ready for that, but it felt good to have their validation.

On this job, the one caveat was that doing good would ensure you the worse assignments nobody wanted. It reminded me of when I tried out for the North Riverdale Baseball League in elementary school. During tryouts, everybody said miss one or two ground balls because if you make every play, you will be put on a shitty team. But it wasn't my nature to mess up if I could help it. In this environment, it might have been wise to take that approach because I was getting the shittiest assignments. If there was a kid nobody could control, I was assigned to that post. There were more seasoned staff who were bigger heavies than I was, but they had permanent halls and never changed their post. If they were reassigned to another hall, they would refuse and go home. I didn't have it like that because I was still considered a new jack even though I was in multiple incidents.

One time, JC Pena was given another assignment and went off, Pena was a short-diesel Dominican dude who always dealt with the worse kids in the building. He was the standard of excellence at

Fairvue. He always worked on C-Hall and all those residents had high profile cases; these kids all had murder cases that made the newspaper.

Supervision did some moving around of the staff and assigned him to G-Hall. You could see on his face that he was pissed. He told them that before the tour was over, they would have to move him. Supervision didn't entertain that and told everybody to go to their assigned post. When Pena got to G-Hall, all the residents were in their rooms for the change of tour. Pena's reputation was legendary, when he restrained a resident, they felt it. Pena said out loud, "If anybody is standing at their doors, they will be violated." The residents weren't allowed to stand at their doors as per the policy. When they heard his voice, they all fell back and sat in their rooms. But one kid was new and didn't know Pena's reputation, so he stood at his door and gave Pena a challenge. Pena walked over to the resident's door and asked very politely for him to move away from the window at the door, but the resident replied by saying, "Suck my dick," and that was all she wrote. Pena went in the kid's room and bent him up so bad that he caught an allegation and had to be removed from the hall. When Pena saw supervision, he said, "I told you that I would have to be moved." They never moved him from his hall again, and the supervisor who sent him to G-Hall got reprimanded by the tour commander.

But me, I had no seniority, so I could be assigned anywhere. One day, they assigned me to a resident who had a reputation for throwing shit on staff. Yes, I said shit, also referred to as human feces. Everybody refused to work with this kid, but because I was on probation, I would get written up for refusing. I didn't want that on my record, so I went to the hall.

The kid was a one-to-one resident which meant that he has mental or psychological issues and needs his own staff to protect him from himself and other residents. When I got to the hall, lucky for me he was in his room with the door closed. In Fairvue, unlike Spofford, the doors lock. He was put in his room for an incident earlier that day. The staff I relieved told me what he did and that he was safer with his door closed. But the policy states that a one-to-one resident must be a hand's distance from their staff, but then there was nothing in the policy about a resident throwing shit on you.

When I went to his door, he told me to get the fuck away from his door or he was going to wipe shit on the window. I said, "I just want your side of the story about the incident." I sat on the floor outside his door to listen to his explanation. He said he got mad because he wanted his medication, but the doctor in the infirmary refused to give it to him so he turned it up. Turning it up is a term the residents use to indicate that they were going to flip out and start damaging things. I asked him if did it bother him.

He said, "What?"

I said, "The smell of shit everywhere, how do you tolerate the smell?"

He said no, he was used to it. He told me that he did it when he was younger because it kept the kid in his foster home from sexually assaulting him. He said the kid was so turned off he never touched him again. I felt sorry for him after hearing that, I thought it was a great tactic to avoid being raped in that setting. He said now he uses shit as a weapon to get his way. Man, is this kid all screwed up? I told him if he kept his shit in his pants, I would ask supervision to speak to the PA (physician assistant) so I could take him to get his medication.

Then I told him the unhealthy truth about shit. It's waste and not meant to be touched, and now that he isn't in the foster home, he didn't have to do it anymore. This kid doesn't know his father, and his mother gave up on him. He was fifteen and has been in foster care since he was ten.

As time passed, he stopped throwing shit around and found other methods to get his way. I was assigned to work with him until he was taken off one-to-one, and eventually placed in population with the other residents. Our relationship grew stronger, the more he trusted me the more he began to trust other people. I taught him how to give people a chance to show you who they are before you judge them. I said, "Give them fifteen minutes and you will know whether or not they are full of shit." No pun intended.

CHAPTER FOUR

+ ◆ ◆ ◆ ◆ +

Lemonade was a popular drink and it still is
I get more stunts and props than Bruce Willis

—Gang Starr
"DWYCK"

T HERE WERE MULTIPLE FACTORS THAT determined a good day: where you are assigned to work, how many people come to work, what recreation is on your schedule, who is your partner, how many residents are on the hall, and even what snack you got. If any one of those things is off, then your day is fucked.

There were ten halls in the building that were divided by two floors. A-Hall and B-Hall were halls that housed girls and intake, the SHU (Special Housing Unit), C-Hall and D-Hall housed boys on the first floor. E, F, G, H, and J- Halls all were on the second floor and were all boy halls. B-Hall was a special support dorm for girls, while C and F-Hall had eight rooms for male residents that needed a smaller setting. D, E, G, H, and J were halls with sixteen rooms for boys, intake has four rooms and was used to house new residents and those needing special support such as one-to-one residents. The SHU located next to the infirmary was used for sick or injured residents and, sometimes, those residents on PC (protective custody), and those residents who were too scared to be in general population. They would get their lawyer to make up some bullshit story, so they could be isolated.

Because I was new, they assigned me everywhere. It got so bad. There were days I didn't even want to go to work for fear of my assignment. It was more like anxiety because I never knew where I would be assigned, but I could rely on supervision to send me where I didn't want to go. Wherever I went, I knew something bad was going to happen. I always hoped for the best but expected the worse. It's not always fly to be the new guy. The male staff were ultrawelcoming, but I wasn't surprised because my presence meant another able body to deal with these little monsters. Plus, it kept them from being stuck to do a double. Yeah, that was something else that sucked, I could be stuck whenever somebody didn't come to work, which blew my social life. The female staff were a little standoffish. I guess they didn't want it to look like they were sweating me or something. There were no hurt feelings. I'm just trying to pay my bills like them. I never understood why seasoned staff would want to make it hard on new people, shit they were new once too. Plus, if they help me be efficient, it gave them more support in the long run. Each one, teach one—that's my philosophy. At the end of the day, you're a bitch ass if you get off making life hard on new employees that says more about them. You get no cool points for that. I got my dose of those people in the beginning. Anytime I asked a question, they would tell me, "Didn't you learn that in training? What are you asking me for?" Well, okay, then. I know not to ask you for shit. It was bad enough the residents are going to take shots at me, why would you pile on? But folks are grimy. I had to be careful how I maneuvered in this place, one false move and somebody could put a hit out on me. Shocking but true, Boo put me on to the bullshit that went on where staff would put Chinese food on other staff's heads. When I heard that, I told myself to not create enemies. I wasn't trying to tell on anybody or get in anybody's way, I was there to just work and go home. It was everything I could do to not be labeled an IG (Inspector General). These are people that the agency hires to spy on the JCs disguised as JCs. That would be a good way to get set up and jumped by the residents. After a while, they realized I wasn't one of those people because I wasn't a busybody. I was so envious of the senior staff that had a steady hall; their days were like stealing money. Despite how bad the residents are, they had a level of loyalty to their regular staff. They didn't know me, and they didn't want to know me. Sometimes, the only way I had a good day was to be a dick.

One day, JC Carter, one of the biggest JCs in the building, called out and they assigned me to his hall. Carter looked like an NFL tight end, was six foot three, with zero body fat. His days at work were a walk in the park—those kids wouldn't do anything to make him work harder. His hall was H-Hall, and most of these residents were sent to him because they were a problem somewhere else. His residents were the residents nobody could control but him. He was known to smack fire out of any kid trying to violate; his backhand was wicked.

When they told me to go to H-Hall as an assignment, I immediately asked if I was just holding for Carter, but supervision said he called out. My next thought was I hoped the building got evacuated from a fire. It was so bad on H-Hall that the other staff would call Carter to see if he was working because if he called out, they would too. I didn't know him like that and I wasn't in any position to skip work. But I looked at it like this, the harder it is now the easier it will be for me later.

So when I got to H-Hall, most of the residents were in the day area sitting on the bricks just waiting to see who was covering Carter's shift. Most of H-Hall knew he wasn't coming in before we did, he would always tell his group to prepare them. But it was more like when the cats are away the mice will play. When I walked in, they started laughing and jumping on the bricks like third graders, acting like it was time to do whatever. I felt like the substitute teacher that nobody respected. The staff that I relieved said to the group, "Chill the fuck out. If y'all don't give my man respect, tomorrow will be hell."

They chilled while he was there but when he left, they got on their bullshit again. At that point, I had enough. I turned the radio and the TV off and told them to sit on the bricks for a rap session. Rap sessions were important to establish the tone, this way you prepare the group for your tour and explain to them what you expect. Some of them weren't with it and wouldn't sit down. One kid even went to turn back on the radio. Just as I was going to turn it back off, I heard keys open the door and the smell of cinnamon filled the hall. Then I heard the sexy voice of Ms. Sanders screaming, "Sit your asses down." She was their regular staff on the AM and she was assigned to work with me on a double. All the residents had a crush on her like I did. I get a hard on just thinking about her, that's how bad she was. She had a coffee complexion and was definitely light and sweet. With a body to die for, all the kids respected her and would never violate her. Once a kid got his jaw wired, for calling her a bitch by a resident that was sitting next to him on the bricks. She told them to hold it down for me and to show me respect or tomorrow would be a bad day. Somebody must like me because to be working with Ms. Sanders was a reward, not a punishment. I thanked her for getting stuck even though it wasn't her choice; I just knew if she didn't get there when she did, I was going to have an incident.

I would get nervous talking in front of a group, but for some reason, I was comfortable talking to the residents during a rap session. It was like an anxiety disorder or something I had. In school, I could never speak or read in public without getting nervous. I would start sweating and stuttering like I was going to explode. One of my worse subjects in college was speech, but for everybody else, it was an easy A. Too often, I would allow my fear of speaking in public keep me from sharing valuable information, but in this environment, I quickly realized how crucial it was to the growth and development of these young men. I was the messenger.

With the help of Ms. Sanders, we sat them down so I could give them a rap session. I started by telling them why I was there and how I went from a clothing designer to working at Fairvue as a juvenile counselor. I told them that I didn't grow up in the hood like most of them but, like most of them, I was raised by a single parent and that I never had a father. I spoke on being a father and what it meant to me. I asked if any of them had children, and two of the hall leaders raised their hands.

After my rap session, one of them stepped to me and told me how what I said changed his view of fatherhood. It just so happened that those two residents were members of the Crip gang from Brooklyn and they had the hall. To have the hall meant they ran things and all the other residents listened to them, so getting in good with them gave me instant credibility.

The next day, when I saw Carter, I told him, "The next time you call out, call me so I can join you." He laughed.

H- and C-Hall were the most difficult halls in the building. What made C-Hall difficult was that it housed the residents that were looking to do hard time. They were like the sinister six, they were the worse residents of all three facilities. Most of them were the OGs (original gangsters) of Fairvue with high-street credibility. There were five of them, and all of them but one were members of the Blood gang.

A day after working H-Hall, I had to give Pena a duty free on C-Hall which was like going from the frying pan into the fire. When I walked on the hall, it was like walking up on a pack of wolves. Four of them were playing cards and the one that was the leader was in his room listening to music on his headphones. His name was Supreme, and he was there on a murder charge. Out of the others, three were there for murder and one was there for rape. This was a tough crowd to entertain for one hour.

As I approached the desk, Pena gave me an update on their day and said they were good. Before I sat down, I introduced myself, but only one of them acknowledged me by saying, "What's up" while still playing cards. When Pena left, I could feel the cold in the air of young men with blood on their hands; I've never been in this setting. These kids were killers and weren't fazed by anything, not even my presence. They knew they were doing hard time and didn't care what you had to say to them.

The entire hour they didn't say anything to me, they barely spoke to each other. They just kept playing spades, and Supreme stayed in his room listening to music. It was the easiest hour I ever had working on a hall.

When Pena returned, he asked me how it went, I told him that they held it down. As I left, I said peace, and that same resident who said what's up said peace back; they just kept playing cards. I realized real fast that on first impressions, it's better to observe in this place than run my mouth like a know-it-all. Some situations flow better that way; you could add fuel to the fire if you don't see what's going on first.

I also felt that I needed my own hall that reflected my personality, but that wasn't going to happen anytime soon because all the halls on the PM had consistent senior staff. A and B were out because male staff can't work the girl halls, C-Hall had Pena, H-Hall had Carter, D-Hall had Mr. Lucas (an older grandfather figure who was very stern), G-Hall had Mr. Hoffman (the only Caucasian JC in the building), J-Hall had AZ and Ms. Willis (she was an AM staff that always volunteered plus she did the evening programs), E-Hall had Mr. Digga and Ms. Mays, the SHU and Intake rotated staff, while Mr. Ford worked F-Hall. The only thing I could do was give duty frees and partner up with one of them to get experience. It was frustrating because all I did was move around while most of them had their feet up.

Because of my size, supervision thought I would be able to handle any hall. The physicality was never an issue for me, I was a gym rat and I saw restraining as a workout. If a resident tried to assault one of us, he was taken to his room and given the business. It was easy to provoke them into a restraint; as soon as you got in their face, they would start swinging which justified us restraining them. They were so predictable; we knew if we poked them, they would flinch. To get into the mindset of restraining, I approached it like a sport, almost like something out of the TV show *Gladiators* where it was us against them, then it became fun. We were the gladiators and they were the contestants trying to win a prize. To see it any other way broke my heart because at the end of the day, these were children we were bending up. Where are the cool points in that?

What scared me most was the unknown, where I was working, and who I was working with? These were factors that determined how your day would go. But the more halls I worked, the more confidence I got. This gave me the opportunity to know the kids and which staff I could rely on. The more I engaged with the residents, the better I got at communicating with them. I never tried to be like them, I stayed true to who I was. Sometimes, they made fun of the way I dressed and how I talked because I really had no street swag. To them, I was like a suburbanite, which was sort of true. Growing up for me was going to school and being on time for football practice. I knew nothing about their world.

Most of these kids had to worry about being shot or stabbed, whether or not they would have a home to go to, and where their next meal was coming from. For some, being locked up was a security blanket because to them home was hell. Here, they got three meals and their own room, which was more than where they came from. The more I interacted with them, the more they respected that I was honest to who I was. I never tried to be down with their lifestyle. I would always point out to them that it's their lifestyle that put them there. I dressed more Banana Republic than thug.

Early on, when I spoke in the rap sessions, I expressed how important it was that I set a good example for my younger sibling and how being a single parent raising two young children was a major sacrifice, giving up my dream being a designer to provide for them. After my rap sessions, some of them wanted me to adopt them because nobody in their lives has ever made sacrifices for them. My message to them was if they can one day be positive contributors in society and have jobs and take care of their children, that was enough.

In this age of instant gratification, young people get caught up on the lifestyles of entertainers but don't see that it's the everyday person that makes the wheels turn in life. I would tell them to get a job, a car, and a girlfriend and you will never get in trouble again like this. I would say, "Your friends are the reason most of you are locked up, and they can't do your time for you nor will they. The harsh reality is that you got caught, they didn't. They're living and now you're not. So let's lose that loyalty to your friend's shit and have loyalty to your future—be your own man." They would be so focused on what I said, it felt good. I was motivated to give them hope, which was something most of them never had.

When I was in high school, I remember my coach would have these pep talks at halftime that would almost make us cry. I began to have that effect on the group.

CHAPTER FIVE

＊◆◆◆◆＊

And let the management work for me
Because I don't need the unnecessary hostility

—Pete Rock & C.L. Smooth
"Straighten It Out"

THE HIERARCHY IN THE BUILDING was very understood. Just to give an overview of our roster, there was one executive director and one deputy director who would oversee all operations of the facility. Each tour has two TCs (tour commanders) who were the overseers during the tour. Under them were the supervisors, and there were three for each tour. Then under the supervisors were the JCs; there must have been twenty of us on each tour to cover a shift. We were at the bottom of the totem pole. Each supervisor would have to supervise between twelve or fifteen JCs, sometimes more. It seemed like a complicated system, but it worked only if people came to work. I learned real fast who was in charge and who not to fuck with. After having a high-profile career as a designer, I was looking forward to going under the radar and being an average Joe. I started to realize I wasn't alone; there were more than a few people that I knew from the outside. I saw Ms. Floss, a JC I went to high school with. She was on the PM tour and worked on B-Hall. Then one of my childhood friend's wife was on my tour also. Later, I found out that one of my college dorm mates had a brother who knew me; he worked on the night tour. But the one that made the most difference was a TC who worked on the PM tour who knew me through a mutual friend; his name was Allen Platter.

Platter was a man of high character and he was well connected. At one time, he was president of the union. We quickly hit it off; we were around the same age and both of us graduated from an HBCU (Historically Black Colleges and Universities). He made sure nobody fucked with me because nobody wanted to get on his bad side; he had saved everybody's ass at one time or another. He was the first person who told me not to get involved with the chicks in here. He would say, "Don't shit where you eat." I did have my eye on one or two of them, but after speaking to him, I fell back. I saw what he was talking about because most of them had issues with men having control; more than half of the JCs were females and almost all of them were single parents.

I commend women who have to raise their children alone, but the women I worked with were used to calling the shots. They weren't listening to a damn thing my black ass had to say; they had the experience and the seniority, and I had to stay in my lane.

This was an issue because most of them wanted to run the halls; if they had a problem with a resident, they would tell me to put him in his room. In my head, I would say, didn't you have an issue with him? Why do I have to put him in his room? You can restrain. But I didn't say anything. As the man on the hall, I was always considered the leader during a restraint, even if I didn't initiate the incident. How would it look if I watched a female JC struggle with a male resident? That wasn't my thing. I restrained more residents for violating female coworkers than for violating me. You know how some females can be, verbally taking the manhood out of somebody. It would always lead to an incident.

I remember once, this resident told the female JC I was assigned to work with to suck his dick, and her response was, "It's not big enough." Of course, that didn't sit well with the resident, so he immediately jumped in her face, and it was my job to take him down. In my incident report, I didn't include what she said, and that was my first of many mistakes I made on this job. She needed to be disciplined for inciting the resident. He was wrong, but she was also wrong, and that wasn't the last time she would verbally violate a resident. He learned his lesson before she did. Not too long after that, she got assaulted doing the same shit on B-Hall. There were no men to save her ass down there.

Most of the female staff rarely restrained unless it was necessary. Most of them interacted with the kids and wrote entries in the logbook. Usually, we were paired male and female because there was a shortage of male JCs, but there were five times more boys than girls in the building. It was important to work with the right female JC; a real aggressive female JC could raise the tone while a soft-spoken one could be the right formula.

Being too verbally aggressive could be too challenging for the resident and to me. The last thing I wanted was to be working with somebody yelling all the time; that shit doesn't work. Most of these residents were bipolar and had attention-deficit hyperactivity disorder(ADHD), but we wouldn't know because the agency never gave us their medical record. It was confidential. We didn't even know what they were there for. Now, how is that going to work? The only thing we did know is that they were in our custody. We were counselors/correction officers/psychologist all in one.

Our toolbox consisted of our voice and our hands, not a lot to work with. There were case workers and mental health specialists, but they weren't there twenty-four hours, and most of them had off on weekends. So, if a resident had mental health issues at 11:30 on a Saturday night, we had to control them until Monday. Supervision didn't do much; they felt we were well equipped to deal with any situation, and if it got that bad, just restrain them.

It was sad because it wasn't that simple. It was then that I realized supervision was more occupied with what we were doing wrong. To them, they felt that it was something we did to lose control of the resident. If a resident flipped a desk or broke the phone, they wanted to know why we didn't stop them. Stop what? There were eleven or more other residents with similar issues, how were we supposed to be responsible for a kid that went crazy? Those types of kids didn't even belong there if you want to keep it 100, they belonged in a hospital.

I remember once this supervisor yelled at me because I didn't inform him about something I didn't include on an incident report. I told him to watch how he was talking to me. He said, "Well, then do your job right." I'm thinking to myself, *Booker keep your cool, don't go HAM* (Hard as a Motherfucker). But then I realized, because somebody yells at him, he thinks it's okay to yell at me. Later that night, before I left, I pulled him aside and told him that I don't work like that. "If you want to get the most out of me, yelling doesn't work," I told him. He understood my point; but I could tell, if I didn't speak to him, he would have done it again and he probably did it to anybody that allows him. This one female JC wasn't having none of that, but the bitch-ass supervisors found ways to slow her roll. Whenever they came at her, she would go HAM and her Nuyorican nature would spit venom right back at them. But when she was assigned to the SHU with a resident that had scabies, that's when I saw how grimy they can get. It was fucked up because she was a mother of two small children, and to have her work on a hall to be exposed to scabies was criminal. They put her there because they didn't like her attitude. Basically, she had to work there or she would be fired because she was a new employee and didn't clear probation, she was one write up away from termination. Every time I watched her put on that mask and gloves to work with a kid with a highly contagious skin disease made me want to punch the supervisor in the face; that was dirty. Out of fifteen people in roll call, she and I were the only JCs with little children. They could have assigned someone else, but they wanted to put her in her place. She eventually switched to the AM tour to avoid the PM supervisors, which meant that she had to pay for a babysitter to watch her daughter and get her son to school. A heavy price to pay for challenging an ego-tripping supervisor.

Most of the supervisors got barked on by the tour commanders and thought they could do it to the JCs; but homie don't play that. Like most of the residents that didn't have a father, I took offense to another man telling me what to do. I always saw this as them trying to control me for their own gain, like a race but more like a deterrent than a plus. All the TCs were middle-aged black men, very strong-minded but with very weak egos.

You could tell that some of them abused their power and used their position to get what they wanted. Keeping it real, some were using the position to get pussy from the female JCs. I knew of one TC that was dating a JC, and another that fathered the child of another employee. This was a problem when some female JCs were given special treatment if a TC had an eye for them; most were given light assignments and extra days off. I remember one female could take a break whenever she wanted, and at the end of the night get lifts home by the TC.

There was a lot of resentment and bitterness because of this, some females had the freedom to do what they wanted while others were given the worse assignments. This probably happens on other jobs, but not when you have to deal with these kids; it affects your ability to be impartial and fair. It got stressful for a lot of females, and little clicks developed, making them turn on each other. Once the residents got involved, it got ugly.

I recall one of my classmates got it the worse. Her name was Ms. Carmen. Ms. Carmen was a beautiful well-built dark-skinned woman from Jamaica that all the men wanted a piece of, but she ignored them. We were good friends, I treated her like a sister, and she helped me a lot during my custody situation with advice from a mother's point of view. She had two kids and was a single parent like me; and, like me, the only thing more important than her job was her children. A lot of the female JCs didn't like her because she wasn't the socializing type and she kept to herself. She knew this but it didn't faze her. She would tell me, "As long as those bitches don't say slick shit, I don't care what they think." One of the TCs was trying hard to get at her, but she wasn't feeling him and she would constantly turn down his advances. I could tell this hurt his feeling.

At first, she was given the assignment of G-Hall with Mr. Hoffman, but out of nowhere she was reassigned to work with the girls on A-Hall. This made no sense because she worked well on G-Hall with the boys. She was aggressive with them, but they needed that. She had a motherly side and she was very strong for a female. She could restrain any resident, which was never a problem for her.

When the supervisor told her in roll call that she was being reassigned, she questioned the change and was immediately reprimanded and written up for questioning her assignment. She knew what this was about and laughed. As she left roll call, she said out loud, "You can make me, but you can't break me." I knew what she meant and others did too.

When she got to A-Hall, most of the staff on the AM didn't like her, but she didn't give a damn. I thought this move was temporary; but when days turned to weeks, I thought this was too harsh. Her personality didn't fit A-Hall. Even though she had a daughter, she was real tough on girls. These girls had the most fragile self-esteem. If you told them they needed to use deodorant, they would slit their wrist.

She finally got an explanation from a supervisor, and he said she was moved because the boys on G-Hall thought that she was too hard. Too hard? Somebody needed to be too hard on them when they were doing their crime; those kids only respected too hard. She was being punished for not accepting the advances of the tour commander. The TCs were like the *Wizard of Oz*—they decided where everybody goes. The supervisors were just little pawns for the TCs; they only had power over us. What was funny is that if you know the story about the *Wizard of Oz*, you know he had insecurity issues, which is ironic.

What started to happen was that the girls on A-Hall were giving Ms. Carmen a hard time, and when she complained to supervision, they told her it was part of the job. The AM staff didn't help the situation; they were throwing her shade and they also would talk shit about her in front of the residents, which just instigated things. This was fucked up and a recipe for disaster.

One day, Ms. Carmen called supervision because one of the residents named Jackie refused to line up for dinner. Supervision told her to call security, but security said they would only come after she restrained Jackie which was bullshit; they are supposed to assist in anything. When Ms. Carmen tried to escort Jackie to her room for counseling, Jackie attacked her. Jackie wasn't a small girl; she was just as big as Ms. Carmen and a challenge. Ms. Carmen was struggling and didn't get help from her partner. Her partner called security, but while on the phone, Ms. Carmen was losing this fight and committed a cardinal sin on the job. Jackie was pulling the shit out of her hair and the only way to stop her and get her off was for Ms. Carmen to bite her. When you're fighting for your life, sometimes, animal instincts kick in to help you. In this case, it could only hurt.

When security got there, they were able to manage Jackie into her room, but the damage was done. Supervision arrived and were only focused on the incident report which pissed the shit out of Ms. Carmen. She was like, "What about my hair? Do you care about my fuckin' hair? Fuck the incident report. That bitch pulled my hair out."

Jackie went to medical and filed an allegation against Ms. Carmen for biting her. The allegation was accepted by Justice Central. Ms. Carmen went out IOJ (injured on the job) for six months. When she returned from IOJ, she was suspended for the allegation, then transferred to the Wood (Greenwood). But wait, it gets worse. While in Greenwood, she caught another allegation again working with the girls. This time, after being suspended, she was forced to resign or they were going to fire her. Six months after resigning, with no job and no support from the union, she got a call from the mighty Justice Central that she had better turn herself in to the police or she would be arrested for the allegation in Brooklyn that happened almost a year ago. With no union lawyer and no money to pay for a lawyer, she was fucked. She ended up turning herself in and was put in booking like the girls she was paid to supervise. She got out of jail, but to this day, Ms. Carmen is still fighting for her freedom and being labeled a child offender. They offered her six months in jail and one year of probation, which she turned down. The last offer she received was a hundred fifty hours of community service, which was also crap.

How cruel is that? Where's the justice? Ms. Carmen was a good counselor. This whole shit could have been avoided, but instead, somebody's safety and job was compromised because of a shallow ego. What a bitch.

CHAPTER SIX

◆◆◆◆◆

People, people we are the same no we're not the same
Cause we don't know the game
What we need is awareness, we can't get careless
You say what is this? My beloved
lets get down to business
Mental self- defensive fitness

—Public Enemy
"Fight the Power"

IT WASN'T THAT MUCH EASIER for the men. We weren't treated like sexual objects, but we were treated like physical specimens able to scale tall buildings in a single bound. At times, it felt like being on a plantation, can I say that? But the sad truth is we were the field hands—the bigger you were, the more you were expected to do.

If a JC had size, he was assigned the roughest and worse group of residents in the building, but if you were a man of smaller stature, you got a lighter assignment. How fair was that? We all made the same money, we all got the same training, and we all wanted to get home safely to our families. This unfair assessment of our ability did more damage to the credibility of the smaller male JCs and made their work environment hell. In some ways, supervision made these men look like pussies, and they were called that every day by the kids and other JCs. These dudes got abused by the residents. They were the ones getting spat on and getting threatened by the kids to bring in food or they would get jumped.

I even witnessed a JC allow a resident to go in his pockets and search him for money, and that stunned me. You're a grown fuckin' man, how do you let a child violate you like that? I didn't say shit because he didn't want to say shit. I would ask him if he wanted to report it, but he was too embarrassed to say anything; and then when I realized that this happens to him on a regular, I said fuck it. I wasn't that big, but because of how wide I was and my ability to communicate with the residents, I was considered a heavy and viewed as a bigger JC.

I started to resent getting hard assignments while these other guys supervision had no faith in were assigned to work with Carter or Hoffman or they got to take one resident at a time to medical. That was a woman's job. I would ask supervision why can't I get those assignments. They would be like, "Oh no, we need you somewhere else. We see your value better than that. You're a tough guy." I would say, "Better than what? Better to get spit on? Better to restrain a six-foot-two resident?"

This wasn't a compliment; this was an insult to my safety. I had a right to go home in one piece like everybody else. So many bigger JCs lost their jobs from injuries or just quit from being drained and worn out. The turnover rate was huge with men who left the job because of this, that's why there were so many female JCs. Most of the men didn't last that long.

I would think to myself, how does the agency not see this? It doesn't take rocket science to see that supervision is falsely evaluating the staff based on appearance. At the end of the day, we were grown men working with boys. If you got hired and received training, you had the ability to work anywhere regardless of your size. I gained my confidence from working everywhere; they were holding these dudes back by protecting them. It was the basic house-nigger-field-nigger scenario. We all came from the same place. Why do I get beaten up while this guy gets to chill out?

I remember this one guy who was so big his size put fear in all the residents, but he was a gentle giant. Mr. Karl was six foot four and played college football as a defensive end, but a knee injury ended his playing career. Prior to being a juvenile counselor, he was a bouncer for a Manhattan night club. I don't think he gave up that gig to become the captain of crisis control, but that became his unofficial title over here. This dude always got the worse assignment and always had an incident. He didn't want to hurt anybody; he really wanted to counsel the residents. He was one of the people who misunderstood the newspaper ad for the job. Like me, he was in court, fighting for the custody of his daughter and needed the job. Every day he got assigned, they put his job in jeopardy because he was sent places where an incident happened or supervision knew was about to happen. As much as he wanted to talk to these kids, he was always forced to restrain them; and when he did, he always would hospitalize them and caught an allegation. He had a heavy hand, his rap sheet as a counselor was that he was injuring them, and I thought he would get fired. He had stupid strength; and even though they feared him physically, mentally they thought he was soft. He wasn't, he was just a nice guy, and most of these kids took advantage of nice people.

As big as Karl was, he might have been better off with a lighter assignment just for his longevity on the job. But if there was a hall with four Crips and three Bloods gang members, Karl would get assigned there; and I would cringe in roll call because everybody knew what was about to happen. It was like they sent him to the shark tank, told him to go in there, and feed the sharks by hand.

His biggest problem was that he trusted these kids too much and believed that what they said was what they would do. These were the most manipulative kids on the face of the world, as I would later be cognizant of. One time, Karl got jumped and was out IOJ for a few months. When he returned, supervision assigned him with the same group of residents who jumped him. At that point, he had enough. He refused to take that assignment and got written up. Later that week, he turned in his badge and his uniform. I never saw him again, but I understood how he felt. An opportunity to save souls turned into a soul-searching quest for me and all of us. We all felt that way. What started out to be about the kids was really about the job and making sure you did nothing to lose it.

Most of the JCs were African-American single parents who were hard working and needed the job to support their families; nobody signed up for the politics, but it was totally unavoidable.

It was unfortunate, but in the end, it's the kids who suffer the most. Counselors like Karl had vital information that a young man could benefit from but never got to hear because he was always too busy separating kids and breaking up fights. Most of the JCs were on their second chance in life because something happened that led them to this job. I was one of them. It's not like we got out of college or, for some of us, high school and said, "I can't wait to be a juvenile counselor." It was like we were babysitting misfits, like the guards in the land of misfit toys. Most JCs like me had experienced major setbacks in our lives and needed a way to make a living. I couldn't be more thankful for the opportunity, but I soon found out that all that glitters isn't gold.

Being labeled a heavy irked me, it was fool's gold. If a new resident just had a fight, they would assign me to remove that resident from one hall to another, which was like moving a mountain lion from one part of the woods to another without tranquilizers—no help, no assistance, just me.

After talking for five minutes, I knew how difficult it would be. Once this resident named Andy told me he wasn't moving for shit. Then plan B was to just physically force Andy to move, which did require assistance. Supervision would measure a situation based on its seriousness, which made sense but was hard to speculate. To them, my situation didn't warrant their assistance. I was told to contact security, but even they had their criterion when it came to a response. For them, I had to be restraining the resident for them to assist me; they were tired of responding to situations just to do the job of the JC.

What a fucked-up situation I was caught in. I had nowhere to turn. My only hope was that I could say something to Andy to convince him to leave the hall.

I told him, "Listen, you're not going to like this, but I have to pack your shit and take you to J-Hall. If I were you, I would cooperate because if you don't, the ninja turtles will be here to drag you out, and if that happens, the other residents will think you're scared."

Andy said, "I don't care, I'm not moving."

Then I started to pack his stuff. He thought about it and then told me not to touch his stuff. He then tried to remove his items from my hands, and forced me to put my hands on him and I managed Andy to the floor. The staff on the hall was so fed up with Andy's crap they did nothing until they saw me restraining him, that's when they assisted and security arrived to mechanically restrain the resident with handcuffs and shackles. This could have totally been avoided, but some things have to be done the hard way.

Andy was put on J-Hall where there was a female JC who always had her group in super check. Her name was Ms. Willis. Ms. Willis ran that hall like those were her own kids, and whatever she wanted, she got. At this time, J-Hall was like the Yankees are to baseball, they had everything. When we dropped Andy off, she said, "I don't want him here. He is nasty to females and rude, and if he stays here, I can't promise that he won't be jumped." She told me to get his shit out of there. I called supervision, and after they spoke to Ms. Willis, Andy was packed up and sent to D-Hall where he got jumped anyway.

Some days were like playing musical chairs with the residents and the staff. I would work nine different places before the night was over. I started to totally hate coming to work now, but I guess I had to earn my stripes. With Morales and Ms. Sanchez running the building, I have faith that things would fall into place. Every now and then, I ran into Boo and he would check on me to see if I was okay. I had enough people to watch my back, but then there were people who resented my connections; and when my allies weren't around, these haters would throw a monkey wrench in my flow.

During this time, I was in court fighting for the custody of my children. The job was a good look; it showed that I had stability and financial security. I hired a paid lawyer, a friend of mine from high school, Sebastian Tavares. He was on my high school football team and became a big-shot family lawyer after college. Sebastian had an office on Madison Avenue in New York City and told me he would get me custody of my children. I was so nervous at this time, the thought of not having my children in my life scared the hell out of me.

In court, Sebastian did his thing. When the judge granted me custody, I felt like Rocky Balboa when he finally won a match. I wanted to drop to the floor and kiss the judge. Finally, justice was served. I wasn't trying to take their mother out of their life; I just felt that I provided the best situation for them, and the judge agreed. Men getting custody of their children is rare. I was very lucky, and with the help of Sebastian, we were always prepared.

After getting that monkey off my back, I didn't let much of what happened on the job bother me. I had an extra bounce in my step and had another story to tell during my rap session because the only thing these young men needed to hear was how to win in life. I was a winner. Not just because I got custody of my children but because I never gave up. I hate going in court buildings as much as I hate going in hospitals, but I never stopped going to court because it was my soul purpose in life to be with my kids.

So many of the residents were happy for me because they never stuck to anything long enough to reap the rewards, and they just appreciated my honesty. I told them, "Now, when you go to court, say a prayer, hold your head up high, and represent your life." And I told them that doubters should fuel you. I told them that while I was in court, it was important to sit up straight and look people in their eyes when I spoke. Most of them talked with their heads down and never looked an adult in the eyes when they spoke. We practiced that; we would have a staring contest to see who would flinch first and the winner would get an extra snack or get to stay up later than their level permitted them to.

I said that good manners and appearance is something the judges considered when making their decision. They were so motivated by my words I empowered their hopes. Some of them saw this as rhetoric, but to most it was gospel; and they viewed me as their role model. I can't express how satisfying this was for my psyche. I felt like the conductor of a train leading these kids to better decisions. It's like the movie *The Matrix*, it always comes down to the red or blue pill. Which one will you choose?

CHAPTER SEVEN

———— ◆•◆◆•◆ ————

It's time to motivate, build and elevate,
blind deaf and dumb we have to
change their mind state

—Brand Nubians
"Wake Up"

A S AMBIGUOUS A THOUGHT AS it might have been to say that I had mastered this craft, it started to shape out that way. The one thing I lacked at this point was to have my own hall. Being the newest man on my tour made it seem like pipe dreams; I accepted my role as the go-to-guy. As the go-to-guy I was responsible for all the dirty work—when nobody wanted to go to the hospital they sent me, I gave all the other male JCs duty frees, and I was assigned the one-to-one residents nobody wanted to work with. It was awful, but I gained the respect of my peers because I didn't complain. I took it like a man, but I didn't like it.

I think I got my patience from my mother. She always handled her business and never bitched about it. I don't think I've ever seen her suck her teeth, and in the end, she managed to get what she wanted from hard work. My mother was a college professor. After my father died, her goal was to move my brother and me from the hood and into a more diverse environment because to her, it was always about the quality of life and to be around people who cared about their neighborhood and their neighbors.

I quickly saw that my work environment didn't share those same sentiments. One JC who worked in admissions would always tell me, "You're such a nice guy, just remember the squeaky wheel gets the oil." Once I caught on to what he meant, I started to speak up, but other JCs would tell me they went through the same thing when they started. I just wanted my own hall, a place where I could consistently go and mold a group to mirror my personality. It was around this time that JC Digga who worked E-Hall was dealing with some personal shit outside the building. He got in trouble for selling illegal clothes in the street and come to find out he falsified his paperwork to get the job and gave a fake name, which the agency saw as an opportunity to fuck with him. See, we couldn't get in any domestic trouble or we could be disciplined, so getting arrested was a violation of our code of conduct.

Digga was an African dude with street swagger, even though most of his clothes were bootleg. The residents loved the hell out of him because he wasn't with nothing; he constantly told supervision to stick it. He was a hot head and the administration wanted to get rid of him.

When he stopped coming to work, he was transferred to the night tour and eventually axed; but with Digga off the tour, this was my opportunity to have E-Hall as a permanent hall. His partner was a middle-aged black woman named Ms. Mays. Ms. Mays was in the service and used her military background to work for her on the job. She didn't play with the residents for nothing.

I hate to gain from the loss of the next man, but I had to take advantage of this opportunity. The residents weren't thrilled that I replaced Digga, and I wasn't too thrilled to work with this group either. They were a bunch of ree-rees. This was the same group of residents who turned it up and were responsible for my suspension. They cared only about themselves. Most of them were receiving medication for some level of mental illness: anxiety, ADHD, and bipolar disorder to name a few. And then there were others who took advantage of the free service and made up their illness to get medication to get a buzz or to sell to other residents. They were all followers, and it made them feel tough to appear crazy.

To be normal wasn't normal. It was a form of dumbing down which was contagious in the hood. The reality is that some of them were the children of crack babies, so it was kind of loss-loss. The real crime even worse than men walking away from their paternal responsibilities was leaving these children to be raised by these fucked-up mothers. Most of them didn't have a nurturing bone in their body; they were struggling little girls who didn't even have a high school diploma. "A 40 and a blunt that's all she really wants." Now you can say Cîroc and a blunt. Meanwhile, we take care of their child. As long as her benefits don't get cut, it's a paid vacation from motherhood. Real talk, they're our kids now until they get hurt, then mama sees dollar signs and comes looking for a lawsuit. Then she wants to start acting like she cares. In any event, I had to establish structure, something these kids never had at home.

The first day we worked together, it went well. I knew Ms. Mays was tight that Digga was transferred to the night tour, but she was willing to give me a chance. Working E-Hall wasn't easy; these were the youngest, most mentally challenged residents in the building. People referred to them as the "spider monkeys" because they would never sit still, plus they were the most difficult residents to deal with because most of them had anger management problems. No wonder nobody was lining up to fill Digga's spot, nobody wanted to work there.

These kids on E-Hall generated the most incidents in the building from fighting and accidents. Accidents like a hang nail, a headache, or the ball hit them in the gym. You required extra patience for this group. At this point, it didn't matter to me, I just wanted to lead a hall. The residents would give me a hard time because I didn't have a style like Digga, and I never took chances like he did. Plus, I didn't dress like him or wear jewelry. To them, I was corny. The only thing I had in common with these kids was the same color skin. If they gave cool points for street credibility, I had zero; I wasn't about that life. Imagine Theo Huxtable from the *Cosby Show* working in this environment. Yeah, that was me. Even Mr. Hoffman, the only white JC, had more street cred than I did.

Speaking about Hoffman, the times I worked with him, I learned a ton. He talked a lot, but he knew his shit. Everybody was leery of who he knew, but he was just a white dude from the hood; he didn't know anybody in the corporate office. The suits downtown treated him like white trash and looked down on him like they did us. He'd joke because I was from Riverdale and my life was more sheltered than his. You had to give him props because in this environment, he was the minority and he was never uncomfortable. The residents didn't test him because he was smart and he had combat skills from his time in the service; he was not the one to fuck with. I got called a white boy by the residents more than Hoffman, but I would quickly tell them, "Sounds good, but know that the jokes on you because anytime you make fun of me for talking proper, you're playing yourself."

Whenever I worked the hall, I told the residents, "Don't let the way I talk or the way I dress get you hurt." Sometimes, I had to make examples of some of them because they were always testing me. Soft to them was being nice; they only respected tough, rough, and mean motherfuckers who would throw them around and put a foot in their ass. But that wasn't my style. I tried to tell them that being treated like an animal can't feel good, and that's how society wants you to feel that you only respect being treated like an animal.

This group had a hard time comprehending my counseling. I was forced to restrain them more than I wanted because they just wouldn't adjust to my style. Supervision would question my ability to control the group because it appeared that they wouldn't listen to me. It was a blessing to have Ms. Mays because she wouldn't hesitate to get in their ass. She was a yeller. She would scream on them so bad I would stand up straight for fear that she would yell at me for slouching. The sad truth of the matter is that most of these kids were little boys trying to act tough. Most of my rap sessions were like hygiene 101 because some of them have never taken showers or used deodorant, by that I mean they were so young that they were still taking baths at home. Then there were the bedwetters. Dealing with them involved denial because they refused to believe that the stench of urine was coming from their room. Some other residents would see this as an opportunity to instigate the situation by teasing those kids until it led to a fight. It broke my heart to see children as young as ten put in this environment just to be exposed to everything bad in life by a fifteen-year-old who cared about nothing. After a week, the younger residents were under the wing of the older ones, being used as a pop-off dummy.

These kids would fight over the most idiotic shit. "He keeps looking at me", "I was sitting there first", "That's my shirt", "I had the ball first," and the classic "You think I'm pussy." The reality is that they thought everybody thought they were pussies; there was a constant struggle to prove themselves.

In my rap sessions, I would emphasize the importance of not worrying about what other people thought of you, but it didn't register. Their insecurities were so strong, fighting was the only way they felt validation. Sometimes, it was good to have an older resident on the hall so he could tell them how childish they behaved, plus, the younger residents wouldn't challenge them. But after a while, the older residents would start bullying the younger ones; such goes the circle of life. It was my job to maintain order. With the help of Ms. Mays, we made a good team. She was good because unlike the other female JCs, she allowed me to be the man on the hall and would back me up. Every now and then, we bumped heads. If she thought I made a bad decision, she would overrule me and take it to supervision. She would tell me, "I know you're mad, but I have to save you from yourself." I started to take chances just to be more cool with the residents, but thanks to Ms. Mays, I was quickly put in check, because the last thing I needed was to get suspended trying to make the residents happy. She would say, "I'm not going to lose my job because you want to be like Digga." A lot of times, two JCs would get disciplined for the actions of one. Ms. Mays was not going out like that, and I had to respect that.

Our job on E-Hall was always challenging. Supervision kept sending us older residents who would always take over the hall. These residents would not follow our rules and would try to disrespect Ms. Mays. She was quick to not give extra and take everything away if she felt it was excessive.

When she conducted security searches of the rooms, she would go in each room and remove piles of extra clothes from the residents' rooms. Every resident is supposed to have two of everything, but some would have four shirts or five pairs of socks. She would conduct searches during my rap sessions, and every now and then, I would catch one resident watching her remove stuff from their room.

One time, this one resident wasn't with it and went to take his stuff back, literally right from Ms. Mays hands. They were having a tug of war with his shirts, and I intervened and eventually had to restrain the dude because he wanted to hit her. This was a regular thing. Every day, a resident would try to violate Ms. Mays, and like her little brother, I would get involved and have to drop a resident for calling her a bitch or refusing to listen to her. This was tiring, and it got annoying fast.

As much as I loved Ms. Mays, I got frustrated with her constantly going in on the residents for every little thing. I would never go against her because if they were going to move one of us, it would be me. She had more seniority than me, and very few people wanted to work with her because they thought she was too bossy. Plus, supervision would always lean on the side of harder discipline. I just got tired of restraining kids for talking back. There were days the residents would turn it up if they saw she was there. Nothing was working. I was restraining two and three residents a day.

Any day she wasn't there I got a break from all the incidents. Ms. Mays had two sons in their twenties; she was even a grandmother, I know they didn't want their mother assaulted by any of these punks and nor did I. In some ways, she reminded me of my mother, but she was more like an older sister. She was from Brooklyn, and like the residents from Brooklyn, she wasn't afraid of anybody. If a TC would try to move me, she would get in his ass and get me back to the hall. I don't know what she said, but she had a temper and they couldn't outtalk her—she knew how to shut people up.

The one TC who got on my nerves, she kept him off my ass. When dude would come to the hall to sign the book, he would always look for something wrong to fuck with me about. But if Ms. Mays was there, she would throw it back at him like, "Why would you ask him when I'm standing right here?" He would feel stupid. But if she wasn't there or I had another assignment, this dude would try to embarrass me. His name was TC Herrera, he was from Panama, and he was the motherfucka that nobody liked. This dude was so damn surly it was pathetic. He actually liked not being liked. He's a dark-skinned guy in his early fifties, about medium built, and he ran Fairvue with an iron fist. You would have thought we were a military outfit the way he carried on. Dude swore he was General Patton and damn sure acted that way. Most people would make the mistake and assume that he was black because of his skin complexion, but once he started talking Spanish, you knew otherwise.

Rumor has it that he used to be the TC at Greenwood, and they hated him so much the whole tour refused to work if he stayed there. So they transferred him to Fairvue. He is still here today, and that was more than thirteen years ago. Our tour would never stand together and protest him because our building had more structure and the penalties were more severe at Fairvue. Doing something like that would have had us all in the street unemployed.

The day Ms. Mays retired for greener pastures in Arizona was a sad but happy day. I was losing a good partner, but for the first time, I had complete control of the hall. My days at work were more dictated by my relationship with the residents, not someone else. As much as I relished in the freedom, I regretted not having Ms. Mays there to defend me.

TC Herrera took this time to fuck with my manhood. I say manhood because it was more than just the job; to him it was personal, he just liked fucking with me. You know when somebody goes out of their way to fuck with you, they get pleasure embarrassing you in front of everybody. This dude loved to do this, I think because my bald head was shinier than his or something. People on the job liked me and I don't think he liked that. Sorry, I'm not mean like you. Sorry, I like to laugh and enjoy my time with some of the residents. Get a life.

At the end of the day, these were children, not grown men; so, take that screw face to Rikers Island and regulate the lives of older inmates. Be Burgermeister Meisterburger over there. You remember Burgermeister from the Christmas special *Santa Claus Is Comin to Town*? That was Herrera, grumpy as all get out. He was a real herb; I could never understand how the other TCs bought his act. It was so scripted. But as I continued to work there, I saw that they couldn't stand his ass either. They figured, if this guy wants to go above and beyond the call of duty, knock yourself out. Anybody that gets off bringing people down has issues. It's one thing playing that tough-guy shit on kids, but when you use your position to intimidate people you lead, you're the real loser.

Most of the senior JCs didn't put up with his shit. They were quick to tell him, "We can take it outside." He didn't want that, so he would talk to them in private and his tone would change. I just never saw leadership where you weaken the strengths of the people you lead. He was the worst. There were days I didn't want to go into work because I felt I was going to snap and choke him. He was a master at getting under the skin of people. He would say things like, "Tuck in your shirt, don't sit in your chair like that," or if you were late at roll call, he would lock you out. If he saw that you handled a difficult situation, well, he would give you a harder assignment to find your breaking point, totally exhausting your mental and physical will.

I remember, once he wrote me up for playing ping-pong with a resident. He said because I was the only staff with the group, I need to be watching them and not playing with them. How wack is that? I would tell Platter, "Tell your man to back off." He laughed and said, "Herrera is Herrera, don't let that bother you."

I will give him one thing he was consistent because everybody hated him. He would micromanage everything—from the color of your sneakers to the time you turned off the lights for bedtime to the minute you returned from a break. In his narcissism, he just assumed that everyone was in awe of his presence, but none of his shit fazed me. I just saw him as another dude pumping his chest. He was the genesis of most of our frustration, and there was always a general air of malaise whenever he was on duty.

But if you bent up a kid and hospitalized him, he was your best friend. He loved to restrain the residents and had a reputation for hurting them. This dude must have had over thirty allegations for restraining residents. He ran the building like a dictator and called his tour IHOP (International House of Pain). Really? Dude, these are kids. It's not that serious. To him, if you didn't make a resident cry during a restraint, you did a bad job. There were times I wanted to pull him off them because he wouldn't stop until he made them cry; he got off on that. What a douche bag. That's somebody's child.

These were not good kids at all, but there were layers of shit that made them this way. Once you break down the layers, they were more receptive, and you could avoid a physical altercation. TC Herrera only saw it one way—his way, and nobody got in his way.

The agency never would stop him; they would find ways to protect him because they liked how he controlled us. We were scared to fuck up because we didn't want to be disciplined and have it affect our money. To him, a good resident was a resident in fear. He treated the supervisors like his little cronies and treated us like punching bags; he would even reprimand us in front of the residents. How can the residents respect the JCs if the TCs speak to them like children? These were young men who looked up to us. How can they respect us if they see us being sonned by supervision?

Some residents would say, "You gonna let him talk to you like that?" As a leader, when your team shines, you shine and when they fail, you fail. That do-as-I-say-not-as-I-do shit doesn't work, that's setting people up to fail. Shaming people and embarrassing them is poor leadership. I don't know how they do things in his country; but in America, success is accomplished by building up your team, not breaking them down. He knew he had our balls in a sling because most of us needed the job, so we ate his bullshit. The supervisors weren't any better, they followed his lead. They had a way of zapping your pride as a person and always criticized but rarely complimented the JCs.

It was difficult to take orders from people who had less education than me, but that was just my reality. They got off on embarrassing you; I started to tune them out because I knew that the only way they felt better was to make other people feel bad. It felt like, sometimes, we were being punished for all the suffering they dealt with growing up and having people better than them. It was so fucking childish. Man the fuck up.

The residents saw them as player haters, always stopping the flow of the JCs. Most of these supervisors and TCs weren't even from this country. To be a leader of men, you have to inspire others to want to follow your lead. It just seemed like they were more threatened by us than wanting to lead us.

They looked down on African-American men and boys, and loved to take shots at them. Black people do discriminate against other blacks. Most men see African-American men as lazy and cocky, this definitely influenced how they treated the male residents. In their country, boys didn't speak to their elders the way American kids do. In Africa or Panama, you might get tied to a tree and whipped for disrespecting an older person, so they had no patience for slick-talking boys or slick-talking men.

Most of the JCs were older street cats who related well with the residents and got their respect without all the tough talk and bravado. The cultural divide was very prevalent, but the agency ignored it because what these guys had over everybody else was good time and leave. They came to work and never took off; it's hard to try to make a point if you don't show up to work.

Most of the African-American men didn't have good time and leave, and if they did, they were never on time. That CP (Color People) time shit wasn't a myth. I needed my dough; taking off wasn't an option, but there were some people who never showed up and the agency rarely disciplined them. Hard to believe with an agency that profiled itself on structure. I didn't get it. People were getting stuck every day just because some people wanted to work only three days a week.

I hated this in the beginning because I could never have a life. I would be so fuckin' tired after working three doubles in a row, I would fall asleep on the hall while the residents were in the day area. The residents would say, "Mr. Geez, wake up." Some would try to put paper in my mouth if my mouth was open. I was fortunate none of them took that opportunity to pop on somebody or else it would have been my ass. Most of my coworkers would get suspended for this reason, and the agency never considered the workload. There were days I would go to roll call and I would be the only man on my tour who came to work. I wondered why didn't anybody give me the memo that everybody was banging out. Some people took this opportunity to get paid.

JC Carter changed my view of overtime. He looked at it like we don't need a second job and we can buy nice things for our families. With overtime, Carter was making more money than the supervisors and the TCs. Once, he clocked over one hundred thousand in one year. He wasn't alone; there were several JCs making bread with overtime, but this was short lived.

When the agency saw that the parking lot was full of luxury cars owned by JCs, they put a cap on their salaries, restricting them from volunteering for overtime. What creeps, I guess they didn't want to see black people living large and phat. This was a slick tactic to regulate our incomes. The flip side of this was that there were people who didn't want to get stuck, but were forced because of the cap. This made no sense. You make people stay who don't want to, and you send people home who want to stay. This could only happen to black people. Anywhere else, staff would be rewarded for working extra hours, but on the job that was predominantly black, they saw us making more money as a threat.

In the beginning, I never wanted to get stuck. It wasn't about the money. To me, I just didn't want to be in the building all the time. As hopeful as I was that I could be helpful to these kids, I could not ignore the feeling of lost dreams that resonated in the building. It became depressing to watch these young black and Hispanic kids living like this, and the more hours I spent there, the more I felt locked up too.

Standing outside was definitely a better feeling than being inside, it felt like real life. Sometimes, I just had to get way from Herrera, but as much as I tried to avoid him, it was impossible. He was my tour commander, and we had the same days off. He would even take his vacations when I did. Talk about cock blocking. I just wanted dude to get off my body. For real.

One day, I got a duty free, and who do I see in the staff lounge on his duty free? You guessed it, Herrera. I couldn't act like I wasn't going to sit down because I just heated my food, so I sat with him. He said some things that were reminiscent of something my high school football coach once told me. He said that if he didn't think I had potential, he would never critique me, and then he said something that might have been the best advice I ever got. He said, "Work the job, don't let the job work you." That was deep because the job was working me in ways I couldn't control. I told him that I appreciated the pep talk. I still thought he was a fake tough guy, but I gave him props for the advice.

Sometimes, I forgot where I was. Even though they were kids, this was jail and I always had to remind myself that this was a detention center and not a youth camp. Despite everything, some of them were so likable. When I connected with one of them, I felt like God put me here to be the messenger and to help guide them in the right direction.

One kid who stood out more than the others was Dayvon (Day). Day was a fifteen-year-old kid from Harlem, and I could tell that he had no experience in this environment. He got arrested for a crime that he said he didn't commit. It was obvious that he came from a good family because he had good manners and he was well-groomed, like his nails were clean and he didn't have any cuts or bruises on his hands, arms, or face.

His case was high profile, and we couldn't talk about it because it was all over the news. Day and his friends were accused of a crime that they didn't do, but it didn't matter. They were in the wrong place at the wrong time. He was stressed, he had no priors, didn't hang with the type of kids in the building, and he had ambition. His dream was to attend college and start his own business.

Most of the kids on the hall were proud to be locked up, like it was a badge of honor or a rite of passage. Like the fat ugly guy saying he's pretty, they swore their incarceration made them valid. Totally making something bad good. It's the sickest shit I've ever seen. These kids would talk about going to the Rock (Rikers Island) like it was Disney World. For the life of me, I never understood that mindset neither did Dayvon. He was ashamed to be in this position. He felt that having this record would hold him back, but I tried to reassure him that when he turned sixteen and was found not guilty, his record would be good. But he wasn't buying that, he was stuck on everything being bad and would stay in his room. Some staff thought he was suicidal because he wouldn't interact with anyone.

His codefendant on the other hand was having the time of his life. His name was Joseph, and he bragged about their case. I realized that Joseph wanted acceptance from the other residents and fabricated his story for personal gain. All this did was damage the relationship of two good friends; Day knew that he was lying, but instead of blowing up his spot, he let it rock.

When Joseph joined a gang, Day had enough. He flipped on Joseph and called him a bitch-ass follower. He said, "You're fucking up my shit. If you want to stay here, that's on you, but stop talking about the case." I had to separate them, and at that moment, most of the other residents sided with Day. As more evidence surfaced, it started to look like they didn't do it.

The other residents respected what Day said about wanting to leave. You weren't a pussy for saying you were homesick. Joseph was transferred to J-Hall because codefendants can't be on the same hall.

While Day waited for his court date, he got more comfortable on the hall and raised his level to closet boy. As closet boy, he was responsible for getting all the laundry out and restocking the clothing inventory. His privileges allowed him to stay up the latest and he could attend special programs. If Fairvue had elections for student government president, he would have won it hands down. He had an electric personality and his candor was trustworthy, it was hard not to like him. I just imagined, if they would have labeled him suicidal, that would have made him suicidal.

He flourished as a leader on the hall, and what I liked about him is that he was neutral, meaning he wasn't in a gang. He wasn't a punk and he wasn't a bully. Nobody had anything bad to say about him. His likability was on high, and even his haters had to admit he was a cool kid.

I felt bad for him because his case dragged for no reason. Well, there was a reason. The prosecutor didn't want to look bad, so they had to blame somebody. The press likes to paint a grim picture for inner-city youth. I knew Day was getting tired of the same ol' same, but I would tell him that this too shall pass. It's not easy being in a building you can't leave when you didn't do anything.

For six months, Day stayed at Fairvue before he was found not guilty and went home. Joseph wasn't so lucky; he caught another charge being a pop-off dummy for the gang he joined and stayed longer. When Day left, I was happy for him. Rarely do these kids experience happy endings, but in Day's case, that was an accurate assessment.

I wasn't always a good judge of character, I will never forget the time I got close to this one resident that I didn't know why he was there, but when I found out it changed everything.

CHAPTER EIGHT

$\diamond\diamond\diamond\diamond\diamond$

You see my aura's positive I don't promote no junk
You see I'm far from a bully and I ain't a punk

—Phife Dawg of a Tribe Called Quest
"Check the Rhime"

His name was Jerry. He was an African-American kid who was very polite and well-mannered. He didn't blend well with the other residents mainly because he was from Long Island. He didn't know anybody from Harlem or the Bronx, which was where most residents were from. He wasn't the average kid who came from a gang or a kid from the block. He enjoyed football, and we talked all the time about the Jets and different players. He told the other residents that he got arrested for punching his teacher in school, which made them like him more because they respected rude boys.

Later on, during the tour, Jerry asked Ms. Gordy, the case manager on the hall, if he could make a weekly call to his mother, and in an abrupt way, Ms. Gordy explained to him in a real nasty tone, "Give me a minute. I'm doing something right now. Give me a minute."

At first, I didn't quite understand at the time where the negativity was coming from; and because I liked the kid, I asked Ms. Gordy why all the shade. She gestured for me to come step into her office and closed the door for privacy. I then asked again why she wouldn't give Jerry a phone call. Ms. Gordy then explained on the resident's arrest record and the real reason why he was here. She told me that he was arrested for raping his four-year-old sister, and his mother threw him out of the house and reported the allegation to the police which led to the arrest, and not the reason that Jerry said at the beginning.

My mouth dropped to the floor and my hands began to sweat. So many thoughts were racing in my head. I stood in Ms. Gordy's office for nearly five minutes to gain my composure. I was so disgusted, I wanted to puke and just go home so that I wouldn't have to face Jerry. He was only fourteen years old and his sister was four. My daughter Rosemary was also four.

I couldn't handle this; I was expected to act like I didn't know about his record. It was difficult to hide my emotions. When I stepped into the dayroom area and the same young man walked up to me and asked, "Mr. Geez, why you have that look on your face like you saw a ghost?" the only thing I could say was, "Please, give me a minute." I was sitting and talking with somebody who enjoyed taking advantage of a little girl.

After I left Ms. Gordy, I went to the bathroom and washed my face; I put my whole head in the sink and opened my eyes. I just wanted to feel the pain of the water burning my eyes to escape the thought of this punk violating somebody she should trust.

When I left the bathroom, I tried to avoid him the rest of the night, but I sensed that he knew that I knew. Now I know why the agency didn't want us to know because of how I was acting. It was a policy that we don't ask them what they were accused of—the quote stating, "Don't ask don't tell." We weren't even told of their medical condition, unless it was visible. Even if a resident came in close contact with the Hepatitis B virus, we wouldn't know. Sometimes, it was like working with live snakes. Who was protecting us? This was a union issue, but the union dealt with other situations like pensions and salaries, but our right to know was just as important.

Back to Jerry, I had a real hard time communicating with him after I knew why he was there. When the other residents found out that he lied about his arrest and that he was there for the big R, they beat him up. I came to work one day and found out he was moved to the SHU for his protection.

I never spoke to him again, and a part of me felt bad that I couldn't help him. But I couldn't come to grips with what he did.

I was human and I wasn't trained to separate my feelings from something so close. I felt over my head. Counselors need counseling too. Sometimes, this agency expected us to be so robotic and not catch feelings, but that was unrealistic. We weren't impervious to what some of these kids were here for. The agency didn't have time to help me, I had to bottle up my emotions and keep working.

I hope Jerry got the help he needed because Lord knows he needed it. Protecting him wasn't the answer; he needed to be in a hospital to find out why he did it. If I could be fooled by his personality and charm, how many little girls will he schemed in the future? Being locked up would just make him worse. In this environment, he would learn more criminal behavior. He needed help—real help.

After Jerry was smoked off the hall, that was just the beginning of the many challenges I would encounter as the lead JC on E-Hall. A day later, I was confronted with one of the most disruptive personality in a resident. His name was Tarik, but he went by the nickname Scoop. He was a Crip and from Brooklyn. When he was brought to the building from Greenwood, he was wildin' out from the gate, it took two admission staff and three security guards to get him out of the van.

Scoop was five foot two and stocky like Mike Tyson with a snarl like a pit bull. His disposition was staticky; and when he was put on G-Hall, he came in the door throwing up Cs like he was at a party yelling, "Cs up." The staff on G-Hall locked all the residents in to avoid an incident because most of them were Bloods. But Scoop didn't care. He told the staff to let them all out so they could get it in. He said, "This is now a Crip-Hall," which infuriated the other residents to the core.

It was amazing how gully most of the kids from Brooklyn were, it was like there was something in the water. Their mentality was to always take over, it never failed. I went to college with a lot of cats from Brooklyn and they were the grittiest. They moved like they were bulletproof.

Scoop was the same way; dude wasn't afraid of anybody. To avoid a riot, supervision moved him to E-Hall. All I remember was seeing this man-child with a personal escort of four security guards to room 215. I looked at my partner and we had that look like, *what atomic bomb did they just drop on us?*

While in his room, Scoop just paced back and forth like a caged lion waiting for the door to open. I realized that this was the assignment of my JC life—if I failed this test, it would be front page news in the building. We would have to let him out eventually. He was talking crazy in his room; he would say, "You're going to need more than two COs to handle me." I was saying to myself, *what kid talks like that?* A kid who fights men. And secondly, who refers to counselors as COs? This kid was groomed to the ways of jail mentality from birth, something passed down from multiple generations.

He was shadowboxing with his shirt off, working up a sweat. We were leery on how to approach this kid without getting ourselves hurt. The other residents were shook. They had never seen a resident take on an entire building.

Before we had to make a decision, TC Platter and Supervisor Cook came to the hall to see Scoop. They didn't hesitate and went in his room; they didn't need the cavalry. To them, he was a small fry in their kitchen. They made him sit on his bed and they gave Scoop the scoop on how things are done at Fairvue. Scoop was accustomed to the freedom of Greenwood; he wasn't used to a structured environment. Cook took off his jacket, rolled up his sleeves, and said, "Let's do this."

Scoop was shocked that a supervisor was that gully, but Cook used to be a boxer and he was about that life. In Greenwood, Scoop was used to the staff being afraid of him, but Platter and Cook weren't fazed. Scoop turned down the opportunity to tussle with Cook and just heard them out. They told him what they expected from him and if he didn't comply, he would be on room confinement every day. It's funny how when you show no fear these kids will back down.

Scoop quickly fell in line after that conversation and became a positive leader on the hall. No resident came to E-Hall trying to take over or turn it up or they would have to deal with Scoop. He couldn't interact with the other residents on other halls because he was the only Crip in the building, and all the other residents wanted his head. Nobody forgot how he punk'd them on G-Hall; they were totally embarrassed.

Once, one of them saw Scoop sitting in the cafe as they were exiting the visiting area, they punched their fist as if to say, *we're going to get you.* But Scoop found it comical and would laugh. He would say, "Yo, Geez, peep this clown playing with himself." Then he turned towards the glass to address the kid. He said, "Do you know who I am? You better ask somebody. I will slap dog shit out of you, bitch-ass fuckboy. Fuck off before I put my hand through this glass and snooze you." Then he would go back to eating like whatever. He wasn't even daunted by this dude banging on the glass. You could tell this kid was on another level; his sarcasm was infectious. He would say the slickest shit straight out of the gangster chronicles, the type of shit Jay-Z says to embarrass his foes.

Scoop was a lone soldier, and pound for pound, he might have been the strongest kid in the building. When I would arm wrestle him, I would struggle to win. Nobody wanted to give him a fair one because one-on-one he would have ripped them to shreds. Scoop was built like a bulldozer; he would do twenty-five push-ups in ten-second clips. He's been shot at, stabbed, and jumped before; this kiddie-jail shit was child's play to him.

Being Crip was passed down from his father who was Crip and was in jail on a murder charge. His brothers would visit him and tell him who to pop on in the building, and Scoop would carry out that assignment like a hitman. For all his tumultuous ways, he never violated my tour and in a rap session in front of thirteen other residents, I asked him about it. I said, "For all the turning up you do, how come you don't turn it up on me?" He said, "Because I know you care, some of the staff are here for the check but you want to help us."

I never saw it like that, but Scoop broadened my view of what my purpose was. Scoop and I talked a lot, and being with him was like hanging with one of my boys; he was real mature for sixteen. We would talk about everything from females, to cars, to clothes, to music. It reminded me of those boring weekends in college sitting on the dorm just chopping it up with my dorm-mates.

Scoop outgrew Fairvue, and his case sent him to Rikers Island before he went home. We never spoke again, but for the time he was there, it was fun to have a big dog control the puppies. That wasn't the first time a resident validated my counseling.

Nothing made me brush my shoulders more than the time I took my own children to City Island for dinner. City Island was like a night on the town for a family from the Bronx. While I was sitting at a table, this man approached me and asked what I was drinking because he wanted to buy me a drink. He said, "My son over there told me you looked out for him when he was locked up." His son came over and we embraced. I was surprised because I restrained him a few times. It was a happy moment that could have turned ugly if I was an asshole to his son. Moments like that negated any negative feelings I had about the job.

It was around this time that the word was that Spofford would be shut down and that we would be forced to wear uniforms. We still wore street clothes, and the agency wanted us to appear more unified. Greenwood was making some changes too and transferred a JC that they didn't want there anymore. His name was Mr. Luke.

Luke was an OG from Brooklyn in his late fifties. He was removed from Greenwood for several suspensions and they were just tired of his bullshit. Luke did what he wanted when he wanted whenever he wanted. He was quick to tell supervision to go fuck their self. He was with the agency so long he remembers when Iron Mike was locked up. He's been working for the agency for over twenty-five years. When he started, the residents were detained on a barge, and there the staff used to beat the shit out of them.

Nobody could tell him shit. TC Platter would try to give him a post, but wherever he worked, there was a problem. It got so bad in roll call that all the other JCs refused to work with him. Carter didn't want to work with him because he would have everybody's door open, Pena didn't want him on the hall because he'd have all the residents doing push-ups in the day area, and Hoffman didn't want him because he once punched a resident in the chest and sent that resident to the hospital. From the gate, he rubbed everybody the wrong way.

When they tried to give him a smaller hall by himself, he complained that it was too stuffy and he couldn't breathe. Once, he was so mad that he got stuck he called 911 and said that he was having a heart attack; and unknown to supervision, an ambulance showed up to take him out on a stretcher. He was faking the whole time; he just didn't want to get stuck.

One day, when I was bringing E-Hall from the gym, he met us on the staircase and tells me that he is going to be my new partner; I didn't know what to say. I was at a loss for words. Platter spoke to me at the end of the night and said they literally had nowhere to put him, and because I was flexible, they felt it was a good fit. What could I say? It was a backhanded compliment; I didn't want to be flexible, but I never complained like everybody else.

Luke was a character. When we worked together, they would call us *Sanford and Son* because he looked like he could pass for my father. He was short and stocky with a bald head, and he would come to work in a suit, a baller hat, and gator shoes. You could tell that he was a gambler, drug dealer, and a stick-up kid at some time in his life. Luke was a true-to-life-old-school hustler; he looked like a pimp. He told me that on the side, he arranged bachelor parties which meant he was about that life.

When he got to the hall, he would remove his suit jacket and shirt and worked in a white tank. For an old dude, he was pretty brollic. He would out push-up all the residents, and he would play basketball with them in the gym in his gators. Once in the gym, he got under the skin of one of the residents; Luke would always cheat to win. He kept fouling the resident in a game of three on three. He would say, "Stop being a pussy and just play ball." It got so bad I had to separate them. I was saying to myself, *why is this old man ready to fight a fifteen-year-old kid?*

His methods were straight old-school. He got to Fairvue before they installed cameras on the halls, so he was very lucky because he broke all the rules. He would line the residents up and whoever could take a punch from him in the chest, he would let them stay up late.

People would tell me he's going to get me fired with his bullshit, and I started to see their point. Working with Luke was like my training day every day. I felt like the rookie in the movie *Training Day*—Luke was Alonzo and I was Jake. He would always take like six cigarette breaks and refused to get stuck. He would walk out the building at the end of the tour and dare anybody to stop him. He didn't care and would only listen to TC Platter. He would tell me all the other supervisors could kiss his ass.

It would just be my luck that I would go from a structured environment to an unstructured one; Luke got respect from the residents, but he had no respect for the supervisors. He was the type of dude you didn't want to fuck with on the street. He had enough shit in his car to be locked up himself. He had enough booze in his trunk to run a liquor store and cartons of cigarettes that he transported from down south, he even had a gun in his glove compartment. This guy was trouble on wheels. He knew all the thugs and the grimmest people on the street, all the older inmates locked up on Rikers Island or in upstate correctional facilities knew Luke and loved him—because he pulled the man out of them when he was their counselor.

Luke had good ideas, though he instituted rules that were of a boot-camp nature. He would write these positive messages on poster boards and tape them all over the hall for the residents to read. On our tour, he would make them recite his twelve rules together and taught them a song about being locked up. I can't lie, the shit was inspiring, but on the flip side, he was a motherfucker to the residents too. If they acted up at dinner, he would make them stand in one line until one by one he allowed them to sit down. This went on for over an hour, and every day we restrained a resident for refusing to keep standing.

Luke was intimidating; he always wore these terminator shades that made him like a drill sergeant. Once this kid refused to stay in line and recite the rules, and he got two other residents to follow him. He said, "Fuck that. I'm sticking it up, I'm sitting down," and he went to the bricks and was followed by the two other residents. Luke went behind the bricks, flipped it, and dragged the two residents to their doors. He'd say, "Geez, I don't have all fuckin' day. Open these motherfuckin' doors. These pussies are done for the night." Then he'd tossed them in their rooms like duffle bags. After seeing that, the third resident just stood by his door because he didn't want to be next.

Luke never used any of the restraining techniques we learned in training. Matter of fact, he told me he doesn't do training. He grabbed the residents like rag dolls and would use methods I can't begin to describe. I spent more time pulling Luke off a resident than actually restraining them; he was a walking allegation. Now I knew why most of the old-timers refused to work with him—because he always did shit to get you in trouble. He was a liability, and even the supervisors avoided him.

When they came on the hall to sign the logbook, Luke would ask them to hold so that he could get his medication for a heart condition. But this motherfucker would just go sit in his car to smoke a cigarette. After five minutes, the supervisor would leave and tell me to call them when he returned. I didn't want to get involved, but I would get stuck in the middle. I would always cover for Luke, another one of my bad choices on this job because Luke only cared about Luke.

Sometimes, he would return from his cigarette break and bring me hot tea. He would say, "I brought you some medicine." When I took a sip, it was lemon tea mixed with Hennessy. I would say, "Luke, you're a fuckin' wild boy." And the rest of the night we would get our sip on. When I would tell him supervision wants me to call them, he would call first, tell them to fuck off on the phone, and then hang up. They would write him up, and he would rip the write-up paper and throw it away.

His biggest nemesis was TC Herrera. Luke was on the job so long he remembers when Herrera was a JC. Once in roll call, TC Herrera told Luke to remove his hat, but instead he removed himself and left the building. This happened every day for two weeks. After talking with Platter, Luke started to remove his hat in roll call; but the asshole that Herrera was, he wanted to fuck with Luke and told him to remove his shades. At that point, Luke had enough and invited Herrera outside like men to handle it. Luke had to be removed and got suspended for his behavior.

When he returned, Herrera would find ways to annoy Luke for every little thing; it was like Herrera enjoyed the confrontation because he would try to put Luke in check in front of everybody. Luke would laugh at him; and whenever Herrera would call the hall, Luke would hang up the phone. Herrera would try to involve me by telling me to write an incident report about Luke refusing to answer the phone. I would call Platter to have him pull Herrera off my back and he would.

Herrera would hurt Luke in his pockets because every time he got suspended he lost money. Once, Luke showed me his check and it was for .35 cents. It cost more to make the paper his check was on, but Luke was good. You knew he had a side hustle because he always had money. Sometimes, he would just give me money and say do something nice with your kids. I would refuse, but he would say, "Take it. I would end up wasting on some bitch anyway."

He would tell me he had a lousy relationship with his son and regretted not doing more with him. I believed Luke had a few kids but he only mentioned one.

One day, Luke met Herrera outside and Herrera never fucked with Luke again. I don't know what happened but he stopped even saying his name. Luke was like a triple OG; he had goons everywhere. Those were the perks working with him. Supervision didn't bother me, and after his meeting with Herrera, he even left me alone.

The flip side is that Luke was just a pain in the ass. Once, he asked this resident who was on his way to visiting to see his mother if his mother was as pretty as he was, and the resident went ape shit and lost his mind. The resident wanted to fight Luke, and I had to restrain him to keep Luke from punching the resident in the face. It was fucked up because that resident ended up missing his visit.

Female JCs refused to work with him because he would talk down to them and would tell them to sit down and don't say shit. He got written up by them for sex discrimination. His write-ups were endless, and the agency wanted to get rid of him.

I don't know who he knew, but it was like he had nine lives. He never accepted fault; he always justified his actions. It was like trying to teach an old dog new tricks. I got tired of his act, and whenever

I attempted to take control, Luke would get in my way and kill my vibe. Some days, he would suck the life out of me and totally not respect my flow; and when I spoke to supervision about moving him, they wouldn't respect me either. I was stuck with him and we started to have a power struggle for the hall.

We even battled for the lights to be on at night. Some residents complained that they couldn't sleep with the lights on, but Luke wanted them on so he could read. When I would turn them off, he would turn them on. This would go on every night. I started to feel like the Lamont to his Fred; that *Sanford and Son* joke became a true prophecy. He even walked with a limp like Fred and talked like him too.

I got so fed up one night I just pulled him aside and said, "I was here before you. To make this work, we have to work together." He said, "When you grow balls and stop letting supervision push you around, then you can talk to me." I laughed. I said this old fart is crazy. He said, "I don't play second fiddle to nobody."

I would say to myself I'm not going to get him to understand anything I say. We agreed to disagree, but later I saw him fall back. Without saying anything, he started to say less, and told the residents before a rap session, "From now on, he's Batman and I'm Robin."

That was his way of saying he understood me. I realized that some people can't admit when they're wrong, and Luke was one of those people.

CHAPTER NINE

◆◆◆◆◆

You're a disgust, you know someone
that I can't trust, you'd
Steal mom's welfare and you'd run
and buy some dust and
Plus, I must say…bigshot you're not

—Slick Rick
"Hey Young World"

NOT ALL THE SUPERVISORS WERE assholes. Mrs. Rooney and Mr. Cook were two of the nicest and most supportive people in the whole agency. Mrs. Rooney was the sweetest thing, too good for Fairvue. She was a light-skinned black woman who looked like one of those throwback sisters from a Sidney Poitier/Bill Cosby movie. The job drained her, and you could tell she was asked to do too much; most of it were things she didn't agree with.

She always wore a yellow bandana to keep her hair together, and you could smell her through the hallway; she always smelled good. I loved when I got stuck because she supervised the night tour and I would get to see her. She was constantly fighting to keep her job and rarely had good things to say about the agency. Her morale was usually down, and when I talked to her, she would tell me to get out if I could.

At this point, I had redirected my life and totally abandoned my designing career. I felt my calling was to help these children find themselves, but Mrs. Rooney told me this agency would never allow me to do that because it's about the agency not the kids. She would tell me how the city was profiting off these children being locked up.

At the time, I didn't see it that way because I saw that these residents got what they deserved—you do the crime, you do the time. She then said, "So then why do they keep coming back?" I was confused, but she made me realize that it was a cycle that kept making a profit off them being arrested.

Nothing we did at Fairvue deterred residents from returning; it encouraged them. A part of me selfishly didn't want to agree with her because at the end of the day, if they kept getting locked up, I was employed. Mrs. Rooney just broke it down in a genocidal way. I appreciated the insight, but a part of me wasn't there yet.

Another good person, Mr. Cook was completely the opposite. He didn't give a fuck. He came from the school of hard knocks, and would tell me stories when he used to break kids arms for laughing on line. He was around the same age as Luke, and like Luke, he would wear a suit one day and a velour sweat suit the next.

Back in the day, he used to be a boxer and had the wit of a comedian. He looked like he could pass for the comedian Paul Moonie's brother. I liked him because he was brutally honest. He would tell you like it is and didn't care if your feelings were hurt. He told this one JC that he sucked as a counselor, and if it was up to him, he would be working in the kitchen. He would say, "How good do you make collar green because you don't know a damn thing about counseling children."

He knew which JCs were afraid of the residents and would pull their card in a heartbeat. He would tell them, "I hope you cashed your check because the kids on H-Hall are going to expect their Chinese food."

Cook liked me and defended me against TC Herrera. When Herrera would try to come at me for something stupid, Cook would tell him to back off. He would say, "Yo, big head, leave him alone, he's one of the good JCs. Why don't you go harass that fat-ass motherfucka on the SHU that's probably sleeping instead of working."

I loved when he was on duty because Herrera stayed in his office and let Cook run the show. Herrera didn't mess with Cook. When they were JCs, Cook was on the front line with him. Platter and Cook were buddies and they were president and vice president of the union back in the day, the two of them kept everyone off my back. They were like the Robin Hood and Little John of Fairvue, you could rely on them to come to the defense of the JCs before anybody else. It was amazing how much they cared, sometimes they cared more about our jobs than we did.

But as time went by, Cook stopped coming to work. His health started to fail, and he eventually never returned. When Cook stopped coming, my alliances were low and even Boo moved on. He got a job working for the Department of Parks and Recreation. I started to lean on the guidance of a senior JC who worked the night tour named Mr. Mann.

Mann was another old-timer who put twenty years in and knew the ins and outs of the agency. We would talk all night. When I got stuck, he would say, "Dr. Geez, it's relax time, put your feet up. I got this." He would do everything from the security search to the entries in the logbook, he even did the showers. He would always tell me, "If you have to restrain a resident, that's good counseling."

He taught me about my pension and emphasized that I prepare myself for retirement. I never thought about those things until we talked about it—life insurance, the best health care for me and my family. Mann went over everything with me, he made me realize how important it was for my future. He knew that the agency didn't care about us, but to him, that's no excuse to not care about my life outside these walls. He would tell me to work my hours, pay my bills, and live my life. He would remind me that the shit that goes on in here isn't real life, life is outside these walls. He would say, "This building is full of demons, and I'm not just talking about the residents." I couldn't agree more, I started to feel underappreciated and devalued in this place, but Mann made me realize that it was just a job. It didn't define me as a person.

The divide between JC and person was something I struggled with, I mean people shouldn't have to ask to go to the bathroom or eat when they're hungry. I didn't want to admit it, but being a juvenile counselor started to enslave my mind. To make things worse, fewer men were coming to work; and between Luke and me, one of us had to be moved.

Even though I was there first, supervision moved me, and the excuse was Luke had issues working on other halls, and he stayed out of trouble on E-Hall. This reminded me of the squeaky wheel theory—Luke complained too much, and the supervisors catered to that. This sucked, that was my hall. But it came down to who bothered them more and I was "flexible."

So they started putting me on F-Hall. F-Hall at the time was the badass hall in the building. Most of the C-Hall kids got sentenced and left the building, so it got closed. Pena moved upstairs to work on J-Hall. Most of the F-Hall residents fought on other halls and needed a smaller setting, they surprisingly got along with each other.

Working there, I got to meet Lamel, a resident from Brooklyn who had a reputation for assaulting staff. Lamel looked like a younger version of Deebo from the *Friday* movie series. He was six feet tall and never smiled, his demeanor was intimidating, and he had most of the staff shook. I avoided saying anything to him because most of the JCs he didn't know would get violated for forcing themselves on him.

For instance, he would do things to get their attention, and when they would respond, he would use that as an excuse to have an incident. F-Hall required two male staff because the residents were hard to deal with. I would ask my partner to deal with Lamel and I will manage the others, and because he was familiar with Lamel, it worked out. The more I ignored him the more he did things to get my attention. He watched my interaction with the group and started to get jealous, not jealous more like he got tight, because he ran the hall and hated being around people he didn't know.

Some of the other residents tried to test me, but I stood my ground. "No, I'm not getting Chinese food. No, I'm not allowing you to stay up late. No, you won't be smoking while I'm here," were things I would say. I had an extra boost of confidence because the regular staff was an older gentleman name JC Ford. They didn't fuck with him, he was another old schooler who's been with the agency more than twenty years.

Knowing Ford was there to have my back was better than working on E-Hall with Luke because Ford had more structure and he allowed me to lead the group. Ford knew that the only way I was going to be a good JC was to get my feet wet and not sit on the side watching him all the time. He told me, "Work this job, don't let it work you." I heard that before.

I learned a lot from Ford. Unlike Luke, he was a good father; and because he was from Alabama, he had southern values and a laid-back approach to the job. He used to tell me, "They're gonna fight, and when they do, let them get it in for a minute before you stop them, because if you don't, you're gonna get hurt. These young bucks are stronger than you think, let them air it out then stop it. This agency don't give a fuck about you."

Like Cook, Ford used to be a boxer back in the day and had quick hands. He was in his early fifties, was five feet ten and was shaped like a full back with a belly. Once coming from dinner, this resident kept talking on the line and Ford had enough. He slowly walked up on the resident and said with his gentle voice, "Didn't I tell yo ass to shut the fuck up? You don't listen."

In less than three seconds, he threw seven haymakers to the kid's chest, and not some soft shit—bombs. The group just turned their heads and Lamel said, "I told him to shut up." I was speechless, and realized Ford was the heaviest of the heavies. He had the most allegations in the building, and when he got mad, it was like he had a flashback and saw these residents like a punching bag. He was another one not to fuck with.

When we returned to the hall, I asked Ford if he was writing an incident report, and he said, "Mr. Geez, that was counseling." My concern was that the resident would go to medical and say what happened, but he didn't. He was afraid the other residents would smoke him for snitching. Ford had that reputation which is why he was assigned to F-Hall.

On the days Ford didn't show up, I was hoping I would be able to return to E-Hall. But they would send me to F-Hall. Every time this happened, my partner was a weaker male JC, and I would spend the entire tour trying to fend the residents off him. Once, the residents went in his pockets to look for his cellphone, and I had to come to his defense. How does a grown man allow kids to violate him like that? This dude was a buck-o-five and shorter than me. I called supervision and told them this isn't going to work; he can't have my back let alone his own front. But they would say that we were short staff and I had to work with him. This is how supervision gets people hurt.

We had no business on F-Hall together. That same week, one of the residents grabbed the fire extinguisher and sprayed that same JC in the face, it flooded the whole hall. It was irresponsible of supervision to place that same JC with the same residents who assaulted him, but they didn't care. When the residents tried to do it again, it was Lamel who intervened and told the resident to put it back. He said, "How the fuck you gonna violate Mr. Geez like that?" The resident returned the extinguisher and chilled, that's when I saw that Lamel liked me. Even though we never talked, he had respect for me.

From that day Lamel and I were cool. We played a card game that he taught me called "garbage" just to kill time. Every day I was there, he seemed to have a calm about him when I was around. Any chance I got I would try to show Lamel the errors of his ways, but his thirst for negativity kept him on the dark side. His brothers were in a gang and it was in his future; he would have more problems if he didn't embrace the family tradition. He said he liked being the scary one, it felt good that people were afraid of him. I told him that's not going to work if you want a job. But he never thought that far.

He was sixteen and he was planning on being locked up for a long time. It's hard to talk to them when they think like that because nothing you say or do will make them care. They already knew they're not going home and were prepared for it. For some of them, being locked up was a safe haven because there were people on the street who wanted their head. Lamel was one of them, he was on trial for attempted murder, and half his neighborhood wanted him dead. So, for him, this was PC without being on PC.

It was around this time that my wife and I agreed to communicate better, and we returned to court to share joint custody. Around this same time, I met someone who gave me peace in my life. Her name was Claudia and she had a three-year-old son. We met when Rosemary was playing with him at the pool. Her son's name was Jacob and his father wasn't in the picture. For some reason, I was always attracted to women with children, maybe because I never had a father. I had a soft spot for fatherless children.

I never thought anybody would want to share in my drama, but Claudia saw my struggle as a positive quality and respected what I did for a living. Claudia helped me see the impact I had on some of the residents, and I realized that if I can save one of them, that was enough. If anyone knows about being saved, it would be Claudia. She was adopted at the age of four and she knows how it feels to be rejected.

But it was crucial that I inspired the group to embrace their true nature; whatever your situation, be who you are. Not for nothing, this generation lacked individuality, being a follower is the norm. Leadership today is reality show actors, rap artists, and athletes. When I was growing up, if there was a singing artist who looked or sounded like somebody else, that better be their brother; otherwise, if they jacked someone else's style, they didn't even get radio play. But today, it's the opposite. You won't get signed if they can't compare you to someone getting radio play today. These kids are the same way. If you're not a follower, you're alone; and if you're alone, you get violated.

I was always to the left. I tried to encourage these kids to blaze their own trail because if something ever goes wrong, they can blame themselves and not have to suffer from someone else's mistakes. Most of them were in detention because they were with a friend who committed a crime, and to avoid being called a snitch, they took one for the team. Fuck that taking one for the team shit. This is your life, own it. Stop letting the next man control your life. It was hard to navigate through the muck and get through to these kids. They were obsessed with being the bad guy, like they didn't want to be Superman; they wanted to be the guy who put Superman on his neck. I hear that being the good guy isn't cool, but it's cool to have good things. They wanted good things, they just wanted to get them in a bad way. Where did this thought process come from? I'm not gonna front, today's rap music is at the core of this ideology. I go as far back as the battles between the Cold Crusher 4 vs. the Fantastic 5, so I don't need a history lesson on hip-hop and its influence on young people. But now they talk trash and shit gold, it's hard to hate on something that produces dollar signs. But like anything, it will come back and then, maybe when I have grandchildren, they will listen to a better message in their music than my children do. Unfortunately, for now, these kids are attracted to all the bad things in life. They loved guns, they loved fighting, and they loved cursing and stealing. It was like a Quentin Tarantino reality show every day. Nigga this, bitch that, and SMD (suck my dick) were words I would hear so much I became used to it.

Once I was working with another female JC, and she said, "Mr. Geez, you let them talk like that?" I said, "Like what?" She said, "Like there's not a female in the room." The hijinks that went on with the boys was offensive to most of the female JCs. I had to avoid being labeled someone who condoned that behavior. It was straight out of the locker room. Their lingo was so bad they made Ebonics sound like hooked on phonics. They never talked straight; it was crooked English on speed. These were fourteen- and fifteen-year-old kids who talked like drunken sailors. It was crazy some of the things they would say. If I had a dollar for every time I heard them say "suck my dick," I could pay my mortgage.

The N word was something I just got immune to. They said "nigga" so much I stopped hearing it. I mean, it was like it was invisible, like if you say a sentence, you're not aware how many times you say a particular word. Nigga was like that, too. If they say a sentence with thirty words, they would say the word nigga four times. It was a part of their daily vernacular, they say nigga more than they blinked. When people say they want to take it out of their vocabulary, I can't see it because it's part of the culture. They were even saying "my nigga" to the female staff.

When I was a teenager, calling a woman "nigga" was like calling her a man; that was a violation. But these kids didn't care. It's sad that our ancestors fought tooth and nail to not accept other people calling them nigger. My sad reality is in my lifetime, the only people who have called me nigger or nigga (same shit) happened to be black like me.

Black men have called each other nigger since the 1960s and maybe before that. For us, it's a term of endearment or just used in jest. Every ethnicity has a term that other people know not to use those terms because they're not a part of that group. I never realized how bad it was because I spent so much time with Luke and Ford, and their mouths were worse than the residents. Sometimes, it was hard to decipher who was worse, the residents or the staff. I learned from the worst how to cope in this environment; they were survivors and never got taken advantage of by the residents or supervision.

The count on E-Hall was sixteen, and to put insult to injury, instead of them letting me work with Luke, they reassigned Ford to work with him. Ford was in the dog house because the administration hated all the allegations he was getting and wanted to punish him. Supervision had the brilliant idea to have Luke and Ford work together, hoping that those grumpy old men would tear each other up. But those dudes were smarter than that. They saw the writing on the wall and got along well. What they didn't realize was that Luke wanted to do everything and Ford didn't want to do nothing. It was the perfect match.

The biggest loser was me, the hall I waited so long to get was taken from me so that supervision could accommodate one guy and punish another. What a bitch this was, I was back to giving duty frees and working on F-Hall.

But it was a matter of time before Luke would run out of lives.

CHAPTER TEN

I was on 1-2-5 and Saint Nick
Waiting on a cab, standing in the rain
Under my heart three clouds of pain
She got the best of me, what was her destiny?
Maybe I should lick her with my nine millime…ter
My mind is in a blur
Cause you could never pay me to think this would occur

—Nice & Smooth
"Sometimes I Rhyme Slow"

THE AGENCY HAD ELECTRICIANS DRILL holes in the ceilings and walls throughout the building to prepare for the installation of cameras. The days of punching kids in the chest and not reporting fights were over, Big Brother was entering the building. Everybody was on board but Luke; he stayed on his bullshit. He was so set in his ways, he didn't know how to ask for permission to go anywhere.

The policy was that we needed to inform supervision of any movement to and from the hall. Luke never respected the policy; he only applied it when he needed it. I got to go to E-Hall whenever Luke didn't come to work, but that was rare; he loved the job. After his conversation with TC Herrera, he had supervision in the palm of his hand. It was nauseating to watch this old guy take over my hall. I couldn't understand how this agency rewarded bad people and punished good people; I was a good worker, but I just wasn't loud enough.

Luke would turn it up worse than the residents and that's what scared them. They didn't want to deal with him because he pushed them around with his antics. Once, he was so mad that the group on E-Hall was talking on line, he made them stand on the patio in the rain like boot camp. That was child abuse, let's get it straight. On New Year's Eve, everybody got stuck but Luke, they were afraid he would get boozed up and turn the building into a New Year's Eve party, so they sent him home. Man, it must feel good to be bad.

What eventually sealed Luke's fate was that one night when he got stuck, he decided to have an extended duty free. I remember because I was stuck with him. That day on the PM, I was assigned to F-Hall but I got stuck on E- Hall with Luke. They thought they were throwing me a bone putting me on E-Hall for my second tour. But if working with Luke was drama in the day, working on a double with him was twice the drama. He wanted all the lights on so he could read, which was his way of letting me know that he was still in charge. When he went on his duty free, that was the most peaceful four hours I had all night. Did I just say four hours? That's right. It seemed like he was never coming back. It was almost like Luke went AWOL. He didn't want to be there in the first place, he was bitching the entire time.

They could only keep him if they left him on E-Hall; that was his policy. When he returned, he started bragging about all the shit he did and why he took so long. He started his story by saying he met this chick outside and she was open to do anything at 1:00 a.m. What type of chick do you expect to meet on a Bronx street at 1:00 a.m. on a Thursday? Not the type of female you want to bring home to meet your mother.

As he continued his story, I asked myself, where does this old man get all this energy, it was like his battery never went out? Then he said she gave him head for two hours in his car. When he said that, I didn't want to listen anymore. Who gets head for two hours at the age of fifty-six? Impossible. Maybe he had one of those little blue pills; but even if that was the case, there was no way he met some chick and she give him head for two hours. But then my question was, "What were you doing for the other two hours you were gone?" But then he said, "Can you shut up and let me finish the story?"

Then his story took a drastic turn. He said she stole his wallet and he fought the chick in his car, but she got away.

The more he told his story, as tired as I was at four fifteen in the morning, the more I realized that this dude hooked up with a prostitute. When he said, he met her on Hunts Point, I knew the deal. At one o'clock in the morning on a Thursday, the only thing walking the street on Hunts Point were drug dealers, drug addicts, pimps, prostitutes, and Luke. I went from being impressed to being embarrassed for him. His thought process was always to outdo someone, but now he just out did himself with this bullshit.

When the supervisor on duty questioned where he was, Luke said he had car trouble and he walked from 125th Street. If that was true, his old ass would have still been walking. The supervisor wanted him to write an incident report and produce paperwork on what happened to his car, Luke was like whatever and shrugged it off. If that was me, the supervisor would have written me up on the spot.

The next day, the police were in the building looking for Luke. Supposedly, he got robbed by the wrong prostitute. They told security that she claimed he raped her, but they figured he probably refused to pay her and she took his ID and reported him to the police. How do you like that, even prostitutes deserve to make a living. The chick basically cried rape, and she was able to identify him with his ID. This was just the bullshit the agency needed to get rid of Luke. His goose was cooked.

After meeting up with NYPD, he came to work the next day like nothing ever happened. There was no shame in his game, but after roll call, he was called to the TC's office and was asked to leave the building pending an investigation. When I spoke to him, he stuck to his story and claimed that she robbed him. I didn't know what to believe. All I knew was that Luke never returned, and he was asked to retire, or they were going to fire him.

Luke had unorthodox methods to reach the residents, but it was effective because as hard as he was, he made them hate being there. He once told me, "To beat the devil, sometimes, you have to be the devil." I didn't see what he meant at the time, but the longer I worked there, the more I realized what he meant. With Luke gone, the floor was mine. I could work E-Hall with no interruptions. One man's loss was another man's gain. I never want it to end like this for Luke, but I had to take advantage of another opportunity.

When Spofford finally closed, they moved all the staff over to Fairvue and some to Greenwood. It was a rough transition. The staff at Fairvue didn't necessarily roll out the red carpet. Keeping it real, they pulled it right from under the staff transferred from Spofford. Supervision expected them to know everything and had little patience when they didn't. Some of them were assigned to halls and didn't even know where to go. The TCs and supervisors enjoyed having the JCs struggle for help, which some of us were too proud to say when we needed it. It was a form of power and it gave them the upper hand. Talk about crabs in a barrel. This place was the epitome of that.

We are the only group of people who get in each other's way, and I'm not just referring to black people. I'm talking about the people in charge and the people under them who work in this environment. I never aspired to be a supervisor because it wasn't a promotion; it was a way for you to feel like you were better than others and let them know about it. They can keep their extra 10k, I was making that in overtime.

As our staff grew, people were fighting for permanent spots. I was lucky that things turned out the way they did for Luke; otherwise, they would have been playing musical chairs with my black ass. I worked a lot with Ford, and unlike working with Luke, he let me run the show.

Hoffman became a supervisor at Spofford and returned to Fairvue along with two other supervisors a lot of old-timers had no respect for. One became my supervisor, and his name was Mr. Ebo. Ford told me when dude was a JC, he always had to save his ass from the residents. He was an older African guy who was shaky and always looked nervous on the job. He was more like a paper tiger, whenever he tried to flex his muscles nobody ever flinched.

The other supervisor was Ms. Flores. She looked black, but I don't know if she was black or Spanish, but she was fine for her age. A little outdated though, she looked like the old chick at the club. You know, that forty-year-old chick who used to be a dime but now trying to compete with twenty-year-old chick wearing tight shit all the time. That was her, but I respected her gangsta because she would tell you if she was wearing a wig.

Whenever they came to the hall, Ford would practically throw them out. You would have thought they stole his money. Ford never liked supervisors, let alone supervisors he had no respect for.

I was in no position to react like that, I didn't know them. On first impressions, I gave everybody a chance. In the case of Mr. Ebo, he didn't look like he was going to last another day, he was so old. I could barely understand him from his accent, and he always misplaced my doctor's notes. This group was the most incompetent bunch of supervisors ever. If it wasn't for Hoffman, I would have had no faith in them.

I couldn't escape the fact that Luke was no longer there, he would have had a field day with this group. As much of a bad influence Luke was, he did teach me what not to do. What I missed was his ability to not be jerked around by supervision. Luke told me once, "If you allow them, they will chew you up and spit you out." He said regarding the residents, "The ass you save might be your own." What he meant was stop looking out for these kids because they're takers and never givers. I understood that, but it was up to me to educate my group on the philosophy of karma. I told them during a rap session that karma is that what goes around comes around and do unto others what you want them to do to you.

These residents had the proclivity for negative behavior. It was something they yearned for like candy. It's hard to get respect from kids who don't respect themselves. The only thing I would try to do was keep them from killing each other on the hall. This was a never-ending struggle of tug of war. What bothered me more were the residents who, no matter what you said, would just do what they wanted. One resident made me so mad I almost killed him, literally. This was before the installation of cameras. This one resident named Benji was forever playing games, and it really pushed my patience. His story was the diary of a knucklehead. This kid was such a pain in the ass, but more irritating was his annoying habit of calling everybody a bum-ass nigga. "Fuck you, you bum-ass nigga", "Suck my dick, you bum-ass nigga", or "Give me my snack, you bum-ass nigga," would always be his last words. He talked this way to the counselors, supervision, and any kid who spoke to him. I even heard him call his grandmother a bum-ass nigga. Respect was never in his upbringing; lack of fathering will do that. He would always stand at the doors of other residents during showers and spit on the windows of their doors or, even worse, he would draw a penis on the glass with a marker, so when they looked out the door window, it looked like they were sucking it.

In a private moment, my partner and I thought it was funny at first, but it would always instigate a fight. One day, I caught Benji at another resident's door and I ran up behind him and fiened him out. He completely passed out and fell to the floor. I thought he was playing, but he was unconscious, and with all the residents on their doors watching, I went into panic mode. I thought I killed him. But before I had to include my partner who was on the other side of the hall, Benji gained consciousness. He got up talking shit like nothing happened. When the other residents told him that he was out, he was in denial. I was just relieved he got up. I had to give them all Pop-Tarts to keep them quiet. Pop-Tarts were like money in the building; it was always a valid bargaining chip. After that, I never wrestled, arm wrestled, or slap boxed with any resident again. That experience shook me up; I stopped playing with them physically. At the end of the day, their motivation was to test our strength, and when they got on their bullshit, they wanted to know our weaknesses. It was always to our advantage to never horseplay with them because these young bucks were strong, and if they got hurt, that was your ass. Even in the gym, I would just stand on the sidelines.

Whenever I had a kid with leadership potential, I leaned on him like a partner to help me establish control. One resident who stood out more than the rest was Jose. He got locked up for protecting his brother. His brother was in a fight, and he took the rap for him to keep his brother from being arrested. Jose was in the fight, but his brother stabbed someone, and he said he did it. That's love, but it was also stupid because now he was doing time for attempted murder.

He earned his credibility on the hall for staying out of trouble. In less than a month, he was on level three, and he accumulated so many points that he was entitled to certain privileges. He wasn't a bad kid, he just had a temper and had anger-management issues. I loved him because as small as he was, he wasn't afraid to tell the group to hold it down.

There was a ponderous cloud that hovered over the hall from Luke's departure. Most of the residents weren't used to taking orders from me and only respected Luke putting his foot in their ass. That wasn't my style. I tried to treat them with respect, and when that didn't work, I put my foot in their ass too. Jose's brother was an OG in a Dominican gang called Patria, also known as Trinitarios, so most of the residents in the building showed him respect because he was also Patria.

Growing up in the Bronx, I was familiar with the Dominican gang DDP (Dominicans Don't Play), but Patria took things to another level. Jose took that shit seriously, and I was fortunate that we got along because to show me respect he never pumped any gang activity on the hall. If a resident tried to violate me, Jose would get in his face and say, "If Mr. Geez gets in trouble, I'm fuckin' you up." This made my job easier and kept me from putting my hands on them.

When the cameras were installed, it was a new day. We were subjected to discipline if the camera showed that we didn't use the proper technique to restrain the residents. It was a scary thought because I rarely used the proper technique, none of us did. We were trained to restrain in slow motion; in live speed, these residents weren't standing still like in training. We argued all the time that we were susceptible to injury and suspensions because the technique didn't work, but it was the only method we had.

During this transition, it was rumored that we would be merging with BCW, and major changes were going to happen. I don't think any of us were ready for this takeover.

CHAPTER ELEVEN

◆◆◆◆◆◆◆

Hey what we gonna do in '92, even
though we had fun in '91
Quick to turn my day, all things comin down
Run up on the new sound, leavin cracks in the ground

—Tribe Called Quest feat. Busta Rhymes
"Scenario (Remix)"

I WANTED TO START OFF this chapter with excerpts from the movie *Poltergeist* with the scene when Steve, the father, was yelling at his boss, the realtor, for selling him a home that was located on top of a graveyard. But Busta Rhymes's lyrics were more apropos to break down this "scenario."

When Mayor Bloombean took over, he placed our agency under the watchful eyes of BCW, an organization whose job was to protect children, but protect them from whom? Protect them from us? We were being watched and scrutinized for how we treated them. Our ED at the time was Mr. Morales, a man who earned his way to that position from the ground floor up. He went from JC to supervisor to TC to deputy director and to executive director. He was a good man who cared about us as much as he cared about the residents.

As they chipped away our foundation, he was one of the casualties, and he just retired. Our commissioner was fired along with the deputy commissioner and anybody else who had an appointed position under this regime. The commissioner of BCW became our commissioner, and they changed our name from DJJ (Department of Juvenile Justice) to DCFS (Department of Children and Family Service). They changed everything. We were issued uniforms, and the residents went from jumpers to khakis and polo tops. They wanted us to look professional. Our obligatory responsibilities were so erroneous it became a joke what we were expected to do on a daily basis.

It was hard enough trying to control defiant children, but it was worse doing it without making mistakes; and for any mistake, there was a price to pay. People were getting suspended left and right for the dumbest shit. We were informed that cuts were being made and people would be let go. The concern was that the city spent too much money on overtime and they needed to cut back on the staff; but by cutting the staff that would create more overtime. What were they thinking? BCW had no idea what this job was about, to them we were making too much money and we were costing the agency money in residents' injuries. They changed our restraining technique from Handle with Care to SCM (Safety Crisis Management) which was a method that was supposed to prevent injuries and was less aggressive. It brought down injuries to the residents, but it increased injuries to the staff performing it. It was so bad a method, and it was shocking the union approved it.

Speaking of the union, that changed too. We had to switch to BCW's union which at the time I was opposed to, but I'm just one dude. I was happy with the old union because they had no ties to the agency. When Morales left and they got rid of the commissioner, I assumed our new executive director would also be someone from outside the agency.

The building still had the stench of Spofford, and it was time to separate us from that stigma, but it didn't happen. Our new ED was Spofford's old ED who also was the ED of Greenwood. Her name was Ms. Nebula. She was in her midfifties, wore glasses with a box-cut hairstyle, and no personality. When I say no personality, she never spoke. I think, for her first month on the job, I never saw her. To expect a meet and greet would have been asking for too much. She never even introduced herself to us at roll call, and if she popped on the hall, she wouldn't even say hi. We called her Evillene, like the witch from *The Wiz*, she rarely smiled and always had a serious look.

She was of West Indian descent, and like most of supervision she had a different upbringing than we did in this country. She had manly features and somewhere between leaving her country and coming here, she forgot the true definition of family because nothing in her make-up said man, woman, and child.

For the agency to promote people like this was just as neglectful as hiring suburban cops to work in urban neighborhoods—they don't relate to the people they served.

To make matters worse, Ms. Nebula never was a JC, or a supervisor, or even a TC. She was the secretary of a former commissioner at Spofford years ago. This was type nepotism if I ever saw it. That's like a water boy becoming the commissioner of the NFL. How egregious is that. She was good with paper but terrible with people. She knew us from the incident reports and badge numbers. If you had no incidents, she might not know you. When I spoke to Platter about it, he said she will ruin this place because she did it to Greenwood and Spofford where incidents were at a record high. He wouldn't say it publicly because as a tour commander, he had to tow the company line; but in confidence, he told me it was downhill from here.

Gone were the open-door policy of Morales and the family atmosphere created by Ms. Sanchez; it became us and them. If you Google the history of Spofford, it was a hellhole for the children detained there. Why would they have those same people running things now? The name changed but not the people. We weren't the problem, they were. Any successful organization is concerned with the well-being of its employees, and they motivate them to maximize efficiency.

But in this instance, the people in charge were never put in the hot seat for their managing tactics. If something went wrong, it was the JC's fault—not because they didn't fit that hall, not because they were tired from too many doubles, not because they didn't get a break or not because they were assigned to a hall with one staff and eight residents. None of those factors were a viable excuse for something going wrong. It was times like this I wish Luke was around to slap a resident or curse out a supervisor. Never have I worked somewhere

where the people in charge were so incompetent when it came to leadership. They weren't leaders; they were rulers or that's what they tried to be.

The counterintuitive thought was that things were fine, but the people in charge labored under the illusion that all the JCs should be talked down to.

They believed that you motivate people by belittling them, but common sense is that you motivate people by encouraging them. Maybe common sense was not international; I mean, maybe what's common sense in this country isn't common sense in another.

Their practices were so slave driven. It could have been a European philosophy of discipline or something; but instead of building us up, it was breaking us down and it resulted in more mistakes. This was a case of the powerful abusing their power on the powerless. We were all black, but my ancestors were slaves; and my supervisor, TC, and new Executive Director's ancestors were never slaves in this country. Jim Crow wasn't in their DNA, to understand the history of this country you must have lived it. They didn't know how it felt to grow up black in America nor did they care. Could that have something to do with how we were treated? For all I know, their ancestors might have owned slaves or sold them; they were closer descendants of kings than I was. Or maybe they just saw us as peasants because they damn sure treated us that way. Looking down on us seemed okay to them, nothing they said or made us do was wrong to them.

When I flashback to my time in China, it reminds me of how Maylyn treated her employees. I felt like I was a prisoner on my job in America. Where Maylyn ran an assembly line of clothes, this agency ran an assembly line also; everything Ms. Rooney spoke about started to make sense. Maybe that's why you must be an American citizen to work corrections or work for the NYPD because our justice system isn't run like a third-world country.

Don't get me wrong. I love my brothers from the motherland, but these people I worked for treated us like shit. There were times in roll call we were told that we were lucky to have the job and that we can be replaced at any time. Who wants to go to work and hear that? It was demoralizing; we were adults. They were so caught up in talking down to the residents that they did the same to us. Human nature is such that if you show common decency, I have no choice but to return the favor.

The people I worked for could never do this. The kids had BCW looking out for them, but who was looking out for us? Nobody would listen to us. We had union delegates, but they were focused on other issues, like our pay. If a JC cried foul, they made it worse for themselves and would get the worst assignment or get days off denied or get stuck more often than anyone else. Supervision had their favorites, and they knew who were the troublemakers.

If you complained, you caught hell. But at the end of the day, it always comes down to money. If we had peace officer status, these people wouldn't be managing this building. The city wouldn't give us that status, which allowed these people to sit on the throne. If this administration was a sports team, the entire coaching staff would have been fired years ago because statistically, their numbers were horrible.

I once attended a goals meeting because I was honored for working during a hurricane, and I watched as the ED and deputy director struggled to explain why the incidents in the building were so high. I was embarrassed for them, but it was good to see them in the hot seat. But somehow, they finessed their way out of it and found ways to blame us. When they returned to the building, we were put in the hot seat. If Platter was there, I was good, but we didn't have the same days off. When he wasn't around, I was treated like a troublemaker because when I needed something I always went to him.

TC Herrera saw this as an opportunity to get under my skin. I didn't have Ms. Mays or Luke to protect me. I had to start defending myself. I never was the type to make a movie to get my way, but the longer I worked there, I realized that this was the only thing that worked. The first time I tried it, I got the opposite result. I got assigned to F-Hall because there was nobody available to work there. When I expressed my displeasure, the TC got involved and told me to report to my post or he would give me a write up. As I left roll call,

I said bullshit under my breath, and I was told to stay back because he wanted to talk to me. When roll call was empty, he said, "You better get comfortable on F-Hall because I prefer to have Ford on E." I smiled and said, "Okay," and left roll call.

I wanted to say, "Thank you. May I have another?" with sarcasm, but that was a way to get my feelings hurt. I knew he wanted me to spazz, but I wasn't going to give him that. They loved to make you beg only to turn you down. What an abuse of power, I wasn't used to this. I felt that I came to work, I did my job, and I was a team player. Why is this guy coming at me like this?

After Lamel got sent upstate, F-Hall was led by this sixteen-year-old Hispanic kid named Charlie Reyes. Charlie was a beast. I knew jail food puts weight on you, but damn. When he was on G-Hall, he was not this big. It was a combination of push-ups, bread, and potatoes. He looked like he played linebacker for the All-City team. Charlie had a menacing demeanor; like Lamel, he got a kick out of people getting out of his way. When I got assigned there, he showed me love because he always remembered how I treated him during his brief time on E-Hall before he was transferred to G-Hall. So many kids crossed my path, I didn't even remember when he was there, but I just played along.

Charlie had the other residents in check; they were afraid of him and did whatever he said. They were truly a wolf pack and Charlie was the alpha dog. He told them what to do and when to do it. Charlie was smart, in that he would have the other resident do his dirty work. Once, he had the group barricade the door so that staff wouldn't come in. It was so bad it took the fire department to help us get in there. They terrorized everybody they didn't like or didn't know. I hated working there because they usually assigned me with someone they would violate. I would tell Charlie, "Have your boys lay off dude today, it gives me more work." He would say, "Say no more I got you."

But there were days Charlie was spaced out. This had something to do with the psychotropic medication he was taking because I would see him go through mood swings whenever he returned from medical. He was bipolar, and on those days, it was like he didn't even know me. I tried to get through to him but I would get nowhere. Sometimes, the only remedy was a phone call to his family. When the case manager was there, I would beg her to give him a call. She would lookout most of the time, but she had to be careful because Charlie would expect it every day and residents are only allowed one phone call a week. Supervision didn't care if he got extra phone calls; there were perks to being a badass.

Unlike Luke, Ford didn't come to work every day, and when he was out, I could return to E-Hall. After working on F-Hall, my credibility skyrocketed; the other residents in the building gave me extra props for surviving on F. Only real seasoned JCs worked F-Hall without an incident. I had incidents on F-Hall but never where I got assaulted; they were notorious for assaulting staff.

The more I worked with the older residents, the better I was to work anywhere. When I returned to E-Hall, the residents behaved because they didn't want me to tell Charlie that they gave me problems. Sometimes, Charlie would stand by the door and point to a resident and ask me if he was good. The resident would be shaking in his boots, praying I said something positive and I would. I wouldn't want to be the staff that got him fucked up.

During this time, Ford went out IOJ and never returned to the building. It would have been hard to take E-Hall away from me now, and I was glad to not have to work on F-Hall because they were completely out of control. They were the thugs of the building, and only a handful of JCs could control them. There was one female staff that Charlie treated like his mother, and because of that, they would assign her there.

There was a look in Charlie's eyes that made me think he was losing it, he started to block everybody out and went out of his way to cause havoc. When I was on E-Hall, I would see him through the glass doors and he usually greeted me with a fist to the chest, but now he would just look at me and stare with no reaction. I think it had something to do with his age; he was about to turn seventeen and that meant we would be shipped out to Rock. Fear started to seep into his head, and for the first time, he would be treated like a man. Being the biggest resident in the building gave him certain privileges—everybody got out of his way, even some supervisors. This wasn't good because this allowed him to premeditate his actions; he wanted to turn it up every day.

That look in his eye was the look of wanting to hurt somebody. One day, I was in the café with E-Hall, and F-Hall entered the café loud as shit. I knew my supervisor was as soft as tissue when the residents of F-Hall disregarded him trying to tell them to settle down. There were only six of them, but they sounded like there were twelve. Charlie who, wasn't even talking, took offense and told Mr. Ebo to suck his dick. Then again, to make sure he heard him, Charlie said, "Yo, Ebo, suck my dick." I acted like I didn't hear him because I was embarrassed for Ebo who acted like he didn't hear him either. Even the staff who was working with F-Hall played deaf because Ebo shitted on so many people; we wanted to see what he was going to do.

Of course, he didn't do shit. It's easy to bark on the staff that you supervise, but to a kid with nothing to lose, you don't say anything. Fear is a motherfucker; it has ways of controlling your actions in ways you'll regret later. I say that because the other residents were watching a man afraid of a child and taking notes. By the third SMD, the JC working F-Hall pulled Charlie out of the café before he got restrained. I was just glad E-Hall behaved because I know Ebo wanted so bad to bark on us instead. That's just like a bully, always abusive to the people they have power over.

I guess Ebo avoided saying anything for fear that Charlie would attack him. He wasn't stupid, he saw in Charlie's eyes—he didn't care. Later, when I saw Charlie, I said, "Where's the love?" He said, "What do you mean?" I said, "Sometimes, when you see me, you look at me like you don't know me." He said, "My bad." I just shook my head. There comes a point that you just have to move out of the way before you get run over; this was one of those times.

It amazed me that the agency kept this kid on this hall with all those followers; somebody's going to get hurt.

A week later, Charlie was about to have a visit and got word that a male JC violated his mother in the visiting room. JC Parrish was a counselor on the AM with mad juice. He worked in a liaison capacity during school and got to float around the building unlike anybody else. I always envied his position because he only answered to upper management, and like Luke, he wouldn't hesitate to tell supervision where to stick it. He had a Charlie Murphy-type sense of humor and enjoyed violating the residents both verbally and physically. He never held any punches, he would say shit that would make these kids want to fight him, but they knew better.

Whenever he went to visiting, he had a reputation for bagging the numbers of the residents' mothers. Most of the male JCs were jealous of his freedom in the building; we would have all done the same shit given the opportunity. Parrish was a bald, dark-skinned dude who stayed in the gym and was fit with a god-body. Despite being in his late thirties, he was the strongest staff on the AM. The dude was ripped. I'm glad we were cool, but I always knew he wasn't right. He did shit to the residents and said shit that would have gotten me suspended or fired, but the powers that be always gave him a pass. He was one of their goons.

He hated Charlie and Charlie hated him. When Charlie got down to the visiting room and found out that Parrish told his mother to suck a dick, he lost it. It took five security guards to hold him back, he wanted to get at Parrish but Parrish wasn't fazed. Parrish wanted security to let Charlie go so that he could spank him in front of his mother.

As they escorted Charlie back to the hall, I just knew this was going to end bad. At the same time, there was an event being held in the multipurpose area which was located in front of F-Hall. As they brought Charlie through, you would have thought they were walking with Charles Mason. It took four people to take him to F-Hall. But Charlie showed no emotion because he knew if he would have sneezed, they would have pounded on him. While this was going on, the residents on F-Hall were tight because they didn't have lunch yet, and all the other halls did. Supervision was afraid to take them to lunch with the event going on, so they promised them that their lunch would be brought to the hall.

When Charlie got there, he had the group turn it up, knowing that the only JC who could respond was Parrish. He was salivating at the possibility of getting a piece of Parrish. But Parrish wasn't stupid.

He knew that they were turning it up to get his attention. Instead of him responding, it was the security sergeant doing his rounds at the time who responded. When the sergeant got there, he was immediately attacked by all six of the residents. These residents had so much rage, they were like a volcano erupting. They kicked and punched and threw chairs while the sergeant laid helplessly on the floor.

Again, the agency took a chance with the safety of the staff by assigning one JC with these monsters. He was so outnumbered he wasn't able to control the group while they stomped out the sergeant to submission. It was so bad they locked down the building and the cops arrived to arrest all six residents. The sergeant was rushed to the hospital in critical condition, fighting for his life.

After that incident, F-Hall was never opened again and a shitload of rules and policies were created to protect us against workplace violence. It was all bullshit. The incident cost the city money, as well as the embarrassment of trying to explain how this could happen. Nobody in charge got disciplined, not for the F-Hall residents not being fed, not for one staff assigned to F-Hall, and not for having only one guard respond to the incident. Even Parrish escaped ridicule for not responding to the incident.

If three more guards would have responded, those residents would have been put in check, but that never happened. Someone almost had to die for them to fix things. Everybody knew that F-Hall was a pot about to burst, but supervision never listened to us. The more I thought about it, I realized that could have been me that day. Those residents had the proclivity for violence and crime. Staying out of trouble was against their nature, and every night before I would get relieved, I would glance over at F-Hall and see that yellow crime scene tape covering the door and say to myself, *what the fuck am I doing here?*

CHAPTER TWELVE

—◆◆◆◆—

In this world of all diverse/ like u used
2 talk proper but now u curse
The sun used 2 shine from day 2 day/ now
the whole universe is filled with grey
No friends, children, family nor wife/
and disrespect is the way of life

—Doug E Fresh
"Play This Only at Night"

EVERY NIGHT, WHEN I CAME home, I would leave my drama at the door. I never shared with anybody the drama that happened on the job. The F-Hall incident had me totally perplexed, it never should have happened. I was just glad the sergeant was recovering and getting his life back. I prayed every day for his recovery.

By now, Claudia and I were living together, and it was difficult shaking the Jekyll and Hyde personalities I developed. I could never be happy at work and I could never get mad at home. What I mean is that I started to ignore problems at home because they became almost trivial compared to the shit that went on at work. I needed to relax. When Claudia complained about one of her nails breaking, I wanted to tell her, "Well, today I almost got my finger chopped off from a kid slamming his door on me, and I got punched in the head seven times from breaking up a fight." But I wouldn't say anything; I suppressed my emotions and totally disassociated myself from the job. Just going through the motions became my daily routine because it didn't require much effort and it allowed me to ride the wave of indifference.

I never really associated with my coworker outside of work because it was easier to accept the shit that went on inside if I left everything there. But by doing this, I became completely desensitized to everything around me, almost numb. There were some staff who were able to deal with the stress level because they were spiritually connected and came to work with Bibles, and there were others who were just dirty dogs, and being around this environment was more structure than their own lives. Then there was me, smack dab in the middle. I was swaying all over the place like a roller coaster.

I came from a good upbringing, but to say I had no ghost in my closet would be a lie. I smoked, I drank, I watched pornography, I did blow in my college days, and I even fell in love with a stripper back in the day. But when MJ was born, the thought of my demons snatching him up terrified me. I had to change my life and show accountability for my actions. Seventeen years ago, I believed my son will live healthy if I lived healthy. I couldn't continue to do things I didn't want him to do.

I will never forget the time MJ saw me smoked out on the living room couch with my homeboy G. MJ was five at the time, and he came to me while I was drinking and smoking and asked me to help him do a crossword puzzle, but I fumbled while doing it, and G and I laughed about it. MJ broke out in a hysterical cry, demanding that I help him; but in my moment of indulgence, I was no help at all. While G sat there laughing, I had a blank stare as MJ threw down the book and ran off. It was then that I asked myself, *what kind of father are you?* That was the last time I smoked weed; it's not for everybody.

This was the message I would relate to my group—it's not too late to change. There is a higher being, and it's not Santa Claus, and he is watching to see who is naughty or nice. I wasn't perfect but I never went out my way to hurt people, and because of that, I benefited from some of the blessings in life. Sometimes, my message fell on deaf ears. They heard me, but I couldn't force them to listen. I made myself believe that I deserved the crap on this job because of my indiscretions. Sometimes, I felt like a wounded bird with one busted wing just stuck here surrounded by little birds that were never taught how to fly.

I had Jose under the wing to hold me down. He was a good kid that I could trust. He was there to hold down Luke and Ford, and now he was there for me. Our relationship grew stronger with me gaining more control of the hall. I could see how Jose got himself locked up—he was a great right-hand man. He would do whatever he could to please the people he cared about. He was like my hall monitor. Having someone like him on the inside was crucial to establishing control because these kids were always scheming. They would throw the ultimate subs all the time, and make you think that two residents are fighting so that we can respond while they are intending on jumping someone else.

This happened all the time, but Jose killed all that noise. If he got wind of a fight brewing, he put them on blast and had it dead before it got started. If there was a resident on the hall who had weed, he would tell me; if a resident had markers and was tagging graffiti on the walls, he pointed him out; or if someone took an extra snack, he would take it out of their hand. He wasn't a snitch; he took care of the hall like it was his house. I loved it because he kept me from getting in trouble. I couldn't see everything.

By doing this, he did create a lot of enemies, but he didn't care. He would tell them during my rap sessions, "If you think you're going to come over here and make it hot it ain't gonna happen."

He was small, but he wasn't afraid of anybody. Some of the other staff who worked E-Hall weren't fans of Jose either. They felt that he thought he was a junior JC. And the first person they blamed was me; they thought I gave him too much freedom. I gave him the same amount of freedom that Luke and Ford gave him, but they came at me because they were afraid to say it to Luke or Ford.

When I got word that they were trying to move Jose off the hall, I told him to fall back, which he did. Was he cocky and a little arrogant? Yes, but he had the most Aspire points in the building, and he stayed out of trouble. That didn't last long because in less than a week, he lost all his points when he was spit on by another resident. Someone had the brilliant idea to have a resident that Jose had beef with moved to the hall. I was pissed because I felt it was done intentionally, they had it out for him. When he got spit on, he immediately fought the kid and got zeroed out. I told my supervisor that Jose was set up. I said, "I hope you guys are happy. You got what you wanted." He said, "What?" I said, "You guys wanted to move him. Now you got your wish."

That was the first time I spoke up, but I was fed up with the set-up games this building played with these kids. When Jose was moved, I struggled to get motivated to work with the group I had. After a year seeing a certain resident every day, it was hard to accept him being removed. It was all politics. There were residents who had multiple fights that I couldn't get rid of, why did Jose have to be transferred after one fight?

This didn't sit well with Jose; he was a shell of himself. His confidence was gone and he refused to eat. I would have to go speak to him just to get him to care about his life. He felt he let me down, but I told him it wasn't his fault. I said, "You were blessed on E-Hall because you stayed out of trouble, and to whom much is given, much is expected. So, you have to behave better than everybody else or you will lose everything."

He was so engrossed with pleasing me, I felt I let him down. I realized the power I had over some of these kids and it was hard accepting because I didn't even have power over myself in this place. I did everything to get Jose back, but supervision was trying to send a message to both of us that they ran shit. Supervision never considered that these residents never had consistent people in their lives, so when they got close to someone it hurt when they were taken away. It was pointless to let a kid rot because you didn't like his bravado. Fuck if he was too happy on E-Hall. Let him be there.

It was amazing the ego trips these supervisors went on. You would have thought I took their basketball and didn't let them play. It wasn't until the mental health staff wrote an observation report that said Jose was better on E- Hall because of his age that they sent him back. They just wanted full control.

It was around then that my main partner was Ms. Vega, she was part of the newest class of JCs assigned to the building. She was gay, and she believed she had bigger nuts than most of the men in the building. She wasn't one of those dainty gay women. She would go

HAM on any resident who tried to violate. Supervision didn't fuck with her because she knew the policy like the back of her hand. She would tell them when they were wrong and she would usually be right. They hated JCs who acted like know-it-alls, but it was obvious she had friends downtown because they didn't fuck with her.

She was rugged but cute for her size. She could get it, but whenever one of the male JCs tried to holler at her, they got their feelings hurt. She would tell them, "Nigga, please. You better go somewhere before I take the only girl you do have." She wasn't lying, she could do it too; she had game.

She was getting more pussy than I was, she was a tall Hispanic woman who had skin as soft as a baby. I always wanted to ask when did she knew she was gay, but as close as we were, it just wasn't appropriate. It was an advantage working with her because the residents couldn't try to flirt with her, which was a common thing in the building. She was obnoxiously professional to the point it rubbed people the wrong way. We had a good system working together, she was very meticulous and covered all bases to make sure we had everything done. We played good cop bad cop. It reminded me of when I worked with Ms. Mays, but a little better because she loved restraining. Sometimes, I had to pull her back from taking a resident down. I never worked with somebody who was so focused. Her work ethic was twice everybody else, and she had a habit of making people look bad.

On the low, most of the staff felt that she would dry snitch and would refuse to work with her because they thought she was an IG. It was like she wanted to be a supervisor without being a JC first. She would tell the residents during a rap session, "When I'm right I'm right and when I'm wrong I'm right." I would say to her, "That doesn't make sense, stop power trippin' like supervision, that's some shit they would say."

She had height on her and would use it to intimidate the residents. She would stand over them and say, "Say something." They would shut up and just walk away with their tails between their legs. But on the flip side, I never had it so easy. She would cover the logbook, do the searches, and even conduct the showers.

I spent most of the time playing video games and having conversations with Jose, and I could tell this didn't sit well with Vega. It was almost like she was jealous of Jose. Any time I turned my back or stepped off the hall, Vega saw that as an opportunity to fuck with him.

It got so bad once that when I returned from my duty free, she was changing his room. When I asked her, what happened, she said he was being disrespectful to her and she felt he was too comfortable where his room was located. I was like, "What does his room have to do with it?" But she knew the room was special to him because the last resident who had that room was his best friend who went upstate.

Her petulant reaction to things started to get old. I just didn't see how this eye-for-an-eye shit was teaching these young men how to deal with conflict. This was a common theme with everybody; if you embarrass me, I will embarrass you more. At the end of the day, supervision sided with me, and Vega wasn't happy about that and requested to work another hall. Her reason to be moved was that she felt that I was undermining her authority when she tried to do her job. I didn't think it was that big a deal, but she was in her early twenties and took everything personal. My attitude was that if that's how you feel, then move on.

Trying to understand the multiple personalities of some of my coworkers wasn't easy, and I started to see why some people didn't want to work with Vega. As professional and as hard as she was on the outside, she was really soft and pink inside. I would always give her a lift home, but because of this situation, she would rather take the train. I once stopped her one day and told her, "Yo, Vega stop being a cry baby and let me take you home." She would say, "Nah, I'm good." At that point, I said to myself, let me stop begging this chick to be my friend. If that's how she feels, fuck it.

The next week, to my surprise, supervision left Vega on the hall and moved me. I was like, "Ain't that a bitch." I have to leave my hall because she doesn't want to work with me. When I spoke to my supervisor, he told me that TC Herrera felt that my services would be better used on another hall and that Vega would be able to hold it down on E-Hall. I was puzzled because women weren't allowed to be alone on male halls, but that goes back to policy vs. practice, and Herrera could practice anything he wanted. I wanted to spazz the way Pena used to when he got moved, but for what, that's what they want, so let me just chill. Plus, I knew the residents on E-Hall wouldn't go for it. I knew that Jose would make it hard on her, and she would be begging them to move me back.

But the opposite happened. She was Jose's best friend and was holding down the hall better than me. When I spoke to Jose, he said, "Geez, she thinks she is you." He said, "Everything we did that she didn't like she does with me." This is some *Single White Female* shit, remember that movie? This chick was trying to replace me.

The more I thought about it, I remember once I told her about a Jets jacket by Mitchell and Ness that I was going to buy, and the next week she said she was getting it too. Then another time, I told her about a pair of ACG boots I wanted, and she got those. I wanted to tell her at that moment that if you want to be a dude, we don't bite each other's ideas like that. But then I had to remind myself that she was young, and that it was a compliment to who I was that she wanted to be like me. I took the high road and realized that I was like her big brother, and without saying it, she looked up to me.

Whenever we weren't working together, I have to admit she would be the first person to respond to any incident I had or she would call to see if I was okay. Whenever I was in a jam, she would always look out. When my kids went back to school after summer vacation, she would always bless me with a few dollars. She would say, "Don't act like you don't need it, just consider it an early Christmas gift from Auntie Vega." She was the only person I could rely on to have my back, and without saying anything, whoever had her back started to have mine too. I started to get more respect from the agency; and I was asked by the deputy director if I wanted to implement some of my ideas, like my idea to start a flag football league. Also, I was able to have NBA 2K and Madden Football tournaments on the Xbox with my group. With Vega's help, I returned to E-Hall, and together, we established E-Hall as one of the best disciplined and cleanest halls in the building. But that moment would be short lived.

Around this time, just as summer was about to start in 2012, things got real murky when a night staff, Ms. Caroline, searched J-Hall. Ms. Caroline was an old-school JC that most residents didn't want to fuck with. She wasn't afraid of them, and she was a straight shooter.

At night, whenever we checked their rooms, it was like opening a jack in the box—you never know what you will find inside. A resident could be jerking off, reading a book, or doing push-ups; but as night drew long, most of them would be asleep. One night, while doing her rounds on the J-Hall, she saw a light coming from one of the resident's rooms. As she goes in to investigate, she noticed the resident was hiding something. When she asked him what he was hiding, of course he said, "Nothing." Not trusting him, she told supervisor Cribbs, a supervisor who was very unreliable. How he got promoted to supervisor was a mystery to everybody.

Mr. Cribbs was one of those people who came to work to do nothing; if there was work, he was nowhere to be found. Cribbs was an African-American shifty little character from Brooklyn who looked like Freddie from the movie *Super Fly*, you know, the dude that got smacked up by the cops. That was Cribbs, always looking smacked up. Having him respond wasn't helping Ms. Caroline. When she told him that she saw a light coming from the resident's room that she believed was a cellphone, supervisor Cribbs believed the resident more than Ms. Caroline. After he searched the resident, Cribbs thought Ms. Caroline was buggin' out. Ms. Caroline, not one to be called a sucker, wasn't letting it go. She insisted that a second search was necessary; and with a second look, they found a charger. Phone chargers and cellphones go together like a belt and pants, but still no luck on finding the cellphone. At this point, Cribbs just wanted to go back under his rock; Ms. Caroline was probably interrupting his sleep. When the resident asked to go to the bathroom Ms. Caroline didn't want him to move, but Cribbs said, "Caroline, let the boy pee."

As the resident leaves the bathroom, Ms. Caroline went behind him and searched the bathroom and found the cellphone behind the shower curtain in the soap dispenser. The resident tried to say it wasn't his, but he was caught red-handed.

While Ms. Caroline was writing her incident report, the resident was in his room making threats, hollering, "Snitches get stitches, bitch." Totally unfazed, she just continued to write. He said he was going to have her shot when she goes home. But she wasn't the one. She told him that if something happened to her, they know where to find him. She said, "Trust me, you're not going to like what my people do to you." She came from a family of drug dealers and real gangsters.

It was mind-blowing that supervision left her there, but they did; and when the other residents found out in the morning that she turned in their jack (cellphone), they threatened her too. Ms. Caroline was a tough cookie. I would have been out of there, but she weathered the storm. Her concern was how did they get the phone, but the real issue was who gave it to them? The rumor was that the cellphone was given to another resident on the hall by a staff member. But who? When she asked security about the cellphone, they said, "What cellphone?" The protocol was that all contraband was submitted to security and then to the authorities for further investigation.

After the cellphone was removed from the hall for evidence, nobody knew where it was. So, where is it? What happened to the cellphone was a mystery, some real *Spygate* shit. Just like in *Spygate*, the evidence was destroyed. It was believed that there were some incriminating things on the cellphone like pics and text messages that somebody in the administration wanted to hide. Whatever it was, it was juicy enough for them to act like it never happened.

It's funny when kids are mad; they usually tell the truth. We all questioned what happened, but it wasn't our place to speculate. Talking about it was a taboo in the building, so we all moved on. Even Ms. Caroline dropped the issue because she wanted to avoid having her life turned upside down for their cover up. They were more powerful than she was, and nobody cared. God bless Ms. Caroline; she did her job.

Unfortunately for her, the powers that be closed the door on the investigation before it even got started. The hypocrisy was so thick you could cut it with a knife. In any other organization or company, the people at the top are being scrutinized, but not here. This place was like Las Vegas—what happens here stays here.

CHAPTER THIRTEEN

✦ ✦ ✦ ✦ ✦

*Again we start, let me say my part About the only guy
who has some heart It took some time for the heart
to come But it's HERE, and everybody's in fear*

—KRS-One of Boogie Down Productions
"Jack of Spade"

WHAT THREW US ALL FOR a loop was when one of the best
supervisors was fired for how he responded during a riot. Let's
call him Karate Joe.

Joe was in the juvenile counselor class before mine and he
climbed up the ladder fast. He was a black belt in martial arts and
would always respond to incidents. Like in the KRS-One song, he
was like the Jack of Spades. I used to tell him, "Slow down because
you're making us all look bad," but that was his nature. When he was
a JC in the building, he was partners with Carter, and they were like
Powerman and Iron Fist on H-Hall, if I had to use a Marvel reference
to compare them.

They had the worse residents, but the most disciplined hall next
to J-Hall. After he took the supervisor's test, he was immediately
promoted to supervisor and was transferred to Spofford before it
closed. I was hoping when Spofford closed he would be assigned to
Fairvue, but he was sent to Greenwood instead. At Greenwood, he
responded to a riot and restrained several residents, but his method
ventured beyond what we were taught in training. What was baffling
was that we were never trained how to restrain in the event of a riot.
How can you simulate something like that in training? It's impossible.
In that situation, it's survival of the fittest.

But instead Karate Joe did his job to the best of his ability, and during the melee, several residents got hurt. He got an allegation that led to his firing.

I understand that working for this agency, you can't look in the rear view for anybody, but this dude was special. He would have made a great tour commander because he was a leader, and he wanted to help these kids. I would have run in the fire with him because I knew he was going in first, but they destroyed him. He fought for his job back and got it after being out of work for over a year, but he wasn't happy that they sent him back to Greenwood with a bunch of stipulations. He said fuck this and quit. Today, he runs his own dojo in Harlem, which might be a better way to reach the youth of today.

They hung him out to dry which was discouraging, and that made me never want to take the supervisor's test. It's amazing how the people making the decisions thought they had any clue of the tolerance level involved with managing these residents. Outside the box, it's easy to point a finger and say that a restraint was too excessive when you have never restrained anybody in your life. Too many times, the juvenile counselors are the recipients of career-threatening results, not the residents or supervision. Our backs were to the wall and our feet were in the fire, and nobody gave two shits. It's a thankless job. There were no financial incentive for going all out; as in Karate Joe's case, it cost him his job.

It was shortsighted to think that the people in the house had any respect for the people in the field. I worked with one woman who had put her kids in college only to go to work, and have a thirteen-year-old girl fight with her over a pen, to be stabbed by that girl and eventually be hospitalized by that same girl over a pen is shameful. Come to find out that the agency never pressed charges on that resident because they didn't want her to stay in the building because of a new charge, and even worse, a teacher gave that girl the pen in the first place.

It's all bullshit, where was the discipline for the teacher or the girl? We were getting fucked with no grease 100 percent of the time—that's a fact. This is like when in sports, the players are fined by people who have never played the game. Just like what Richard

Sherman the NFL player said, "They've never stepped foot on the field and understand how you can get a personal foul." If you have never spent five minutes alone with kids on a hall, what qualifies you to decide my fate after I was involved in an incident? You've never walked in my shoes.

The union sucks, let's keep it real. Anytime, you're forced to change unions because management has changed is bad business. BCW picked our union, and don't ask me did I vote. I did but that was for delegates. The union came with BCW, and to be honest, most of us were happy with the old union. Who's the union for the bus drivers? I wish they represented us.

As I watched all this unfold, I realized I had to get in where I fit in. Everybody wants to make everything a black-and-white thing, but there was nothing black and white about this. We were all black and we were devouring each other like piranhas. My assertion was that working in an environment that was predominantly black, I wouldn't have to worry about discrimination. This couldn't be further from the truth, it was blue-collar-black-on-black crime. From the staff setting up each other, to staff setting up residents, to supervision setting up staff with bad assignments, or residents with other residents they had beef with, it was dog eat dog. It was like working with the Decepticons, I didn't know who to trust.

Our lives were made so much more difficult when they changed the residents from wearing jumpers to polo-type shirts and khakis. Not only were we responsible for their behavior, but now we had to make sure their pants were up, literally. Whoever told these kids it was cool to show the backside of their underwear to expose the bubble of their ass must have been a booty warrior. I mean, if my name was Father Sinclair from boy's town, then this would have been a beautiful sight, but every time I saw a resident with his ass out, I wanted to put my foot in it. Nothing disgusted me more than to see five inches of the back of a kid's underwear. Some rapist in some correctional facility somewhere in this country created this fashion statement so he could set up his next piece of ass, and somehow these kids think that shit is cool. What idiots. The ignorance was like the blind leading the blind. That's when you know most of these kids have no fathers because any father who allowed his son to wear his pants like that should get his chin checked.

Now on top of all the things to discipline them for, we had to worry about this. They should have just left them in jumpers, but BCW wanted to get away from the incarcerated appearance. Why didn't they ask us? Now it was easier for the residents to escape the grasp of a restraint because now they would take all their clothes off and get completely naked. Way to go BCW, that's very child-abuse safe.

If I could draw any positives from watching these kids in this setting, it was that most of them were avid readers, always looking for the next series to a book. They would read a book a day. Other than doing push-ups and writing letters, these kids read more books than I ever did at fifteen. Maybe it was because it was the only thing to do, but I was impressed whenever they asked me to get them a book. I would bring them books all the time. My favorite book that I passed on to most of them was *The Art of War*. That book helped them improve their ability to deal with conflict, which was something that put them here in the first place.

But there was never a dull moment in Fairvue. There was staff bringing in weed, residents exchanging medication with each other, and rumors of sexual activity between staff and residents. These kids were crafty. They would make weapons out of deodorant bottles and plastic soap holders; we couldn't give them anything.

I prided myself on having none of the above transpire on E-Hall. Vega wasn't having none of that either, and she never let her guard down. She would go through the residents' papers in their room and find kites (letters) that they were intending on sending out to their homies in the building or to one of the girls on A-Hall. These kites were usually gang hits or thuggish love letters that were considered contraband. When a resident returned from medical, Vega would make them open their mouth and rotate their tongues to make sure they weren't trying to cheek (hide) it. I never went that hard, which was probably why they hated when she was there. I started to feel at times she went too far because it wasn't what she did, it was how she did it, and I would tell her to fall back; we already went down this road. I would tell her, "Let's not go through this again." But for some reason, she was fixated on violating their self-worth and whenever she went in on them, she would drag it. It was like she was out to prove that even though she was a female, they were the real pussies. It was obvious that emasculating the residents was her proverbial obsession.

It wasn't enough that they were locked up, she wanted to embarrass them and treat them like shit. She stopped harassing Jose and put her energy on another resident named JB. JB was older than the other residents on E-Hall, and Vega wasn't wrong when she said he was too old for the hall, but supervision felt he behaved better on E-Hall because he would always fight other residents he thought were bullies. JB was like a bully buster, and he hated watching weaker people get taken advantage of.

He wasn't that big. If I'm five foot eight, JB was five foot four, but he was a brawler. He was half black and half Puerto Rican, and he was arrested for beating up somebody in a street fight and almost killing him. He probably was defending one of his friends. Two years ago, when he was in Fairvue, I had him on E-Hall. I used to wrestle him in his room and toss him all over the place. He loved it, but I couldn't play with him like that anymore; times have changed. Plus, he was much bigger now, and he told me that the tussling we did toughened him up. He would tell me, "Mr. Geez, I will fuck you up now." I would tell him, "See these," then I would kiss my fist and say," Don't get it twisted, light skin. They still work but it ain't that type of party anymore."

Plus, as cool as Vega and I were, I still didn't trust her enough to do anything out of line in her presence. I remember once, I was roughing up a kid and she flipped, she said, "Yo, geez, what the fuck is wrong with you? You will get us both in trouble. Don't you see the cameras?"

How could I not see the cameras? She was right. I didn't appreciate her screaming on me, but wrong was wrong. After that day, I was more careful how I moved on the hall. JB had no respect for Vega, he would violate her any time she came at him. He always went at her sexually, and he never liked how she went at people. Once, he had his feet up on the bricks, and she said, "Nigga, are you crazy? Get your feet off my bricks." JB would say, "Let me find out these are your bricks, not only does this bitch think she has a dick, now she thinks she owns the place." When that happened, she would demand that I put him in his room. Then JB would say, "Don't have him put me in my room, you do it being that you got a bigger dick than everybody here."

Whenever a resident came at her like that, she would get all soft and pink, and instead of going at them, she would call security. The fact is she would bully the other residents, and JB didn't like that. Before security got there, I escorted JB to his room to avoid an incident, but that wasn't good enough for Vega. She wanted him moved, and when supervision got there, he was transferred to G-Hall.

He told supervision if he gets moved, he would pop on somebody, and to his word that's what he did. As soon as G-Hall went to the café, JB punched another resident just to make his point. He was restrained and taken to the TC's office where he promised to do it again if he wasn't returned to E-Hall. The TC and supervisors didn't care and sent him back to G-Hall, he was placed in his room until he was willing to participate with the program on G- Hall. The staff who worked there had a good relationship with JB, so he apologized to the resident he punched and adjusted to the move.

As time passed, Vega was spending more time off the hall and outside the building. She became a trainer and was working more downtown. They were revolving different JCs to work with me on E-Hall which made it difficult to establish consistency, and I again leaned on Jose to be more of a leader.

But things changed for him. The last time he went to court, the judge told him that he was going home in a month. His attitude completely changed. He spent more time in his room and rarely involved himself with the group. Instead of breaking up arguments, he ignored them and avoided confrontation with other residents. I didn't blame him; it was just something I wasn't used to. We were very close, and it was hard to adjust to him being so distant; but he mentally checked out and was focused on going home.

The day before Jose went home, I tried not to cry. It was hard, but I had to make sure I was happy for him and not sad because he was leaving. He served his time and deserved to leave. I gave him my number, even though it was against the policy because I wanted him to know that I would always be there for him, plus I promised to play him in 2K basketball online from my PlayStation game at home.

That night before I went home, we hugged, and he said he loved me and that I was like a father to him. He started to cry and went in his room. That wasn't the last time I spoke to him, but that was the last time I saw him. I had other residents I was close to, but I never had a resident make me want to come to work; Jose did that. We gave each other hope in a place that was so hopeless. With Vega and Jose gone, my attitude on the hall completely changed. I started to be paired with JCs supervision had nowhere to put which felt like having another resident not a coworker.

It was frustrating because I had nobody to rely on. I tried to have JB transferred back to E-Hall, but he didn't want to come back. He told me with Jose gone, the hall was dayroom, which meant that the residents were herbs and corny. I just wanted a big dog to help me control the puppies like Scoop did. Sometimes, the residents fear each other more than the staff, and every hall had one resident like that. E-Hall lacked leadership from the group. On G-Hall JB fit in well because the residents were more his age. The only problem was that G-Hall was run by a gang called 1090 led by a resident named Chaz.

Chaz was from Harlem, and he was emerging as the OG of the building. He would do whatever he wanted, and he knew how to manipulate supervision to get his way. He was a tall, slender, brown-skinned kid with cornrows and a laid-back demeanor. There was nothing that fazed him. He was there on two counts of attempted murder for shooting two men in a gang-related incident. His reputation was well-known on the street. He accepted JB even though JB was neutral. In the building, 1090s were known to attack other residents not down with them.

Things changed when JB jumped in to help another resident who was assaulted by three 1090 members. Maybe he should have minded his business, but that wasn't JB's nature. He hated seeing other people get beat up. But by doing this, he made enemies with Chaz, and became a target of the 1090s. Supervision knew that if JB stayed on the hall, he would get jumped; and when they asked me if I was okay with him returning to E-Hall, it was hard not to smile.

They made JB sign a contract which said that he would not get into any fights on E-Hall, and that he would respect the staff who worked the hall. If he violated the contract, he would be moved off the hall. In addition to being with me two years ago, what made my relationship with JB work so well was our love for football. He played on his JV (junior varsity) team at Clinton High School and always had a football player's mentality. He was fearless and loved physical contact. I wouldn't allow him to play basketball in the gym because he would change it into jail ball and send other residents to the infirmary. When I would tell him that he couldn't play, instead of getting mad, he would run around the gym in full speed for the entire hour. If anybody got in his way, he would run them over. If I had a team, he would be my starting safety. He reminded me of a young version of Ronnie Lott.

JB was from Webster Avenue in the Bronx, and he had a daughter. We would talk for hours about being fathers to daughters and what that meant. Even though he was a Giant fan and I was a Jet fan, we had a lot in common. On Sundays, we would go crazy watching the NFL games. We both missed the contact and camaraderie of being on a team. When there was a big hit in a game we were watching, I would have to keep JB from tackling the other residents. Most of the residents would stay in their rooms when the game was on because they knew JB was on his bullshit, and they didn't want him tackling them. Most of them weren't built like that; they were shooters, while JB was a fighter.

JB was like an old-school kid; he didn't shoot guns, but he threw his hands, which was why I liked him so much. In a street fight, JB was the person you would want by your side. If Jose was a good leader, JB was the best leader. Most of the residents in the building didn't want to go toe to toe with JB. He never wanted to see me lose my cool because a resident misbehaved. If I was having a rap session, he would tell the group, "Don't you hear staff talking? Shut the fuck up," and the group would be silent.

He had eccentric taste; he was infatuated with the *Lord of the Rings* trilogy. When *The Hobbit* came out, he begged me to bring it in, and when I did, he made the entire hall sit down quietly and watch it to create a real movie atmosphere. He was like the tough guy who liked teddy bears or lollipops. His childish nature and enthusiasm were infectious, plus he had his ego in check. If I told him to do something, it didn't hurt his feeling. If I told him to lock in or sit down for a program on the hall, he would listen, which made it easier to control the group because if JB listened, you better listen.

What I also respected about JB was that he had no interest in joining a gang. If anybody asked him what was he jackin' he would say, "I'm NFL—Neutral for Life." He would tell me anybody who joins a gang needs protection, and he could protect himself. Every gang in the building tried to recruit him because they knew he was a warrior, but he would turn them all down. It was like he had a wicked jump shot and a bunch of colleges were offering him scholarships; even Chaz was willing to forgive him if he became 1090.

JB made me care again. I stopped thinking about the people I missed and started focusing on the ones who were there. JB told me it wasn't about the contract; he was behaving because he knew I cared, and he would never give me an incident.

Everything changed one day when JB went to visiting and got assaulted by two residents from G-Hall. All three residents were escorted to the second floor by a female staff who was not equipped to handle one resident, let alone three. Supervision dropped the ball and didn't realize that the two residents from G-Hall were 1090, and they forgot that Chaz put the hit out on JB. The incident happened on the staircase and JB was beat up so bad that he was hospitalized. Even the female JC sustained injuries trying to break it up. It was fucked up because none of the supervisors got in trouble for that decision.

When JB returned from the hospital, he had a head wrap on, a busted lip, and a black eye. When he walked through the door, he was laughing and removed the head wrap to show me his left ear where he lost 30 percent of his hearing. I felt so bad for him, but he quickly said, "Don't feel bad for me, feel bad for them."

At the time, I didn't read much into that, but later, I realized he was on a mission to get them back.

CHAPTER FOURTEEN

Tables turn, suckers burn to learn
They can't dis-able the power of my label

—Public Enemy
"Rebel without a Pause"

JB WAS OBSESSED WITH REVENGE, he stopped watching TV and rarely smiled. He spent most of his time in his room and didn't interact with the group. When I spoke to him, he would just say, "Time will tell." I would say, "Time will tell what?" he would just laugh and walk off. He started going psycho on me. He would stand at the door staring at G-Hall.

Like a hungry dog, he was waiting to run off the hall and try to get at anybody who was 1090. I tried to tell him to let it go, but he wasn't built like that; his mind was set on revenge. Chaz took it all in stride, and he wasn't worried about JB. He was ready to put another hit on JB. This was like something out of the movie *Death Wish*—JB was on his Charles Bronson bullshit. There were other 1090 members on other halls, and JB found reasons to walk past every one of them.

One by one, JB attacked and assaulted all of them, he got them on the school floor and in medical. Once he was in the medical area and heard the voice of one of them in a mental health office, he ran in the office and pounded the kid so bad he was hospitalized. Supervision wanted to punish JB but something about what he was doing was heroic. These were assholes he was attacking that nobody liked. It was like he was doing us a favor because these kids terrorized the building, and now the predators were being hunted.

It was stunning because he was doing this all alone. Other residents wanted to help him, but he would tell them that this was his beef, and he didn't want the responsibility of defending them later. This was totally admirable. I've never seen anybody take on a gang all by themselves. He was like William Wallace from *Braveheart*.

The running joke was that whenever a 1090 member turned it up, the staff would say, "Don't let me have to get JB." In less than a month, JB assaulted seven residents who were 1090, hospitalizing two. He knew they put a hit out on him and he flipped the script and put it back on them, but he wanted to get the head of the snake and go after Chaz. That wouldn't be easy because Chaz always had two of his boys with him. He wasn't stupid, he carried himself like John Gotti in the building. It was like he was untouchable.

One day, JB saw Chaz in a class and he ran in the back door hoping to get at Chaz, but a JC got to him first. As JB struggled on the floor while being restrained, Chaz looked at him and said, "Silly rabbit tricks are for kids." JB said, "That's okay, nigga, you can't run forever." They had to hold Chaz back because he was about to kick JB in the face.

When I think of it, I never saw Chaz have a fight, but his hands worked. Once on G-Hall a big kid was admitted to the hall from Greenwood and was talking shit. Chaz beat him up so bad both the kid's eyes were swollen, he had hand skills. I would have paid to watch him, and JB get it in, but supervision made sure they were far away from each other. As bad as Chaz was, he was a charming kid. Most Harlem cats were the kings of swag, and Chaz wasn't any different. He was a good-looking kid with incredible ball skills. If he wasn't locked up, he could get offers from colleges for basketball.

But he had malevolent eyes and was motivated by control and violence. Once supervision denied him visits because they felt he was receiving weed from his visitors; so, he told them every day he doesn't get a visit, a staff member will be assaulted or as he put it get popped on. To his word, for six days straight, a JC or security guard got popped on by someone from the 1090s. It amazed me the control he had over these kids. They were like suicide bombers; they did anything he said.

At that time the staff was so shook, nobody wanted to work with any resident affiliated with 1090 because those kids were good to do something bad. It was their nature. I asked a resident what did 1090 mean, he said, "Ten percent loyal, ninety percent grimy." Supervision had no choice but to reinstate his visitation rights for the safety of the staff. It was hard to prove that Chaz did anything because his hands were clean, but everybody knew he carried out the order. Chaz and his goonies had a pervasive choke hold on the building; it was a case of the inmates running the asylum. It was a relief to be working on E-Hall now because JB would not allow any 1090 to be on the hall, and just like Chaz, he would have them smoked off the hall.

It was around this time Ms. Willis from J-Hall was promoted to supervisor, and if Ms. Nebula was Evillene, Ms. Willis was Glinda the good witch. Nothing moved without her involvement. Before she was supervisor, most of supervision never did anything without getting the TC's approval, but Ms. Willis would get the approval of the ED and the deputy director. She had access to the kitchen, the school floor, and even the recreation room to change the TV channels.

I was fortunate to have her office on E-Hall, and we benefited from her being with us. She took care of us like she did J-Hall. This was a game changer because now I got anything I wanted as long as my group behaved. TC Herrera would do his rounds and ask me, "Why are all your residents up?" and I would say, "Ms. Willis said they could." Or he would say, "Why are the lights off?" and I would tell him, "Because Ms. Willis said I could have them off." He never challenged her.

She was the only supervisor who remembers how it felt to be a JC, and she was like a player's coach. She had our back, but not everybody was a fan of her methods. She caught flak from her peers who felt she had too much control for a new supervisor; but if they remember, she had too much control as a JC. This was no surprise. It was just that now they couldn't tell her what to do. She even drew haters from some JCs who were mad that she got to be a supervisor, but what they failed to realize was that she deserved it and was better at the job than anybody else.

She didn't hesitate to step in a resident's face or step in a JC's face if they did something wrong. If she barked on me, I ate it because, unlike the other supervisors, she would compliment me for something I did good. She knew how to handle the multiple personalities of the residents and the demands of the job. If it wasn't for her, Chaz and JB would have killed each other a long time ago because she was the only person they both feared. It was more respect than fear.

If she had to, she would use a hands-on approach, and her methods were effective. She wouldn't hesitate to slap the shit out of one of them, and they would take it like men. The administration took a blind eye to her behavior when it got out of control; but they gave her control when they promoted her. Things got heated on E-Hall because my coworkers who worked the AM and night tour weren't feeling how I ran the hall. They felt I allowed the residents too much freedom, especially JB. They all wanted him off the hall. But with the support of Ms. Willis, they were preaching to the choir. She always agreed with me, and told them that I had the most seniority on the hall and that they better handle it.

That didn't sit well with Ms. Kindie. She came from Spofford when they closed. To her, I created more problems because she felt I made them look like bad guys to the residents, and they would turn it up on them for doing things different. But I didn't change, I stayed consistent. I ran a program that rewarded them for good behavior. It was a constant power struggle between me and Ms. Kindie who was strict and rarely gave second chances. Once you were in her dog house, you stayed there. She didn't like how JB tried to do his own thing and how he told other residents what to do.

Unlike Vega, she wasn't afraid of JB's tough talk. She would tell him, "If you don't want to listen, I'm gonna pack you up." She had the power on the AM; the AM tour commander did whatever she wanted. She was a fine-ass middle-age Trinidadian woman who had two teen kids of her own. She would never allow any child in this setting to get the better of her. It got so bad JB stopped coming out his room when she was there. When she asked him why he wouldn't come out, he would say, "I was waiting till the PM staff comes in." I told him stop because it was bringing unnecessary attention to me.

When other residents did the same thing, supervision got involved and forced them to stay out of their rooms. When TC Herrera got wind of the protest, he took it a step further and had me work on another hall. He said, if they want to wait until I showed up, they can keep waiting. I was so fuckin' mad. I thought it was unfair to move me because they can't control their tour. The first day this happened, I passed by E-Hall and JB saw me walking toward G-Hall. He asked me where I was going. When I told, him I was working on G-hall, he freaked out. That same day, Ms. Kindie got stuck and overheard me talking to JB at the door. When she told him to have a seat, he ignored her. He said to me that he was going to turn it up. I said, "Do what you want." That might have been the wrong thing to say because in less than an hour, I heard a security call to E-Hall on the radio. To this day, Ms. Kindie never forgave me. She swore I gave JB the green light to turn it up.

Indirectly, I kind of did. JB had the other residents violate her tour while he stayed in his room. That day, E-Hall got shut down, and I could hear them banging on their doors all the way from G-Hall.

Things weren't much better on G-Hall. It felt like I was in the lion's den. I never worked on G-Hall since Chaz got there. I knew him in passing, but we never had a conversation. I was more familiar with the other residents. In the back of my mind, I was prepared for the worst. There were fourteen residents on the hall, and six of them were 1090. I could see Chaz telling his goons to violate me, but that didn't happen.

When I got there, he was in his room with the door open; he was reading a book. When I walked past his room, he invited me in like he was expecting me. On his walls, he had pictures with different girls, all dimes, and photos of his favorite NBA players. For a young dude, I was amazed at how crispy clean his room was. His bed was made, and his books were organized like a bookshelf. I wasn't surprised that one of his books was the book *Power*, I was just shocked somebody got this crazy motherfucka that book to read.

The first thing he asked me was, "What's up with your man?" I say, "Who? JB?" He said "Yeah, why doesn't he let that go." I said, "Because you had him jumped." Chaz said, "I didn't have anything to do with that." I looked at him, then we both laughed. He wasn't as pernicious as I thought; he was down to earth.

He said he wanted to squash the beef between them; he actually liked JB. I told him, "JB hated your whole crew, the beef will never end." He said he respected JB because he was a true maverick and followed nobody, plus he knew JB was tougher than anyone he was rolling within the building. We talked for two hours, and I realized how smart this kid was. His goal was to go to college and play basketball. He even thought he was nice enough to go to the A (NBA). He said he was the black sheep of his family because most of the people in his family went to college; he was the only fuck up.

I asked him, "So why be in a gang?" He said he was attracted to the lifestyle, and most of his boys were a part of it. To be a part of something that allowed him to move up the ranks based on reputation and not based on race or financial status gave him all the incentive he needed. As much as I detest gang activity, I couldn't argue with him there. His inability to have remorse for his actions was the extreme of being 1090, he didn't care. This made him the most ruthless and gave him power.

In the 120 minutes I spent talking to him, I realized he wasn't as bad as I thought; he knew how to work the system and he would take advantage of people's fears. At that moment while having a conversation with this child I forgot that he was just that, a child. But in this setting these boys moved like men. Criminal behavior ages you, and Chaz was a pro with serious game. Institutional slavery has torched his mind to believe that jail was real life. I told him if he could channel that energy to good use, he could become a millionaire. That's what future entrepreneurs are made of. He actually listened to me and valued my opinion. It was almost like he was waiting to talk to me for advice.

My reputation was pretty solid in the building as a JC. Most of the residents thought I was helpful. He said he heard I was a good dude and that he liked my style. Then we started talking about female

JCs and supervisors, and he ran down a list of them he said were on him. I didn't buy it, but when I thought about it, I have overheard some chicks say how cute he was, and if he wasn't so young he could get it.

In roll call, I would ear hustle and hear the shit these chicks would say. As we were talking, the partner I was working with was replaced by Ms. Hermes.

She was one of the newest JCs who came in the last class. Ms. Hermes was hands down the baddest JC in the building, and I mean bad meaning good. She was Spanish with long hair and a gorgeous body. Her ass looked as soft as a pillow, and it was hard for any female to look good in our work pants, but she made it look easy. Every male staff in the building tried to holla at her, but she was in a long-term relationship and played the faithful-girlfriend role.

As soon as Chaz saw her, his attention shifted from talking to me to staring at her. He said, "I'm gonna holla at you later," and he went in the day area to sit and talk to her. When the phone rang, she got up to answer it, and like a scene out of the movie *Caddyshack,* all eyes were on her ass; it was impossible to ignore.

Chaz then told me that he was getting that. I told him, "Good luck. Everybody tried and struck out." Chaz put that Harlem swag on and spent the whole night talking to her.

At about 10:00 p.m. when everybody was locked in, Chaz asked me if I could get him another blanket, but I knew he was trying to get me off the hall. I laughed and told him he was wasting his time; but he was determined to try. After ten minutes of searching the building for a blanket, I returned, and he ran to the door and told me he needed more time. Just then, there was a radio call for assistance to J-Hall. I stepped in to tell Ms. Hermes that I was going to assist, and to my amazement, she was sitting in his room. I told him he was lucky I had to leave, and I went to respond to J-Hall.

When I got to J-Hall, this big kid who needed a respirator to breathe was turning it up; he attacked the staff and was being restrained by security. As I assisted in the restraint, I was thinking in the back of my mind how foolish Chaz was to think anything could possibly happen between him and Ms. Hermes.

After calming big boy down, I returned to G-Hall to write my incident report, and I heard gagging coming from the staff bathroom. It almost sounded like a cat choking on a fur ball. It was Ms. Hermes; she didn't hear me come on the hall because she was pretty loud. When I went to Chaz's room, he was sitting on the edge of his bed, wiping his boxers with a towel. I know this didn't just happen, I was gone for twenty-five minutes, maybe thirty. His room had the stench of saliva and semen. It was hard to believe, but it was real, this chick really stepped to the mic. Nahhhhh, man, this fuckin' kid got this fine-ass chick to give him a blowjob. There is no fuckin' way. I was dumbstruck. He had cum all over his sheets.

In less than thirty minutes, he was able to get a woman we all thought was wifey material to suck his dick. What the hell is this world coming to? Damn, she bit the forbidden fruit, or in this case sucked it. He said he could have fucked her, but he didn't have time. It was then that I knew this kid could get whatever he wants in the building.

What was crazy was that he was moving like he does this; maybe not to her, but he was a pro at this. When Ms. Hermes came out the bathroom, I played it off like I didn't know, but she played it off even more and started a conversation about nothing. The whole time we were talking, I started to feel bad for her boyfriend. The poor guy was kissing this chick, and if she would do this, what else is she doing? Maybe her boyfriend wasn't piping it right, but that's no excuse to get your rocks off on a kid. You must be demented and be suffering from low self-esteem to do this shit. What a skank or better yet, wench, because she was providing lube service. It's funny how someone so beautiful could look so ugly.

She wasn't who we thought she was. If the guys on the job knew her head was so fucked up, they would have made a power move straight for that ass. She looked like she had it all together, but looks are deceiving. I lost mad respect for her as a woman. On the flip side, Chaz didn't need money or a powerful position on the job to get her to service him. His celebrity in the building got him anything he wanted. I never spoke about it after that night because I was embarrassed for her. I didn't actually see anything, but it was obvious what happened. Plus, Chaz wasn't the type of dude to kiss and tell.

BCW might have looked at this as child abuse. No this was a young predator preying on the naïve and disheveled behavior of a woman, that's it. Sometimes, in a house of sinners, everything abnormal becomes the norm; and as fine as she was, she obviously had serious insecurity issues. Chaz was seventeen, and the way he was acting, this wasn't his first time.

The next day when I saw JB, I told him to stay away from Chaz. I told him, "That nigga will kill you." JB said, "Fuck him, I'm gonna get him."

That situation with Ms. Hermes was an inside joke between Chaz and me until he got sent upstate. When I saw him, we would just laugh and never talked about it. Dude needed to be in advanced juvie for the most-clever criminals.

Not long after Chaz got sentenced, Ms. Hermes got hurt in an incident while working with the girls and never returned to the job. I think she knew that I knew what happened and eventually found a way out.

After Chaz, new policies were implemented to separate gang members from being on the same halls. I thought they would have learned their lesson from what happened on F-Hall, but I guess not.

CHAPTER FIFTEEN

It's unbelievable uncivilized/ and
now I'm starting to realize
Danger in the jungle, the jungle means danger/
tension intense hearts filled with anger

—Jungle Brothers
"Straight out the Jungle"

WHEN CLAUDIA WAS PREGNANT, WE couldn't have had better timing. I went on paternity leave at the right time. When my third child Jordan was born, I had a whole new outlook on life. It completely recharged my battery.

When I returned to work, things felt a whole lot different. As I entered E- Hall after a six-week leave, the residents ran down on me like I was Jehovah. I know the other staff hated that; they would tell me that the residents would say, "Geez this and Geez that. When Geez gets back, we do this with Geez," and some were counting down the days till my return. They even made congratulations cards for the birth of my son. It felt good to be back. After a leave of more than six weeks, there is always a loss and gain in the number of residents on the hall, but the overall sentiment is that I was missed. After a long vacation, you never know what you'll get when you return, always expecting the worse, I was prepared for the bullshit. Gone were two or three residents I wasn't feeling, and in return, I met the most talented kids I have ever seen admitted at Fairvue. His name was Victor, but everybody called him Happy Feet because he could dance his ass off. Victor was from Harlem, and like most kids from uptown, music and dancing was his coping mechanism. It gave him wings and freed him from the negative feeling he had about being locked up. This kid would give Chris Brown a run for his money. He was a natural, and I would tell him all the time that he needs to be a choreographer and in videos, but like most kids at sixteen, his mind was on pussy and money. It's hard to get them to capitalize off their talent at this stage because they don't see tomorrow; they are only worried about now. I've had the best basketball player and the best rapper and graffiti artist in the building, but it was nothing like having the best dancer. This gave us the type of swag we never had on E-Hall. There were times the ED would have city council members visit the building and the highlight of their tour was to see Happy Feet get lite. We were the beneficiaries of this attention, and the perks were extra snacks and special programs, but nothing on the level of reduced time or a letter to the judge to help him go home. To me it, was like they were using him on some chicken George shit to entertain their guest, and like chicken George from the TV special "Roots," all Happy Feet wanted was to be free. He rarely helped his cause because he would always get into fights defending his manhood. The innocuous challenge by Happy Feet against the other residents in the building didn't sit well, they took his confidence as cockiness and did anything to ruffle his feathers. The haters in the building would call him Happy Boy because of how flamboyant he was, and I would try to emphasize to him that they wish they had your talent, but he would tell me, "They called me pussy, I had to pop it off." All this did was keep him in the building and limit his chances of going home. JB was still there and put Happy Feet under his wing to back off the haters, but JB had his own problems to deal with. Now that Chaz wasn't there, JB became that dude in the building, and most of Chaz's crew dropped their flags for fear of being violated with no leader. It's amazing when followers have no one to follow—how quiet they get. There was a sense of resolve in the building with Chaz gone.

All the gang assaults were over, and most of the other 1090 kids who were heavy hitters were removed from Fairvue. It's was stunning how much power one kid could have. E-Hall stayed clean of gang activity— thanks to JB—until Leon came to the hall.

Leon was from Harlem, and he knew Chaz from the neighborhood. He tried to hide the fact that he was 1090 and hoped to get a crack at JB. When he got transferred to E-Hall, JB said, "Nah get this op outta here." JB asked him, "What you jackin?" and he told JB he was neutral.

One day, he was playing the video game which was next to JB's room and JB overheard him say he was 1090. JB asked the staff to open his door and he ran down on Leon and rocked him with a flurry of punches. After that incident, JB got rearrested and was shipped to the Rock. The other residents were so mad supervision had to move Leon because they feared for his safety.

My job got harder with JB gone because he kept the hall quiet. Every time a resident I was close to left, I would promise myself that I won't get close to anyone again. Sometimes, it was easier that way; being an asshole kept me from being nice to anybody. At this point, I would rarely see Ms. Vega in the building after she became a full-time trainer. When I did see her, she was usually responding to incident and never worked on a hall.

There was never any love lost. I understood her mission was to move up the ladder; but when she applied for a position and didn't get it, her attitude changed. She wasn't playing the politics game with them, and they denied her access into their club. It was unfortunate because she would have been a good supervisor or manager, plus she would have been somebody for me to go to when I needed something without the red tape. I tried to get her to return to the hall, but she was over that. When she sustained a minor injury, she applied for a transfer to work downtown and got it.

With her gone, I needed a new partner. I was tired of working with anybody. They started pairing me with Ms. Rosario, a new JC who trained under JC Pena.

Pena was promoted to OM (Operations Manager), which was the same position Vega applied for. He was responsible for training the new JCs and started by putting together a response team. For a month, they would just respond to incidents, which prepared them more than most of us when it came to restraining; it became second nature for them.

Ms. Rosario wanted to be my partner so bad and her ambition won me over. She was only twenty-three, but her maturity made her seem older. Her parents were from Costa Rica, and she was the cutest little thing. She almost looked like a doll, but she didn't want anyone to get it twisted. She was a firecracker. She was like a younger version of Ms. Willis; she would smack up a kid in a heartbeat. I guess she didn't want the residents to take her looks for a weakness. Like Vega, she went to John Jay College and got her degree in criminal justice.

She had hoped to get her feet wet at Fairvue and to eventually climb up the corporate ladder, but I told her not in this place. I said, "Get in and then get out, or you will have cobwebs growing under your arms." Then she asked me, "Why are you still here?" I don't know what to tell her.

For the first time, I realized my life was stagnant. After getting custody of my children and having my bills paid, I was satisfied, and I didn't want much else. I guess I stopped dreaming. I told her, "You're too young to get stuck here. Keep your options open." She appreciated the pep talk and agreed to avoid getting comfortable.

At this time, H-Hall was off the hook, and to make matters worse, JC Carter was moved to D-Hall which left H-Hall without a JC who could establish control. First, they got busted for smoking weed and got most of their staff fired or suspended. Then, whenever they conducted searches, supervision would find weed, lighter, X-rated CDs, and money. It was like a bodega on that hall—whatever you wanted, they had. When the residents found out who did the searches and took their stuff, they would violate them. I was lucky that I was on E-Hall, but when they assaulted our best male JC who covered weekends, my luck changed.

The TC on duty told me that he needed me to work H-Hall because there were no men available. I wished I called out that day. It was so bad there that the residents put giant holes in the walls big enough to walk through, so they could go from room to room without opening the doors. Supervision wanted to close the hall for repairs, but they had nowhere to put these kids; they were that bad. There were only six of them, but they were the worst residents in the building. It was like F-Hall all over again.

Again, the administration ignored their own rules and had four residents from the same gang together, while the other two residents were neutral. For convenience sake, the administration put their words in their pockets and allowed another hall be dominated by one gang. Three of them I had on E- Hall, which made it easy for me to go there without any problems. When I went to H-Hall, most of them greeted me with hugs and pounds, but the one I didn't know was the worst of them all. His name was Archie, and he was a problem.

Archie was a fifteen-year-old Dominican kid who was six foot two, and the one responsible for most of the assaults on the staff. While I was talking to the other residents, Archie walked away like he didn't want to be bothered. When I said what's up to him, he kept walking and said, "Get this nigga outta here before I violate him."

Before I could defend myself, a resident I had on E-Hall named Marko defended me by saying, "Yo, watch your fuckin mouth. That's my nigga. He took care of me when I was a snot nose on E-Hall." Marko was the leader of the group, and he was the shot caller for Patria in the building. Archie just went to his room. Marko apologized for Archie, but I told him, "He doesn't know me, it's whatever."

Marko was on E-Hall two years ago. Yes, he's been in the building that long. He was there for a murder charge. If I remember correctly, I stopped JC Ford from beating his ass once on E-Hall, and he never forgot that.

He missed the cologne I would wear. He said when he smelled it on the hall, he knew his day would be good because I never let anybody pick on him. When he first got there, he was small and didn't speak English. I always protected him, and he felt safe when I was at work.

While I stood there talking to Marko, I heard a banging and kicking noise. I went to see what it was and saw Archie kicking down another wall in his room. I said, "Yo, what the fuck are you doing?" He told me to get away, and before I could say another word, Marko and the other residents told him to stop. He stopped, but he had an attitude. When I asked him what was wrong, he wouldn't answer. When I asked Marko, what was wrong with him, Marko said, "Geez,

I'm not gonna hold you but he's young and dumb," but another resident said he was mad because he hasn't had a phone call in two weeks, and every time he asked a supervisor he gets denied. I told him, "If I get you a phone call, will you smile?" He struggled to avoid a fade-away smile.

I called Ms. Willis and begged her to give him a call. She wasn't with it at first but gave him one for me. When he returned to the hall, he changed his attitude and apologized for acting the way he did. It felt like I pulled a splinter out of a bear's claw. Marko helped smooth shit out when he started talking about the old E-Hall when JC Ford and Luke were there. He told me I was his favorite staff and that he admired my love for my children. He said he missed my rap sessions because they got him through the rough days; he hated being locked up.

Archie was listening, and because he looked up to Marko, he started looking up to me. What opened Archie even more was when Marko asked me to pray with him at the end of the night. On E-Hall, I always prayed with him the night before he went to court. I would always say the Lord's Prayer, and it was something I did with most of my residents the night before their court day. Marko said it always helped him sleep better.

I didn't attend church a lot, but I do believe in God and know the power of prayer. After that night, I would get a call from supervision to go to H-Hall because Archie wanted me to pray with him. I started to feel like Archie's personal pastor. This opened the door for Archie and me to develop a strong relationship.

When Marko got sentenced, he put Archie in charge of their set. I don't think Archie was ready for the responsibility of being a leader of a gang. Some people are leaders and others are followers, and Archie was a follower. He never thought of consequences when he reacted, he always took things to the extreme. When I talked to him, I used karma to help him fully understand that everything bad that happened to him was the result of his behavior. Very few people could get through to Archie—if you worked with him and he liked you, the day was easy, but if he didn't like you, the day was hell.

He once put a JC in the trash can head first, and another time, he spat in a staff's face and then punched him so hard in the eye he thought he lost his vision in that eye permanently. Archie was a human wrecking ball. I've seen my share of bad kids, but Archie outdid them all with the number of times he got into incidents. Archie would turn it up every day. It got so bad security would post by his hall to be prepared for his next incident. This ominous disposition was something Archie reveled in, and he loved to be the elephant in the room.

I started to be assigned to H-Hall just because Archie requested me, but I hated working there because those residents liked to smoke. And no matter how many searches or rap sessions were conducted, if they had weed, they would smoke it.

When he got transferred to intake and then J-Hall, my prayers were answered because they had consistent staff to deal with him. What was puzzling was that the agency kept him in the building, why didn't they send him to Greenwood? But Greenwood wouldn't take him, and the fear was that they would have sent us one of their problems.

I couldn't take credit for trying to rehabilitate Archie. People with way more history with him than me put the time in to help him. One of those people was Ms. Willis. She would have him brought to her office and counseled him for hours. Being that her office was on E-Hall, he did pose a threat to the other residents, but he didn't have issues with them and because both Ms. Willis and I were there, he behaved.

Most of the other supervisors had issues with her traveling him to her office, but none of them had a relationship with Archie or had answers for his behavior. His ubiquitous influence was felt by everybody in the building. Some staff called out of work for fear that they would get the assignment to work with him.

If he was with Ms. Willis, the day went smoothly. Who would argue that? Whenever she wasn't at work, he was a terror; but I couldn't do much, I had a bigger problem E-Hall.

CHAPTER SIXTEEN

◆ ◆ ◆ ◆ ◆

But uhh, a thug changes and love changes and
best friends become strangers, word up

—Nas
"The Message"

ONE DAY, WHILE TRAVELING FROM the gym on the staircase, Archie attacked three residents from E-Hall over some gang shit. Latin Kings were virtually extinct in Fairvue, but there was one Latin King on E-Hall, and his name was Jazz. Other residents took issues with Jazz because he dropped his Latin King flag to become Blood. This happened a lot. Some residents would drop one gang to join another for protection. The false claiming of gangs was a regular thing in this building.

Archie took offense to that and still saw Jazz as a Latin King, so when he saw Jazz on the staircase, he took that opportunity to assault him. When I got to work that day and found out what happened, I went to J-Hall to speak to Archie. Archie told me that they exchanged words and that Jazz was talking reckless, but he agreed to squash the beef because of me.

Jazz was next in line to become the closet boy on E-Hall. He was under the wing of JB before JB left the building, and like Jose, he was very reliable. He was a fifteen-year-old thin Dominican kid with long hair in a ponytail from the Bronx. He became Blood under another resident who was on E-Hall named Doughboy. Doughboy was a Mac Baller and had the building and was beefing with Archie before he got sent upstate. I believe Jazz just got caught in that web, and Archie didn't know Jazz. He was just frustrated because he never got a shot at Doughboy. With Doughboy gone, a lot of the gang responsibility was on Jazz, and I didn't think he was ready for that. After hearing both sides of the story, I told Ms. Willis, and she brought them together to settle their differences, which they did and agreed too dead the beef.

My life got easier when TC Herrera went out indefinitely from an incident on J-Hall. I never wish for anybody to get hurt, but when you encourage restraining, sometimes, you get what you asked for. With him gone, I felt a calm resonated within the staff, and we could shine without him putting a cloud over our progress. It was criminal the amount of power he had over us. The other TCs never took things to the extreme; Herrera did and it borderlines on being inhumane.

Nobody ever challenged his methods because the suits downtown gave him the green light to do what he wanted. What an Uncle Tom. Dude would even kick us out the building if our shift ended to manage the overtime like it was his money. Complaining about him would have been like telling the Death Star that Darth Vader was mistreating the storm troopers. How would that go? This opened the door for us to implement more of our ideas on the halls.

We weren't getting written up anymore for frivolous acts, especially those out of our control. For instance, Herrera would hold us responsible if a resident damaged agency property which was totally unprovoked. Most of these residents were overmedicated, and their behavior was a reaction from what they were taking.

But TC Herrera didn't want to hear that. He felt we got paid to do a job, and we better do it. He even told one staff that because they were there when this resident broke the phone, it should come out of their check for the repairs.

Most of us were glad he wasn't around. This gave Ms. Willis complete control on the weekends. E-Hall became the new J-Hall. We had the most inventory and we would watch movies with ice cream and cake on the weekends. If we stayed incident-free and all the residents had their rooms clean, Ms. Willis let us rock.

The haters came from everywhere. Most of the other residents wanted to be transferred to E-Hall and the other JCs didn't like us.

They thought we had too much and would always point the finger at Ms. Willis. Even the other supervisors thought she was showing them up because she would always do twice the amount of work as they did. They wanted her to slow things down, but she only had one speed. I was just the recipient of her generosity; you can't be mad at us because the best supervisor had an office on our hall.

In roll call, Ms. Willis would take them to task and ask anyone to speak up or forever hold their peace, but nobody would say anything. Things got real catty, and even Ms. Rosario got flack for getting the assignment to be on E- Hall. Who cares? Now y'all want to work on E-Hall?

For the longest, I didn't have a consistent partner. Everybody thought those kids on E-Hall were a pain in the ass and too needy. Ms. Willis helped change that. She made them see the fruits of their labor, and they realized with good behavior came good things. Other tours also resented the special treatment of E-Hall, and slowly, we started getting the worse residents, which was a ploy to ruffle my feathers.

One resident was Ohio. He lived in the Bronx, but he was from Ohio, and he was a Crip. Everybody knew that it was foolish to put Crips and Bloods on the same hall, and E-Hall had more Bloods than any other hall. Ohio was brought to Fairvue from the Rock on a theft charge, and he had an attitude worse than anybody. He was a dark-skinned African-American kid who wasn't afraid of anything or anybody.

One day during my rap session, he was sitting in the front row and got up to tell the group that they could get it. He said, "If any of you motherfuckas wanna get it, let's go." Then, out of nowhere, this one resident got up and swung at Ohio, and he quickly weaved the punch and dropped the kid. Then the other residents went after him, but I intervened and took down one while Ms. Rosario restrained another. We anticipated this situation, and before the rap session, we put Jazz in his room. I could tell when they were plotting to jump somebody. It was like spider sense. When they start moving funny, you know something was brewing.

Jazz was salivating at the mouth, demanding to get out during the melee, but he could only stand at his door and watch as his crew got put on their backs by the staff. He was lucky because all those involved were transferred to other halls, all but Ohio. Everybody was tap dancing around the fact that it was a matter of time before Ohio and Jazz got it in. It got so bad that I had Archie speak to both of them, hoping that he could get them to chill.

There was so much tension because it wasn't working with them on the same hall together. One of them had to move.

All of a sudden, things went from bad to good. The day before supervision moved Ohio, I got a call that JB was in admissions about to be brought to the hall. His bail got paid for the rearrest and he returned for two weeks before going upstate. If there was ever a kid I would consider a savior, it was JB.

He treated Jazz like his little brother, and the word was that on the Rock, he ran with Ohio. They fought side by side against 1090s on Rikers Island. Before he got to the hall, he was updated on the beef between Jazz and Ohio. When he got there, he sought out Jazz and let him know that Ohio was good, within five minutes, Jazz went to squash the beef. JB and Ohio hugged like lost brothers, and JB told the group, "If you have beef with Ohio, you got beef with me."

The hall was at peace again, and supervision let Ohio stay. Those were the smoothest two weeks. JB and I never had a proper send off. We were now able to close the chapter on our friendship and agreed to stay in touch. With JB there on the hall, Jazz and Ohio maintained, and after hearing a few stories about their time on the Rock, Jazz started to respect Ohio. They both had a few similarities, both dropped flags to join other gangs. Jazz left the Latin Kings to become Blood and Ohio started jacking YB (Young Bosses).

Those were the two dominant gangs in the building along with Patria. This allowed them to coexist better than if they were true Bloods and Crips. Jose always told me that jumping from gang to gang was not acceptable on the street, but in detention, it was like musical chairs. It was incredible the bond they formed.

After JB went upstate, it was like having two JBs—one Spanish and one black. They were the ultimate dynamic duo—Jazz was the silent assassin and Ohio was more in-your-face. It was hard to fill the shoes of JB, but together they made it work. They were like BFFs or, better yet, frenemies sharing snacks, clothes, and commissary. They seemed to have a mutual respect despite their differences, but the one thing they had in common was that they both had love for JB, and because of that they could bond.

If Jazz had beef with somebody, Ohio caught them from the back, and if Ohio got into a fight, Jazz had his follow up. It was dope because if you didn't know them, you would think they hated each other, but JB fixed that.

They had a partnership in maintaining the hall to keep it clean and incident free.

I stayed on them to check their behavior because if one of them got moved, it would change the complexion of the entire hall. Most of my peers felt I went from one monster in JB to two in Jazz and Ohio. If it wasn't for Ms. Willis, they would have been moved, but she was instrumental in staying on top of them which helped keep off the haters.

Not really feeling the gang thing, I told them to keep that shit in check. Ohio did a better job of it than Jazz. He was obsessed with recruiting people much to the dismay of Ohio. When Jazz initiated two residents on the hall, Ohio had enough. He stepped to Jazz and said, "You're doing some fuckboy shit. Didn't staff say kill that gang shit? You trying to make this hall all Blood?" Jazz took offense and said, "Do you, nigga. I'll do me."

Ohio took it upon himself to assault anybody recruited under Jazz. After he beat up two residents, he was moved to D-Hall. I told Jazz he was next to be moved if he didn't keep his gang activity to himself. He agreed to fall back because he knew if he got moved, he wouldn't live like he was on E-Hall. He saw how hard it was for Ohio on D-Hall, being at the back of the food chain, he was miserable.

With JC Carter still running the show, he had no sympathy for Ohio. There were bigger dogs over there that he had more history with. D-Hall was a YB hall, and the alpha dog over there was a resident name Mamadou. I had him on E-Hall when he was a puppy.

The kid who put him on to YB, I introduced them, which Mamadou never forgot.

Mamadou was born in this country, but both of his parents were from Africa. He got locked up on a gun charge, and his rep on the street was well- known, plus he had the green light to lead the YBs in the building. Not everybody cared about gang activity on their hall, as long as nobody got hurt. On D-Hall, Ohio became Mamadou's hitman. He was responsible for smoking anybody Mamadou told him to. If he didn't, he would get smoked by the other YBs on the hall; it was a form of earning his stripes. I told Ms. Willis we must get Ohio back on E-Hall because he's a pop off dummy for Mamadou, plus most of the residents over there were sixteen and seventeen, while Ohio was fifteen.

She could move him back to E-Hall using his age as the reason. They set up a contract like the one JB signed to monitor his behavior. I was glad he returned because he got exposed to some negative shit on D-Hall that affected his growth. Plus, Jazz was feeling himself, and Ohio was the only resident that would step in his face and tell him the truth. It must have been an Ohio thing because there was no shame in his game when it came to speaking his mind, but like always, his mouth would get him in trouble.

The day he had a fallout with Ms. Rosario, he almost got him moved again. He felt that Ms. Rosario showed special treatment to the Hispanic residents and violated only the black ones, which wasn't true, but he knew how to play with words. He started to get snippy whenever she addressed him. When I spoke to him about it, he said, "Scrap (he called everybody scrap), you better check your partner. She acts like she doesn't see the bullshit these Spanish niggas are doing, but she wants to ride me." I told him it's not like that. She treats everybody the same. Then he used one of my lines, he said, "Sounds good." I said "Good."

When Ohio felt some type of way about something, it was never over. He wanted to fuck with her. He told her that she was moody because she didn't get any dick over the weekend and said it loud enough for everybody on the hall to hear. She was so mad she said, "My nigga, go to your room. Your night is over." He told her,

"I'm not your nigga, bitch." She got all indignant and looked at him sideways for calling her a bitch. Calling a woman a bitch was like a slap in the face. She grabbed him by his collar and attempted to put him in his room.

At this time, I was on the other side of the hall playing Madden with some other residents when I heard the commotion. I went over there and pulled Ms. Rosario off him and put him in his room. He was livid. He kept saying, "That bitch called me a nigga," and Ms. Rosario was just as upset because he called her a bitch. It was crazy, I was caught in some real he-said-she-said shit. Neither of them would let it go. They both wanted to report the other.

To avoid supervisions involvement, I had Jazz talk to Ohio while I calmed down Ms. Rosario. I told her that my nigga shit is not cute. I said the N word is nothing to play with. Society has gotten real comfortable saying the word, but all black people don't feel that way. I said, "We all hear you say it, and as pretty as you are, it makes you look ugly. Just change your vocabulary. Plus, you don't want that on your permanent record."

She never saw it that way and agreed to let it go. To her credit, I never heard Ms. Rosario use the N word again, and I never saw her talk to Ohio again after that also. Their relationship was never the same. That incident hit home for both of them. When Mamadou left the building, he made Ohio the shot caller for the YBs, which caused friction on the hall. Ohio wanted to have more YBs on the hall, but Jazz was determined to have only Bloods.

When Ms. Willis got wind of what was going on, she violated them both. I watched as she dragged a trash can to both of their rooms and took all their shit and dumped it. Their clothes, snacks, robes, and letters were all trashed. I had to give them new clothes and sneakers; she even took their Bibles where she found gang papers in between the sheets.

She zeroed them out and took all their privileges; they couldn't play the video game or watch TV. They took it like men. They knew she giveth and she taketh away. Everything they got came from her. It was reminiscent of the saying don't bite the hand that feeds you.

Things changed when a resident was transferred from the SHU, and he brought bed bugs with him. The hall got shut down and we got moved to G-Hall. At this time, G-Hall was closed for repairs and now was reopened just in time for us to move in. On G-Hall, our entire flow changed. We no longer had the benefit of Ms. Willis on the hall, and no Xbox either.

This sucked. They merged the group with other residents from other halls that needed a change of scenery. One of those residents was this kid from 8th Avenue in Harlem name Binky. He was a transfer from D-Hall, and he was tall for a fifteen-year-old with incredible ball skills. He had an old-school game like Magic, but his true gift was snappin' or, as the kids say, "cuttin' ass" on other people. If you don't know, cutting ass is how all black comedian get started when cracking jokes. Binky would say some shit that would have me almost pee in my pants, and when he got started, he would go in. He would stand in front of the bricks after my rap session, and row by row, he would roast every kid sitting in front of him. He would say shit like, "And this nigga right here with the beady eyes and the big lips who the fuck told you that you look good? Damn, you're ugly." Sometimes, I would pull him away because it was too embarrassing the shit that he would say to the other residents, and some of his jokes cut so deep it would lead to fights; but he knew who to pick on and rarely would it be somebody bigger than him. But his jokes weren't limited to just the residents. He cut ass on the staff the most. Every day, he would throw a few zingers my way, and he always came at me about the way I talked or how I dressed. I would just laugh and tell him to go somewhere but I never took it personal. He would always call this one staff itchy butt because this man would always scratch his ass in public. Just thinking about how he would say it makes me crack up; Binky was one funny ass kid. If they ever made a New York version of the *Friday* movie series, he would be perfect to play Smokey. I would tell him all the time that he had a talent and that he should do stand-up, but he was another one who just wanted to stand on the block and sling rocks. I didn't get it; these kids did their talent for fun, and they were only serious when doing a crime. But Binky's jokes helped us get through the day. Another resident who was transferred to G-Hall was Steven, a sixteen-year-old Puerto Rican kid from the Bronx who came from the SHU. He was there because he lost a kidney from being stabbed but got cleared by the doctor to be in population.

What a pain in the ass this motherfucker was. He did whatever he wanted on the SHU and thought he would have it like that upstairs. He was Blood like Jazz, and I leaned on Jazz to control him. But because Steven was older, there was very little Jazz could say to him. Together, they reminded me of Jimmy and Tommy in the movie *Goodfellas*.

I would constantly have to get in Steven's face for the dumbest shit; no other resident tested my nerves like he did. I couldn't even restrain him that hard because of his condition. When I grabbed him, I avoided taking him to the floor. I always used a technique standing up.

I tried to get Ohio to put him in check. I even offered him extra snacks if he helped me with Steven, but at this point, Ohio was focused on getting off the hall. He said, "E-Hall is over, Scrap. This G-Hall shit, I'm not feeling this." I couldn't argue with him, I hated it too. He said, "I'm not touching that little nigga for him to drop dead and I get stuck here. Fuck that." He said with Steven on the hall it was dayroom, and he told Jazz he could have it.

This wasn't good because Ohio was my enforcer. I felt my control shifting in a way I didn't want. I was so used to Scoop, Jose, or JB, or even Ohio to hold me down and keep me incident free. Jazz was too quiet to speak up. In some ways, he looked up to Steven because, even though he was put in charge, Steven became Blood outside the building, which held more weight than joining inside.

In a five foot one frame, Steven was a tone raiser. He did anything anybody dared him to. If the residents told him to flip his dinner tray, he would or if they told him to spit on a staff, he would do that, too. He was like Mikey from the old cereal commercial, he did anything for attention. Around younger kids, he was divisive; but around older ones, he was a follower. He was just a punk-ass wannabe.

The day Ohio got transferred to H-Hall for good behavior, things went from bad to horrible. It was like Steven got bigger, the more alliances I lost. H-Hall now was repaired and used as a platinum hall for residents with the most points. For Ohio to be there was a positive and increased his chances of going home. Even Happy Feet was over there at the time, which was a good look for him to. I was grateful that Jazz was still there because he was the only person Steven would listen to. Nobody wanted to be that staff who sent Steven to the hospital because it could mean your job, plus his care plan was as thick as a Bible. I wasn't trying to get an allegation, so we just avoided putting our hands on him.

The day Jazz told me he was going home, I selfishly wasn't happy for him because I was so concerned with who was going to control Steven. The hall regressed to when I first started working a hall. Steven had more control of the residents than I did. It wasn't just me, every tour was sick of Steven; and we argued with supervision to move him, but they felt he was safest on G- Hall.

Before Jazz left, he gave Steven his position as the big homie of the building, and all Steven did was recruit more members to his set. When I would return off my past days, there would be two or three residents who were neutral on Sunday and Blood by Tuesday, even Binky became Blood under Steven. G-Hall was like the old G-Hall when Chaz was there, but Chaz had a method to his madness; Steven was just mad annoying. He popped on anybody they brought new to the hall, and it got so bad I asked Archie to shake him up. But Archie didn't want to touch him either. Everybody was aware of his condition, and he played on that.

When he first got there, Ms. Rosario connected with him, but after he flipped on her and called her a bitch, she was done. She said, "I'm not dealing with him, you can." Ms. Rosario had a stubborn side to her, and when she made up her mind that she wasn't fuckin' with a resident, that was it. No matter how much I tried to look out for Steven, he would always shit on me.

Once I gave him an extra snack if he promised to chill out, but after he got the snack, he got on his bullshit and refused to go to his room. He said he wasn't tired, and if he goes to his room, he would turn it up. I grabbed him by the collar and threw him in his room. He immediately started banging and kicking his door. I went in his room and grabbed his throat and said, "Listen, you little piece of shit. I fucked with you because of Jazz, but every time I bend over for you, you fuck me. Go the fuck to bed."

I might have made things worse because he kept banging until security came to handcuff and shackle him. Steven was really fuckin' with my head. Once during a rap session, he kept talking while I was talking, and when I told him to hold it down, he said whatever. At that point, I lost it, and the male JC I was working with had to hold me back. Steven just laughed and said, "The camera's watching, nigga. If you don't want thirty days in the street, you better do your rap session."

Every day he did dumb shit, I would write it up in an observation report, but nothing changed. Residents like Steven knew the power they had against us because the system was always set up to protect them; I was at a loss. I needed a monster for this monster.

If Scoop, Jose, JB, Ohio, or even Jazz were here, Steven would not be like this. Most of the other residents on the hall feared him because of his health and because of his status as a Blood; three of them were under him. As stupid as he acted, he was very aware of what he could get away with; he was quick to get a counselor caught in an allegation.

He once got another male JC banned from the hall when he accused that JC of touching his private parts. When this JC restrained Steven, he told the doctor who filed the incident report that the JC grabbed his dick; and after that, the JC accused was never allowed to work around Steven again. It was like an order of protection. Why couldn't that have been me? I couldn't shake Steven to save my life.

Then one day, this kid from Brooklyn, who was also Blood, returned to the building. His name was Kofi. I had him on E-Hall a year ago, and he was a terror. Greenwood sent him to our building because they couldn't control him. He was only fourteen and a badass.

Kofi was short like Steven, but strong for his age. When he was on E-Hall, I restrained him, and he fought me back. He even spit on TC Herrera, and I thought Herrera was going to rip his arm out of its socket when he put him in a chicken wing. Kofi told Herrera to break his arm. He was crazy like that and crazier than Steven. I remember last year, Kofi told me that physical punishment didn't faze him because his mother use to beat him like a slave, so getting his ass kicked was normal for him. He was just the person I needed to put Steven on skates, but supervision wanted him on C-Hall by himself. I begged Platter to transfer him to G-Hall, and I promised to control him.

Kofi and I developed a good relationship after I restrained him a year ago, and he loved me. When they transferred Kofi to the hall, Steven got quiet. He knew what I was doing, so he told the other Bloods to violate Kofi. But they wouldn't do it because they were more afraid of him than they were of Steven, plus they knew Steven was making it personal.

What I loved about Kofi is he was buck wild and from Brooklyn. He knew Steven was selling wolf tickets but was really a Chihuahua. I schooled Kofi on the situation, and he went straight to Steven and told him, "First, we're both Blood, and second, we don't violate Mr. Geez. He's like a father to me." Steven was stuck on stupid. He wasn't use to anybody challenging him, plus he knew Kofi didn't care about his health issues. They were the same height, and if they shot a fair one, Kofi would have washed him. Steven always relied on jumping kids with help from the other residents on the hall.

After that, Steven was silent the rest of the day. Unfortunately, Kofi was sent upstate the next day, much to my displeasure. Steven won again, I could not get rid of him.

The day Ohio got sent upstate was a bittersweet moment. He had the admission staff bring him to the hall to say goodbye. We hugged, and I wished him well, and when he saw Steven, he had a look like he wanted to punch the shit out of him, and I was hoping he did. But he did something better. He told Steven, "Stop being a pussy and stop biting the hand that feeds you. Geez and the other staff are looking out for you, hold them down," and then he left.

Ohio always spoke the truth, that's what I loved about him, but things finally changed for me when Steven opened his fat mouth. A JC overheard Steven say to another resident that he was going to have me jumped if I brought Kofi to the hall. I wrote an incident report which said that Steven threatened to harm me, and I didn't want to be held responsible for anything that happened to him when I defend myself.

That did it. It was enough to have him moved off the hall, and from that day on I never had to work with him again. Finally, an allegation worked in our favor. It was true that the pen was mightier than the sword. He was one kid who truly made me earn my pay, he even said that to me once. He said, "Don't get comfortable. You better put on your boot straps, nigga. You gonna work today." Ain't that some shit. I was getting punk'd by a punk.

Steven was sent to Archie's hall where he barely came out his room. He wanted to go on one-to-one, but instead, supervision transferred him to D-Hall with residents his age. On D-Hall, he stayed in his lane, he couldn't bully any of the residents over there. Instead, he behaved and maintained until he got sentenced and sent upstate. Deuces!

CHAPTER SEVENTEEN

I ain't bullshittin, ask my nigga Buff
on the street he was tough locked up he was sweet
stuff Shit is hot, word to Ma Duke get the loot
from the man kick his ass with my timberland

—Black Moon
"Buck Em Down"

WHEN BINKY GOT SENTENCED AND sent upstate, things got real boring. Binky was the entertainment on the hall, and without him, it felt like we were flavorless. But before I could blink, I was confronted with a new state of affairs. This came in the form of a transgender youth who was admitted to the hall. His name was Juan, but he wanted to be called Juju. The rules of the agency were that if any LGBT (lesbian, gay, bisexual, and transgender) resident wanted to be called anything other than their government name, we had to address them as that.

Juju was a fourteen-year-old Hispanic kid from the Bronx, and he never hid the fact that he was transgender. He looked more like a girl than most of the girls on A-Hall. He was tall, thin, and had long straight hair. The designer in me saw the modeling potential in his androgynous look, but as much as I tried to talk to him about that, he wasn't feeling it. Like any time when dealing with young people, all you can do is express to them any positive qualities you see in them and hope that they take advantage of that; and if they don't, you can't press the issue. They have to find out on their own.

The interaction between a heterosexual man and a transgender child is nothing they taught us in training or you could read in books or find support in the Bible. I saw this as an opportunity for me to help a child love himself in an environment that breeds hate.

Most of the male JCs hated working with him, but it didn't bother me. I was comfortable around him, it helped me better understand who he was. When I designed clothes, I worked with a lot of different types of people. They respected my sexuality and I respected theirs. For my last fashion show at the Tunnel nightclub, it was promoted by a transvestite who helped me get the opportunity to work in California. I was always grateful because she was one of the few people in the industry that believed in my talent as a designer.

Juju was good in his skin. He never tried to be anything different. It was hard involving him with the other residents because they would not accept him. I restrained more residents protecting Juju than any other resident I did before. In my rap sessions, I would use the example of how black people were treated during the civil rights movement, so why be like that when it's wrong. But what I think bothered them most was that they didn't know who they were. Juju's presence made them question their own sexuality.

What helped was that I had a hall leader named Moonie who hated seeing people get picked on. He got transferred from J-Hall for slapping a male JC. He had a little JB in him, and when he got to G-Hall, I thought he would be a problem, but he accepted the move because he was told it was temporary.

We were cool because I once went to J-Hall to pray with Archie, which was something he never saw any JC do. Plus, most of the residents on J-Hall I had on E-Hall, and they all showed me love, so he liked me from the gate.

One day during a rap session, he told the group that they were bigger pussies than Juju could ever be because he wasn't a follower like they were. Moonie said, "At least Juju has the balls to be who he is. You niggas need props from each other." Then he said, "If anybody touches him, you're going to have to deal with me."

Moonie hated bullies. He got transferred because he saw a male JC yelling at a female JC. When he wouldn't stop, he slapped the dude so hard it left a mark on his face. Moonie was very close to his mother, and when he saw his mother's boyfriend violating her, he violated him. He got arrested for beating the shit out of him, so if he sees anybody being disrespectful to someone of weaker stature, he's going to have something to say about it.

With Moonie on the hall, I got to breathe a little. I thought he was going to be a problem, but he was the solution.

Sometimes, I would bring in my iPod so they could listen to music. iPods were contraband and not allowed in the facility. This was another bad practice that I developed, but it was the one thing that calmed them down. Moonie would give me a list of songs to download from home, and they would connect the iPod to the Xbox system. They would all sing the songs like the Harlem Boys Choir. Whoever said music calms the savage beast wasn't lying.

They would tune out everything and be entranced by the lyrics. They weren't into today's popular hip-hop artists who get radio play. They wanted to listen to Chicago rappers like Lil Durk, Lil Herb, or Chief Keef. The more I listened to it, the more I saw the correlation. Chicago rappers spoke about real scenarios that actually happened. It was all grit, no glam. They didn't just talk about it; they were about it—everything these kids could relate to. It was all drill music, which is a darker style of hip-hop. It's like gangsta rap on steroids and sounds like a soundtrack to a horror movie, Mobb Deep type shit, just deeper.

I'm not a fan of the violence but it's their reality. I would try to put them on to rap artists from my time, but they weren't with it. Sometimes, I felt out of touch; but for the most part, I had their ear and they wanted to follow my lead.

Moonie was the ultimate soldier. He played his part like he was the captain of my team. I could tell that he looked up to me because we would have these lengthy conversations, and he always wanted to know how my day was and what did I do.

On weekends, Claudia and I would hit a few night spots for drinks in front of live bands, but for the most part, we did family stuff with the kids. Moonie would go as far as to ask me how many drinks did I have, what did I drink, and if I got ass when I got home. I would tell him, "Real men don't kiss and tell, you'll figure that out." Discussions like this made life for him normal in an abnormal place.

Moonie loved to hear my life stories and wanted that life for himself in the future. I couldn't have asked for a better right-hand in the building.

He only had one problem and that was that he loved to smoke weed. He hated being on G-Hall for that reason. When he was on J-Hall, he smoked every day, maybe even twice a day. With Archie over there, that was the least of their problems. The staff probably allowed it because that was the only thing that chilled Archie out, but Archie wasn't on G-Hall, and Moonie couldn't control his urges. He told me he would never smoke if I was there, and he was a man of his word.

Ms. Kindie tried hard to get him off the hall and have him moved for that reason, but my argument was that Moonie kept everybody from violating Juju, and that's all supervision cared about. The funny shit was that we could never catch Moonie smoking. All we knew was that he always looked high. He left no smell, no smoke, and no evidence. It got so bad that supervision made us post by the bathroom door and watch him shower or take a sit down. Ms. Kindie didn't like me anyway. That was another thing she used to try to have me reassigned. She never forgave me for the JB thing, and she tried to accuse me of having Moonie sabotage her tour. I knew the stuff she said about me behind my back because the residents would tell me, but I didn't care because as long as Ms. Willis and TC Platter were there, I was untouchable.

The cat-and-mouse game with Moonie was pointless. It wasn't until later that we found out it wasn't weed he was smoking. It was some new shit called K2, something completely hard to detect. Those kids always found ways, criminals are like that. Whenever you think you figured them out, they were always five steps ahead of you.

Moonie was on almost every hall, and wherever he went, there was always a fight or contraband. He was Blood, but he was the antithesis of Steven and Jazz. Unlike them, he wasn't on any look-at-me or look-what-I-can-do kick. He was more laid-back, and I think it was because he didn't take gang activity serious in the building mainly because he was Blood before getting locked up and he saw the juvie shit as kid stuff.

Supervision presented him with a contract, but he refused to sign it. That's when they told him if he gets into anything, he was going to be transferred to Greenwood. Moonie was from Harlem, and the idea of Brooklyn wasn't something he was feeling. He wasn't stupid, he always had two or three residents do his dirty work. When an incident happened, supervision always implied that he was involved but they had no proof.

But for the most part, they left us alone. Their main concern was that Juju was treated right; the LGBT issue was a sensitive topic.

It was hard having a transgender resident in this environment. Juju wasn't happy on the hall, and Moonie was about to return to his old hall. I started to stress because I knew when Moonie leaves, the other residents would pick on Juju. Juju didn't help the situation. He demanded to wear a girl's uniform which was orange, as opposed too dark green for the boys. I told him it would never happen, but much to my surprise, the administration approved it.

This made the other resident more infuriated, and other halls made fun of them, which didn't help. When we traveled through the building to dinner or to the gym, there would be a gap between Juju and the next resident on the line because they refused to walk next to him. I would have to put Juju in the back of the line to avoid an incident.

The day Moonie left, he told the group if they touched Juju, he would smoke them. Juju had fun with this and did things to antagonize them. Sometimes, most of the residents would go to the patio to get away from Juju, and Juju would follow them and sit on the card table like a car ornament daring them to do something. They would just get up and leave, they were well aware of the ramifications for assaulting an LGBT resident.

I pulled Juju aside and asked him why was he fuckin' with them, and he said that he wants them to pop on him so that he can be moved to the girl's hall. I told him again that he was asking for the impossible. I didn't want him to get his hopes up to be let back down. I told him to just chill until he gets sentenced or goes home.

What I found out later was that he was taking hormone pills to help him look more feminine. His appearance started to change.

He started to look like he belonged with the girls. To insinuate that the agency was providing him the pills, I couldn't say. He was taking them, somebody was giving them to him.

I could see that some of the other residents were acting like they weren't looking at him, but they were. He was hard to ignore, he was developing breasts, and I could tell some of the other residents were getting turned on. When nobody would assault him, he started to assault himself. One day, I caught him slashing his arm with a broken deodorant bottle. I stopped him and reported it to supervision, and they put him on one-to-one, but that didn't help because he had his door open and it was like he was on stage.

Supervision gave in and transferred him to A-Hall with the girls. His behavior improved, but several parents of the girls had issues with a boy being on a girl hall, but there was nothing they could do. The agency's policy allowed it. I said to myself, what if a girl identified as a boy, would she be able to live on the male hall?

It was such a double standard. Who made these rules? Is this agency so subservient to an ideology that you can't make adult decisions for children? If I was to let my eleven-year-old son pick what he wants to eat every day, he would have pizza for dinner and jellybeans for breakfast. At some point for the development of a child, you must draw the line. People on the outside can say what they want, I watched this juvenile reality show every day, and it was a train wreck that I struggled to keep from becoming a horror show. The system was a psychological nightmare; the lines between fantasy and reality were blurred.

To satisfy Juju, they sacrificed the psyche of everybody else. How does this help the girls? How does this help the other boys or Juju? As much as the agency claimed to care about the kids, it didn't look that way. It seemed like they were more concerned with avoiding lawsuits from the LGBT community than doing what was right. If they really cared, most of them wouldn't be detained in this environment in the first place. It was like mixing oil with water.

It was irresponsible to assume that these children had the same quirks and tendencies. They needed a detention center for criminals, one for runaways and another for psych patients and transgender youth.

Juju never belonged there. His crime didn't qualify him to be in the same room with murderers and gangbangers. Unbeknownst to us, Juju suffered from gender dysphoria, something none of us in the building had the training to counsel. Another misdiagnosis by the medical staff, just throwing this kid to the wolves. The way it was structured was a zoo, but even in a zoo, they don't have the birds with the big cats or with the reptiles. We all know how that would turn out, and that's just how it was every day in Fairvue. Chaos.

Anytime I saw Juju, I was happy that he was happy. He seemed in his element on A-Hall, and he got along with all the girls. It befuddled us that the agency allowed this because not all the situations worked out like Juju's. There were transgender youth who were sent to the girls' halls who would pull out their dicks and sometimes assaulted the girls. How do you explain that to a parent?

I guess they will change it when one of those girls gets pregnant. It was like everything bad that happened was a result of the agency taking chances like we were all test monkeys in a lab. I started to question the methods of the agency.

But it all came to a drastic low the day someone told me Jose was killed. When I got to the hall, one of the senior female JCs asked if I heard about Jose. I said, "Jose who?" She said, "Don't act stupid. Your boy, your closet boy on E-Hall." I said, "What about him?" Then she told me he was killed in a gang-related incident the other day.

My heart felt like it was sinking in my chest. I was speechless. I started to tear up and excused myself to the bathroom. I had my phone with me that day and attempted to call him from the number he gave me. On the other line, somebody picked up and then hung up. I called back desperately, hoping it was him but a woman speaking Spanish answered the phone, and she spoke like she was scared. I didn't speak Spanish, but I could tell something was wrong. The guy that relieved the female JC spoke Spanish, I asked him if he could speak to the woman on the phone because I wanted to know if Jose was killed. He agreed and spoke to her. He said the woman on the phone was Jose's mother, and she said Jose was alive, but he was on the run.

I was relieved but still worried. He said that Jose killed somebody, and that the guy he murdered was a member of a gang, and his boys were looking for Jose along with the police. Jose's mother was getting death threats, and the family didn't know where Jose was. I couldn't believe he did this. I swore when he left, he was going to make it. I didn't know to be more happy or sad, I was just glad he was alive.

It hurt because I hoped he would stay out of trouble. He called me once when he first got home, and we played a game of 2K basketball online. The more I thought about it, I remember my oldest son MJ told me a few times that Jose was trying to contact me through his profile on the PlayStation game. I didn't take it seriously because I just thought he wanted to play me again, but that was months ago.

This news of him murdering somebody stunned me. To go from the worst news to the second worst news wasn't a huge boost of emotional relief. During all this, I still had to work and act like nothing happened. It helped to have someone to talk to, otherwise, I would have needed a sick call.

Everything got so heavy, it felt like I was weight lifting my emotions. Jose was hands-down my favorite resident. My feeling for him surpassed my feelings for any other resident. I had him on E-Hall for two years. He was like a son or a little brother to me, and he was the only resident that I cried about when he left.

What a failure. I failed him, and he failed himself. Maybe if I got back to him, this would never have happened. I always told him about his temper. He was a little guy always trying to prove how big he was. His favorite words were, "I'm not pussy," and I would always tell him, "Anytime you say that you're not pussy, you sound like a pussy."

I later found out that it was over a gang beef, and that the guy Jose killed called him a pussy, how ironic. He never liked to be disrespected and supposedly this guy dissed him. This was even on the Channel 12 news where they showed a wanted poster with Jose's face on it, and there was a major manhunt for his capture.

How many people could say they were close to somebody on a wanted poster? Not a good feeling. I went from feeling bad for Jose to feeling sad for the guy's family he murdered; dude was only twenty-five. If I could speak to Jose, I would tell him to turn himself in; it's only getting worse that he is hiding.

As time passed, I had to put this in the back of my mind. I knew that God would take care of Jose.

Four months after the murder, Jose was found in a small village in Puerto Rico's Cordillera mountains by the US Marshal Task Force. His family got him out of the country, and he was with his father who lives in PR. The eerie part of this was that when they found him, all he had was a learner's permit for ID, and when he was here, I got him the DMV manual for him to study to get his learner's permit. My life felt like a bad movie.

If I was low before all this, my mind was in the gutter at this point. Everybody at work wanted to tell me about Jose like they were rubbing it in. It was one of those I-told-you-so moments. They knew how close I was to Jose, and I always defended him. There was no defending this. Jose was a murderer. Never would I have thought this would happen to him, but if you live that life, this is what happens. I told him years ago when he turned eighteen that I would try to get him a job working for my mechanic, but now that ship sailed.

Most of my peers always questioned my counseling acumen. Now I did too. I was done trying to save lives. At this point, I only cared about my family, my money, and my health.

As my professional life seemed hopeless, my personal life was promising. My relationship with Claudia was flourishing, and my children were growing older and smarter. I couldn't deny the blessings. I had a lot to be thankful for. But on the flip side, my heart was hurting. Claudia and my kids never knew how much I cared for Jose, I spent more time with him than my own children. But he sealed his fate, I had to move forward.

At work, everyone could see my lack of interest. I started to let Ms. Rosario do the rap sessions and take the lead. I would just sit on the side and watch. I became one of those people who just collected a paycheck. I stopped having closet boys and stopped praying with them before their court date. I even avoided praying with Archie. It just didn't matter anymore. The whole purpose was to give them good luck for court hoping they would go home, but they always came back.

The day I tried to get my boy, Chuck, a job, it put things in perspective. Like Boo did for me years ago, it was time for me to help a friend in need of stability. I offered to help him get a job as a juvenile counselor, but he said no thanks. It was puzzling because Chuck had a month before he was getting evicted.

He was married with two little daughters, and he just lost his job. He said they were going to live in a shelter until something came through. Something came through? Am I missing something? I told him, "Bruh, are you crazy? Who does that? I can get you a job with overtime, you'd be doubling your salary. It's easy money. You're a real dude from the city. The kids would respect you and make your day smooth." He said, "It's not about the kids, it's the system that runs the place. It's corrupt. It's the devil that makes money off the mistakes of young black and Hispanic men that get locked up."

I never saw it like that. I told Chuck, "It sucks, but I'm employed because stupid kids want to do stupid things. It's not my fault they got arrested. If I could share my experience with one of them and it changes their life, then I did the work of God."

He said, "But it's the devil's workshop. I'm not trying to change who I am to adjust to a place I don't belong. It's not me. How could I look my daughters in the eye and be good with myself?" The notion of what he said seemed all too real. I stopped looking my kids in the eye. I would look right pass them because, without saying, it I wasn't good with myself. The evil around me became my norm. I convinced myself that I was good because I was being responsible, but I knew I wasn't happy. I said, "So you're getting evicted, and you, your wife, and two daughters are going to live in a shelter? Who's doing better for their family, you or me?" He didn't answer, but there was truth in what both of us were saying.

But not even a week later, when I watched a resident rip up the Bible, that made me see his point more. There was a demonic feeling in the building; no ghost or anything, but just bad people who do bad things. There was a chapel in the building, and whenever I took the group to the chapel, there was always one or two kids who saw this as a time to turn it up.

What kind of person turns it up in church? Even real gangsters don't do that. I had to reflect back to the people before me who worked this job and never let it work them, like Luke and Ford. Those two old cats were OGs who mastered this job. They set the tone and did what they wanted. Maybe I needed to incorporate that attitude in my approach.

It had to be a balance of good and evil. As Luke once said, have a little devil for the devils. Most of these kids were diamonds in the rough and just needed a positive voice or message to help guide them in the right direction. But at this point, it was hard for me to do that.

As I struggled to keep a positive outlook on the situation at work, nothing could prepare me for what happened next.

CHAPTER EIGHTEEN

◆ ◆ ◆ ◆ ◆

He say, she say, I heard it through the grapevine
No static got an automatic, too much of anything
makes you an addict
Teasing, skeezing, all so pleasing
Don't ask why I got my own reasons

—Nice & Smooth
Sometimes I Rhyme Slow

WE WERE SUBJECTED TO THE most unbearable conditions, and it's amazing nobody died. We weren't given the benefit of the human element. There was staff getting spit on, getting piss thrown on them, and getting cursed at by people half our age, and it took a lot of patience.

I went black (shocked and enraged) once when this resident told me that he was going to rape my daughter and cum in her face. I lost control of myself and smacked the shit out of him, which was borderline, a punch, then bent him up and almost broke his arm. I had to be pulled off him by my coworker. I completely blacked out because at that moment, the job didn't mean anything to me. I never had my emotions brought to such a vulnerable place, it was like a reflex. Like any loving father, his baby girl is at the center of his world. I wasn't any different.

Some things I could overlook, but my daughter was my weakness. That resident took me there. Most of the caseworkers and administrators didn't have children, so how could any of them relate to my feelings for my daughter? I have feelings just like these kids, but I guess because I'm an adult and I have a job to do, I should

170

know better. Fuck that. Most of these residents were young men, and when they got mad, they went after everything you loved.

When you're dealing with an element of society that has nothing to lose, you're going to lose; and most of these residents would take you there. If supervision would have seen this, I would have been suspended or fired because I tried to hurt him. It was embarrassing the lengths they would go to protect these kids. If a JC got punched in the face or almost choked to death by a resident, the agency concerned themselves with the health and the physical condition of the resident to avoid potential lawsuits.

I've seen a coworker get punched in the face, and the resident get sent to the hospital to have his hand checked, while my coworker had to continue working. They looked at it as a workplace hazard. This is what we signed up for. It was a business, like selling furniture; it was our job to make sure none of the merchandise got damaged. We had to juggle multiple personalities, and most of us needed more mental health attention than the kids.

I know we suffered from some level of PTSD (post-traumatic stress disorder). There was a time I had eleven residents on the hall all diagnosed with ADHD—three of them with bipolar disorder, two murderers, and one rapist. That shit was a Molotov cocktail; I was lucky nobody killed me.

Supervision never concerned themselves with our safety, all they care about was their coverage. The only person I could count on that had the power to make changes was TC Platter. As the tour commander, he had the authority to move residents; and if I was uncomfortable with a certain resident or who I was working with, I could rely on him to make adjustments.

One day, I arrived at work and got the news that he resigned from the job. I didn't know if it was a rumor or fact. He changed his number, but he eventually called me and told me that it was true. He said he was done. There was nothing left to do because the building was falling apart and the new administration was to blame. He told me to hold my head and to watch my back, but as he was talking, I was saying to myself that he watched my back.

He said he was going to work for the union, and that he would have the freedom to help us more in that setting. After hearing that, my feelings about the union changed to positive. I felt relieved that he was still affiliated with agency, just in a different capacity.

What he said next I never forgot because it sounded like déjà vu. He said that they're all snakes that will eat you and spit you out if you let them. I heard the same thing from Luke when he retired. Damn, all my teachers, bad and good, had the same message. The only ally I had to hold me down was Ms. Willis, but her power was limited, and to add insult to injury, they promoted a tour commander from Greenwood to take over the PM tour who was a no-good SOB. This dude made TC Herrera look like a saint; he was the epitome of grimy. His name was TC Okeke, and he was from Nigeria, and you would have thought his power gave him the license to ill (make sick choices). He would transfer residents to halls that he knew they had beef on, and he would pair the staff with people they didn't work well with. It was self-defeating, it never made sense, but he didn't care. He let us all know that he was the new sheriff and he made the rules.

Where everybody was required to wear uniforms, Okeke said fuck that and wore his leather blazer like he was Richard Roundtree in *Shaft*. With him in charge, incidents went up and more staff got hurt. They transferred him from Greenwood because of an EEO (equal employment opportunity) report from a female employee. Supposedly, he had womanizing issues, and he had just as many allegations as Herrera, if not more. Dude was a snake, he even looked like one, no lie. I guess when Platter was schooling me, Okeke was one of the people he was referring to.

When Greenwood was at its worst, Okeke was the TC and Ms. Nebula was the ED. How did we get so unlucky? Now Ms. Nebula had one of her goons to help her ruin Fairvue. Any time I went to her to complain about something he did with the coverage or on the hall, she would say, "Why are you talking to me? Follow your chain of command." I would say to myself, *"I'm coming to you because, my chain of command sucks."* But I just made things worse for myself because she would call him and tell him that I was complaining.

Time to shut up and watch my back. The one thing I had was my seniority. I was good at holding my hall down, so Okeke respected my counseling skills, and he knew that I rarely had incidents. With us back on E-Hall, I stayed under the wing of Ms. Willis, she kept the heat off me. Okeke and Ms. Willis didn't like each other, but they coexisted, and they both had a good relationship with ED Nebula.

With most of the gang activity under control, the only elephant in the room was Archie. He became more violent because he had nobody to fight, so he took his anger out on the staff. The residents now in the building weren't as belligerent as in the past. It was almost like every four months a new monster was born.

Archie was the last of a decade of defiant and unruly residents who would leave a trail of destruction. He had hospitalized countless JCs and sent a number of residents to the infirmary. He was the only rude boy left. Whenever I tried to talk to him, it would go in one ear and out the other.

One day, I responded to a call on the radio for assistance, and I knew it was for Archie, this would go on all day. When I got to the hall, I entered through the back door and Archie was standing there with his shirt off, clinching his fist. I ask him, "What are you doing?" only to see as I stepped around the corner of the hall that there were four security guards, three JCs, two staff from admissions, and a supervisor ready to pounce on him. Ten people for one kid. I felt like Moses when he parted the sea because everybody moved out the way as I escorted him to his room.

He was lucky that Okeke or Herrera weren't there, otherwise, he would have been kissing the floor. He knew when to get on his bullshit and who to act up with; he only respected senior staff. If you were new, he would violate you. Ms. Willis was the only supervisor he would listen to, but the more things she did for him, the more people questioned the nature of their relationship. It wasn't rare to find Archie in her office for hours because I was there. Her office had windows surrounding it, and she never closed her door unless she was yelling at him, which I saw as a form of counseling.

I gave up trying to convert Archie to sainthood. As much as he attempted to refrain from his urges, his pedigree was to turn it up. A few days later, he took it to the max. There was a call for assistance on J-Hall, and as much as I hesitated to leave my hall, this was a code blue. Code blue was the equivalent of man down. When I got there, it was chaos. Security guards were restraining Archie, and in his room, Ms. Willis was laid out on the floor. From what I gathered, Archie was fighting another male JC; and as Ms. Willis got between them, Archie punched her and knocked her unconscious. While he was being restrained, his only concern was with Ms. Willis, but the damage was done. His precipitous behavior got the best of him. Ms. Willis was taken out on a stretcher.

Archie was rearrested, and he was hurt when Ms. Willis pressed charges on him, but what he didn't know was that because of the severity of the incident that was the protocol. He had to know that an incident of this magnitude would have catastrophic results. When he returned to the building, he was placed on two-to-one, and only the most seasoned staff had that assignment. I worked with him on my doubles and he was torn; his feelings of remorse turned to feelings of redemption. Not to the good redemption, the bad one.

Archie and Ms. Willis never crossed paths again, and not too long after her return from IOJ, Archie was sent upstate. If when Chaz left it felt like euphoria, Archie's exit felt like paradise. You never knew what he was going to do next. It was like he always raised the ante on his bullshit trying to outdo himself. He accumulated over one hundred incidents, injured over fifty staff members and residents, not to mention the property damage he caused.

Only here could someone wreak so much havoc and successfully do it with arrogance like Archie. If this was BCW's idea of children and family service, we were lame ducks; our leash was much shorter. If a JC would have injured Archie in an attempt to defend themselves, there would have been a high price to pay. Days in the street or termination would have been in order. We always fell on the sword. Where was the justice?

With Archie gone, it was hard to believe that our troubles were behind us because we always had to look over our shoulders for the next catastrophe, and we didn't have to look far.

The day Ms. Hendricks passed away changed all our working lives forever. Ms. Hendricks was a JC in her midfifties who was too good for this place. She was a grandmother, and the residents respected her like one. Everybody loved her, and nobody violated her because she was such a peaceful woman. She had a kind heart, but she was a Bronx girl and rough around the edges, which was mandatory if you want to survive in this environment.

She had two sons and grandchildren the age of some of the residents at Fairvue. Because she was diabetic, it was important that she took her medication and ate at a certain time. There was a policy that the staff wasn't allowed to eat on the halls; and on this day, Ms. Hendricks, like most of us was very hungry. I have gone more than ten hours without eating and sometimes, two tours.

It's a shame when grown folks can't fill their stomachs when they want, and in Ms. Hendricks case, she had to have food along with her medication. To avoid being written up, Ms. Hendricks shared some food that was ordered and ate it in one of the empty rooms on B-Hall to avoid eating in front of the camera. On this day, I was working on E-Hall with Ms. Rosario and another JC. Ms. Rosario had an annoying habit of floating around the building, and it would piss me the fuck off. Sometimes, she would leave me by myself with all the resident for hours. I never reported her, but I let her have it when she returned. She always said she was responding to other incidents around the building, but I knew half the time she was on a cigarette break or chopping it up with one of her friends working on other halls.

It would get so bad that I would hide her radio so that she wouldn't hear the call for assistance. I was selfish like that, sometimes, but she was a good JC, and I didn't want to lose her because she had to clean up somebody else's mess.

That evening, there was a radio call from A-Hall, and like always, Wonder Woman ran out the door. I told the other JC, "Watch her take an hour." After four hours, I was so tight I was going to let her have it when she came back, but then I started to worry because it wasn't like her to take that long.

Within that fourth hour, supervisor Gill came to the hall and told us we lost Ms. Hendricks. I said, "What do you mean we lost Ms. Hendricks?" She said Ms. Hendricks passed away while working on B-Hall. I just stared at her, and we both just stared at each other for two minutes until tears ran down our cheeks.

I was physically distraught; there was nothing to say. I couldn't believe it and I didn't want to believe it. I said I was just in roll call with her, teasing her, and saying, "Where's my snack?" because she always had the goodies. Ms. Gill didn't know enough at the time to say what happened, but when Ms. Rosario finally came back, she told us because she was there.

She said that when she responded to the incident on A-Hall she heard screaming coming from B-Hall and then ran over there, and when she got to B-Hall Ms. Hendricks was unconscious and not responding. The staff who was with Ms. Hendricks was hysterically trying to revive her but without luck. She said the medical staff arrived, but it was too late. Ms. Hendricks died before the ambulance got there, and Ms. Rosario went with them to the hospital where Ms. Hendricks was pronounced dead.

Ms. Rosario said they believed Ms. Hendricks choked on her food, but there were so many factors that led to her eating on the hall in the first place. That night, I rode home with Ms. Rosario because she was so traumatized from the experience. It was too much for her to handle. She was very close to Ms. Hendricks, and to watch a friend die in your arms was very debilitating.

Now twenty-five, Ms. Rosario was a vegetable after this, we all were. While I was talking to her in the car, she couldn't stop crying. It was then that she said she was done. She said, "I can't go back there, I can't work there anymore." She felt that if Ms. Hendricks didn't have to hide her food and was able to eat like normal people, she would still be alive.

I didn't know at the time that Ms. Hendricks was diabetic, but supervision did and because of her condition she had to get her medication and eat at a certain time. We were never told by the administration how Ms. Hendricks died. It was like they all took an oath of silence. But absent content can't fool the eye.

In roll call the next day, Ms. Nebula spoke to us and addressed Ms. Hendricks passing, that was the first time I heard her say more than two sentences in the building. She commended the staff for how we handled the situation and acknowledged Ms. Rosario for being there for Ms. Hendricks in her last moment. I felt bad because before I knew what happened, I wanted to flip on Ms. Rosario, but I realized that Ms. Hendricks wanted her there.

Ms. Rosario would always drive Ms. Hendricks home after work, so it was only right that Ms. Rosario could say goodbye.

Ms. Nebula became more of a presence around the building. She would say hello and would smile when she spoke, but most JCs weren't buying it; we found her whole act forgasi. We felt the administration failed Ms. Hendricks, and all the smiles and hellos weren't bringing her back.

As a group, the JCs became closer, and we started to show each other more support. Sometimes, we as black people can be so endearing, I hate that about us. While other people are stepping on everybody's throats, black people are ready to sing kumbaya and hold hands, forgiving those who kick them around. Just grateful to get scraps, like when we have pig's feet and chitlins for the holidays. We know where that tradition came from, that's more insulting than us calling each other niggas.

I'm not excluded, I was the epitome of this. I was a good worker, but deep down, I developed resentment for the administration, and every now and then, I took chances with a laissez faire attitude. Like, "You want to shit on me? I'm going to spit in your cup of water," not literally, more figuratively was my attitude. On some Kizzy shit; Oh, I forgot, not everyone saw the original *Roots*. Well to clarify, Kizzy was a character who spit in the cup of a white woman who told her to fitch her some water. Classic shit.

But for Ms. Rosario, she had enough. She said she didn't want to be in a place where she got no support or respect from the people she worked for, and that she didn't want to be the next person to die on a hall, so she started looking for a new job.

The vicarious trauma that we all suffered from Ms. Hendricks' death was taking a toll on the entire staff. The agency offered counseling, but the reality is that the tours' coverage proceeded anything else. So we weren't encouraged to take advantage of that service, and we all suppressed our feelings and went back to work.

My coping mechanisms took over me and I reverted to smoking cigarettes like I did before MJ was born. It felt good to escape the stress level I was under, but it wasn't helping anything. It was just something else to add to my daily routine, chipping away at my self-esteem. As good as it felt, did I really need this?

Claudia knew I was smoking, but the kids were in the dark. What stopped me before was MJ at the age of four who said, "Daddy, please stop. I don't want you to die." That's all it took, and I stopped.

Prior to fatherhood, I developed this bad habit from being around photographers and models during photo shoots every day. A steady diet of coffee and cigarettes, not cool, but that was my world then. I went from Lucky Strikes to cloves to stopping, back to some other shit called Al Capones. They looked like cloves, but they were cigarettes dipped in cognac, kind of reminded me of honey blunts but they weren't. It was a weakness, and just like back then, my self-confidence was shaky. The more I think about it, I should have taken advantage of the counseling service the agency was providing. I could have got the mental help I needed to put me back on track, but instead, I surrendered to temptation and the psychological pat on the back the job gave me for being a team player.

Within a month of Ms. Hendricks' funeral, Ms. Rosario got a new job working for corrections. I was happy for her, but sad for me because my allies dropped to nil. The only person left in my corner was Ms. Willis, even Pena resigned from his position as OM.

As badly as I wanted to leave, I was stuck believing that things could get better, like a crackhead trying to get that first high again. I didn't have the problems most JCs had. I had my own hall and all the residents in the building respected me. I never had to worry about being assaulted by any of them, which was something that I thought about every day in the beginning. The hardest thing was putting on the uniform and showing up.

I was as comfortable as a resident on platinum. At forty-five, where would I go and not have to worry about budget cuts and being the first to be let go? I was at the top of the food chain on my tour. Out of twenty male JCs, I was top five. In a despondent attempt to salvage what was considered my bread and butter, I tried to make a bad situation good.

Sometimes, what I'm looking for comes when I'm not looking for it, but I didn't know what I was looking for now. There was a time the job was worth it, but now it wasn't worth it anymore. It wasn't a team anymore because all the good players were getting fired, injured, or walked away. Ms. Hendricks's death left a bad taste in my mouth, and it never went away.

I got a call on my past days that Ms. Willis just cleared out her desk and left the building, nobody knew why. She practically lived there. She never took a day off unless for health reasons. We later found out that she wasn't allowed in the building because of an allegation.

The administration was good at keeping secrets; they never shared decisions like this with us. We were completely in the dark. I never saw so many people pile on. The haters were in droves and all of them were females. I was the wrong person to talk to because that was my girl, and I only saw her bend over backward for everybody. Ms. Willis could never ingratiate the female JCs, she thought they were lazy and catty. She came from the AM where the female staff held down halls like the men, but on the PM, most of them complained a lot.

Whenever she thought they were out of line, she let them have it. I've seen her tweak on them so bad it made some of them cry. She was hard on them, but she was hard on everybody. I caught her wrath more than anybody because we shared a hall, and she held me up to a higher standard. When she talked crazy, I took it like a man.

The news of her leaving got to me. I was spent, I tried to call her, but she wasn't answering my calls.

First, Ms. Mays then Vega then Platter then Ms. Rosario and now Ms. Willis. I lost all my resources and my support was gone. I didn't have anybody I could turn to when I needed help to remove a resident or get a day off. Suddenly, my immunity shield was no longer there.

CHAPTER NINETEEN

◆ ✦ ◆ ✦ ◆

Now come one come all we about to get hectic
If my crew don't get in than the X makes an exit
To the rear, I'm outta here I don't front on my brothers
I take care of them before I take care of others

—Brand Nubians
"All for One"

I MADE A LOT OF enemies hiding behind Platter and Ms. Willis. It felt like open season on my ass, and the first in line were Okeke and Ebo.

Ebo never forgave me for always getting my timesheets approved by Ms. Willis. I started getting commissioner checks (this is a check with no overtime when the supervisor forgets to include it), and most of my requests for days off got denied. It was a price to pay for being so arrogant. He even conferenced me for being late two minutes. This was nothing compared to what Okeke did. He saw this as an opportunity to ruin E-Hall for good. I was afraid they were going to shut it down, but thanks to Ms. Kindie, she wouldn't let them. Ms. Kindie and I never really saw eye to eye, but when it came to E-Hall we came together like Cookie and Luscious on *Empire*.

Okeke assigned me with the worst staff and gave me the worst residents. I became very reclusive, and I rarely engaged in conversations with my coworkers. I started giving fake smiles and hellos, and I became real shady which was against my nature; I didn't trust anybody. My attitude as a counselor went from confident to cocky.

I felt that my seniority allowed me certain privileges on the weekend. I had the most seniority out of eighteen people, and I started feeling myself. I've seen the crap this agency dished out, I wasn't with none of it. I started to get on my Luke shit. I knew their closet wasn't clean, and I wasn't trying to be another one of their casualties. At this point, trying to decipher the semantic of this place was stressing my brain. I do have a life outside of here that was being neglected, it's not all that bad, but it was. I couldn't separate myself from the madness, it just all started making me mad.

Any time they transferred a resident who was a problem on other halls to E- Hall, I would tell my group to pack him up, and by the next day, that resident got smoked off the hall. I took care of my group, and they took care of me. If any of them had a birthday, I got them a slice of cake from the carrot cake store and a soda. Normally, this stuff had to be approved by the administration, but I would just bring it in anyway. They treated me like a gang leader, but I wasn't "about that life," but my experience and reputation took me there.

My behavior mirrored Luke's last words to me when he said, "To beat the devil you have to be the devil." Never in my life did I believe I could be like this, but I was. If any of my past residents returned to the building for a parole violation, I gave them the hall if the hall lacked leadership. This didn't always sit well with all the residents, but I didn't care. I wanted to clean the hall of weak and untrustworthy kids and just surround myself with those who would hold me down.

Once a week, we held an E-Hall meeting with just the JCs and OMs, and during this meeting, the entire time was spent critiquing my leadership on the hall. I stopped going because I wasn't trying to hear it. Give me a break, my credibility was cemented on that hall, "I was E-Hall." But in reality, I was out of control. My soul was tainted with wicked thoughts. It was the weirdest feeling because I didn't start out this way. Here I was, the same guy who was afraid to see someone run over a cat, now plotting to have kids jumped. Tom Dudley had nothing on me. I was a sinner.

I went to church, sometimes, with my mother. We attended Riverside Church in Harlem. At the end of service, I would go to the columbarium where they stored the cremated ashes of my father on the left side and my grandmother on the right side, and I would kneel in between both and ask for forgiveness and guidance. Constantly being around murderers, rapists, and thieves who were children torn my spiritual fabric and made me punch drunk with negative power like a supervillain. I was getting off on being around badasses who only listened to me. To control these uncontrollable kids was a power rush for me. At this point, I really didn't know where my mind was going. It was like I lost it, and it started to make me a bad guy because I just don't give a fuck.

Whenever I was Mr. Nice Guy, I got pushed around by the kids or supervision. From day one, most of the people who made decisions held me down, but those days were gone. I became the monster of monsters.

But the day I almost caught my first allegation slowed my row. On this day, I was en route to the dinner with E-Hall, and when we entered the café, the girls from A-Hall were there having dinner. This was a bad idea because a resident on my hall named Gregski (pronounced Gretzky) had a run-in with a girl on A-Hall in the town. When I say he had a run-in, I mean before they were locked up, she gave him a blowjob, and he posted her doing it on Instagram. All the kids in the building saw it and would tease her about it. Supervision never listened to us, and when I got to the café and saw them in there, I tried to tell my supervisor, but he said, "I don't have no time for that, these are the last two groups to have dinner and I have to be in visiting in twenty minutes." As we entered the café, all the boys started laughing. I told them to shut the fuck up or they would be locked down for the day. One resident named Trigga (I don't have to tell you how he got that name) took it a step further and started calling her out of her name under his breath. Her name was Tatiana, and he was calling her Thotiana. She took offense and jumped out her seat to approach him on the line, but she was stopped by the supervisor and the staff on A-Hall and went back to her seat. Ebo addressed my group and said, "One more word and E-Hall will be eating dinner in their rooms." Trigga fell back, but when he sat down to eat, he kept looking at Tatiana and started making blowjob jesters with his hands and mouth. As I approached him to make him stop, Tatiana ran over to him and mashed her plate of food in his face. I was too late. At this point, they started fighting. I guess nobody told him not to hit girls because he punched the shit out of her and got restrained by supervisor Ebo. Before Tatiana could get up and go after Trigga, I managed to restrain her using the standing upper torso technique. While Trigga was being restrained, the other girls on A-Hall attacked him by throwing food at him and trying to punch him, but whenever they got close he would kick them in the face. It was an all-out food-fight riot between one boy and eight girls. Trigga was a little runt who liked playing with guns, but it was obvious he was good with his hands and feet. When security got there, they got things under control, but as Trigga was escorted out of the café, he and Tatiana exchanged words. He was screaming, "Thotiana the top queen, Thotiana the top queen, stop sucking dick on video, bitch." As I was holding her on the wall, she kept telling me to let her go, and as Trigga was taken out, she spit on him, and he tried to spit back, but it hit one of the female security guards in the back of her hair. As I release my hold on Tatiana, she started trying to swing on me, but the security guards managed her into the medical area. When Ebo asked me if I was okay, I asked him if he was still doing visiting, but he just told me to write my report and avoided my question. This whole thing could have been avoided if he would have listened to me the first time, but what did I know? I just spend every day with these kids and know what they talk about. I was grateful that the other residents on E-Hall didn't get involved or it would have gotten real ugly. When I submitted my report, Ebo told me that I'm going to have another problem. He said that Tatiana filed a sexual assault allegation against me. I told him, "What the fuck is she talking about? I just restrained her." He told me not to worry about it because the cameras will prove her wrong. She said that when I restrained her, I felt her up and rubbed my privates on her ass which was bullshit. For the first time, the cameras should be a benefit, but I was fortunate because the staff on A-Hall had a long talk with Tatiana and convinced her to withdraw her allegation claim against me, which she did. I got very lucky because the way Justice Central goes after people, who knows how that would have turned out. Not even a week later, I had another wake-up call when I took E-Hall to the gym and this one resident busted his head open. It was hard to avoid the temptation of competition because boys will be boys, but the game has changed, and the agency wasn't paying us to prove how fast or strong we were. I tried to simulate a football drill with the group, but it went bad. Whoever said that thugs play football was lying because these motherfuckas were fragile. I had them run a nutcracker drill where three kids were on both sides while one of them ran down the middle with the ball and the other kids tried to knock it out of his hands. As the kid with the ball ran down the lane, he bumped his head on another resident's chin, and out of nowhere, blood started leaking from the seams of his cornrows. I thought I was fried; he had to be rushed to the hospital where they stapled his head.

When they asked him what happened, he said he bumped his head playing basketball, completely saving my ass. That would have automatically been thirty days in the street or more. But I owed a lot to some of these kids.

My idea of a flag football league died with that incident. I relied on the residents on E-Hall more than the people I worked with. I missed the days of open dialogue with the old ED Morales and the conversations I had with TC Platter, even being able to chop it up with Ms. Willis in her office to discuss strategies on how to resolve conflict on the hall.

I didn't need someone to hold my hand; I needed a morale boost. Even though I became an asshole, supervision trusted that I was responsible enough to train the new JCs and rotated them as my partners. This was annoying because it was usually somebody awful. I would be stuck with somebody with no experience. When I say no experience, I mean someone who has never worked with teenagers in this capacity. This agency needed new people to hire the new people because whoever they had doing the hiring sucked. I was that new guy once, but I was never that bad. The more mistakes they made the more I got blamed for it. This was just something else to make me more mad.

I always had a steady partner. This musical JC shit was, as the kids would say, was "dayroom" to me. The residents would always provoke them mentally and physically, they never lasted three months. I watched this one resident take this guy's badge and he did nothing. I had to restrain the resident while this guy stood there and watched. I wasn't a bodyguard. I had less patience for my coworkers than I did the residents.

The newest class who came in was all females, and they looked real weak. They looked like they worked at Bloomingdale's, in the make-up department. I just shook my head as they were introduced in roll call. I kept saying to myself, *please don't assign any of them with me*. The residents will hurt their feelings, and I will have to pick up the pieces.

Out of three of them, two were African-American and one was Caucasian. The Caucasian woman looked like she had no business being here. I'm all for equality, but she's going to get somebody hurt. If she isn't streetwise like supervisor Hoffman the residents will have her for lunch, and she looked like she was from the reality TV show "Jersey Shore." Her name was Ms. Bollerio, and she was blonde with blue eyes and very pretty, but this wasn't a beauty pageant. She looked like Molly Ringwald with blonde hair.

When Ebo gave out the assignment, he thought he spared me by assigning me with the biggest of the three, but bigger doesn't always mean better. What she had in size she lacked in mental toughness. She was too sensitive, and the residents verbally had her on edge. They made her so mad that she cried in anger, which is something you can't take back.

I told Ebo that I would rather work by myself than have one of those new JCs as a partner. He told me because the count on the hall was high, he had to assign me a partner. Ebo thought he was slick. For the past three classes, he would always assign me to work with the weakest new staff, figuring that I would never let the residents violate them.

But at this point, I was done being Captain Save-a-Ho. I hate to refer to men as ho's or anybody for that matter, but the dudes he gave me were useless. He would gas me by saying, "Mr. Geez, that's my man, he is the best I have." Maybe he meant it, but I knew he was just using me. I just saw it as an opportunity to get days off so I would play along.

After the last one cried, I wasn't ready for anything else. When he assigned Ms. Bollerio as my partner, I just knew he was fucking with me. I did everything to avoid my premeditated thoughts that she would be terrible and gave her a chance. I can't front, she held it down pretty good. When she stepped on the hall, I felt like I was in a *King Kong* movie, like when all the villagers reacted when they saw that white chick.

But she dismissed the prima donna treatment and dug into the job. She put on a screw face, rolled up her sleeves, and never allowed them to shake her. What amazed me was her ability to not judge them. She gave everybody a chance to prove themselves almost to a fault. She treated them all the same, but if a resident had issues with women or white people, she didn't fuck with them, which I understood. She was like Ms. Rosario without the diva.

All the residents loved her. She reminded me of the babysitter that they had a crush on, but always treated with respect. She had her admirers, but nobody violated her in a sexual or provocative way. I think this was because she was so nice and generous. Most of the residents were overprotective of her like they were of me. Every time we worked together, it was the greatest day; I mean no drama. No drama from her and no drama from the residents. It was the most peaceful days I can remember.

My attitude started to change. I started to care again, and I couldn't wait to go to work. That goes back to what I said about not looking for something, and it becoming something good. Sometimes, a resident or a coworker had that effect, as long as we worked together, I was good and so were the residents.

Having a female partner who could hold her own was something I was used to. Ms. Bollerio did just that. I didn't have to be her bodyguard. Even though she was only twenty-six years old, she had the maturity of someone much older. She never approached this as a popularity contest, she saw this as an opportunity for bigger and better things. She could restrain and wasn't afraid to get in a resident's face. All the residents were African-American and Hispanic and 99 percent of the JCs were the same. She represented that 1 percent. She stuck out like sore thumb, but it didn't faze her.

She had a criminal justice background, and she knew what she signed up for. We were like Cloak and Dagger, the Marvel superhero team. The residents loved us and we had the best tone in the building.

After Ms. Rosario left, I wasn't sure I would ever have another partner on that level. Ms. Bollerio was just as good, if not better, in some ways. Unlike Ms. Rosario, Ms. Bollerio stayed on my hip and followed my lead. She saw me as a mentor, and in return, she helped me adjust my mindset from bad too good. I never wanted to misguide her or let her down. I felt like I had a responsibility to show her the ropes, like so many good JCs did for me. It was then that I started developing my best rap sessions ever.

Sometimes, I got inspired by something I heard on sports radio or just something I observed from watching the group's behavior, I started getting on them for how they dressed for court. These kids dressed for court like they dressed for the first day of school, it was a fashion show. Sneakers worth $200, $500 belts, and True Religion jeans.

That shit is cool for a party but not for court, but I blame their parents for spending their money on this crap. It's crap when you're fifteen and locked up for a crime. If I was in their position, at fifteen, my mother wouldn't have bought me shit. She would have said, "Whatever socks they give you in the facility, those are the same socks you will be wearing to court. Don't ask be to buy you a motherfuckin' thing."

How can you possibly think any judge is going to give you leniency when your clothes cost more than theirs? Dress conservative and semiformal like a job interview. Oh, I forgot they've never been on an interview. I would bring in my ties and teach them how to tie them, but we would argue about how to dress because they were so caught up with impressing each other. None of them knew how to tie a tie, but I bet if I ask how many knew how to roll a blunt, they would have all raised their hands.

It was pitiful where their mindset was. It was always on chilling and never on working. Every now and then, a kid would wear a suit to court, but most of them felt it didn't help. I would say, "Okay, how about the Russell Simmons look? The sweater vest with the polo shirt and jeans." They were feeling that and some of them took my fashion advice.

When I cared, I was arguably the best counselor in the building, and it would show because my group would think like me. Ms. Bollerio was getting a lesson in counseling, and unlike some people, she wasn't a Ms. Know-It-All. It was refreshing that she wanted to learn.

After several weeks of working together, it looked like we were permanently partners. Before the residents locked in for the night, they all would say, "I love you, Ms. Bollerio. I love you, Mr. Geez. Get home safe." Hearing this felt like we reached another level of counseling, and for the first time, I had a partner who was a female version of me. The synergy between us was crazy good, and we had the yin-yang thing on lock.

Life is funny like that. When you think all hope is lost, something happens to make you change your view. All the residents made a conscious effort to stay out of trouble because they didn't want to disappoint us.

For the Super Bowl, we got approved to have a party, and we were the wave of the building. We had chips and dip, pizza, soda, and Ms. Bollerio had her mother make the most incredible cookies that they still talked about to this day. We had haters, but we understood that if we didn't have haters, we weren't doing a good job. Surprisingly, the females on the PM welcomed her and were glad someone wanted to work E-Hall because they felt that the residents on E were annoying snot-nose little kids who were nasty and disrespectful to females. But Ms. Bollerio changed that. If she found out that any of them were disrespectful to a female, she spoke to them, and then that resident would apologize. When they did something wrong, they didn't want her to know about it because they didn't want her to not like them.

I never seen anything like it. If she restrained someone, that resident got beat up just because she had to restrain him. This was the best time I had as a JC, but like all good things, it came to an end the day we weren't assigned together. When I asked supervision at the end of the tour why we didn't work together, I was told by Supervisor Gill that some things were better left unsaid. I said, "What the hell does that mean?" She said, "No comment."

I wasn't comfortable with that answer, so I called her from home, and she said that it was brought to her attention that we were an item, and that it would be better if we weren't assigned together. When I asked her, who said this, again she said no comment.

Later, I found out that Okeke sent a memo to the PM supervisors to not assign us together because he believed we were fucking. At that point, I went black. Who the fuck did this dude think he was? I didn't want to snitch on Ms. Gill by going straight to Okeke, so I spoke to the OM on the AM tour, and he said it was unethical and unacceptable, and that he would get to the bottom of it. The next day, OM Perez who worked the PM said she was aware of the situation that was passed to her from her colleague, and that she would take care of it and said, "You will get your partner back."

In the meantime, Ms. Bollerio was assigned to work with girls on B-Hall, and to make matters worse, Okeke reduced E-Hall to less than nine residents so that I could work alone. The policy permitted a ratio of eight residents to one JC.

Okeke was slick. He was feeling Ms. Bollerio and didn't like the relationship we had. He used an innuendo to separate us and made sure that we never worked together again. What a bitch. Now I know where I got the King Kong reference from—he was King Kong chasing the white girl. The residents were pissed and started reacting negatively toward supervision, and I didn't care at this point. I understood how they felt, and my faith in supervision went back to zero. If Ms. Willis or TC Platter were here, Okeke would have never gotten away with this. Every time I complained about being alone, it fell on deaf ears.

Ebo would tell me that Ms. Bollerio was better on the B-Hall, but whenever she requested to go to E-Hall, they told her to speak to Okeke. When she spoke to him, he played with her. He would assign her to E-Hall when I wasn't at work or just for one hour to give me a duty free. It was a game to him—he would give her the most bogus assignments. He would send her to the store for coffee and tell her to buy something for herself, and then other times, he would have her sit in his office doing nothing just for his amusement. What a creep. This dude was a pro at *quid pro quo.*

Now I see why he was kicked out of Greenwood; dude was a slime ball. Every time I asked him if Ms. Bollerio could be my partner, he would tell me that I was good with eight residents and that I didn't need help. He would say, "Geez, why are you bitching? Damn, you're getting soft." It was like he was challenging my manhood, and I didn't want to come off as a pussy so I dealt with it. This dude just sucked the fucking nice right out of me, and I was back on my bullshit.

My work ethic changed, and I stopped caring again. Just when I was about to believe that things got better, my attitude reverted back to fuck everything. OM Perez came to the hall and had me write an EEO statement against Okeke. She wanted to help me, but in some way, she was helping herself. She never liked Okeke and wanted to pin something on him. The feelings were mutual; he couldn't stand her either. He would call her all types of names behind her back. She was always going after him for dumb shit, and I guess she thought that this would stick.

In my statement, I basically said that it was unprofessional for a superior to make such an asinine assumption and how unfair it was to remove Ms. Bollerio for personal reasons. Weeks after I wrote the statement, nothing changed. I continued to work alone, and Ms. Bollerio continued to work on B-Hall. Okeke selfishly made things harder for Ms. Bollerio because other JCs would call her the princess because he gave her special treatment.

On this job, being called princess was not cool. It was bad enough that she stood out, but now nobody wanted to be around her because they thought she was a snitch or like a teacher's pet. I was surprised she didn't quit, but she wasn't a quitter. She didn't ask for this; it was making her miserable and because she was on probation, she wasn't in a position to complain.

Now I just wanted any partner because the stress load of managing a hall alone became too heavy. Writing in the logbook, opening doors, entertaining eight residents, taking them to dinner, then to the gym, then doing showers, then getting them to lock in for the night, and then writing observation reports became a lot. The eight-to-one ratio should have been changed a long time ago, especially after that shit that happened on F-Hall. But Okeke didn't care. If I complained, he would use reverse psychology on me and say, "You can handle it. You're one of my best staff."

I had to fall back because the more I complained about it, the more people started believing the memo. It's sad when two people have a great working relationship and other people have their minds in the gutter. I was almost twice as old as Ms. Bollerio and nobody was happier than Claudia that I finally had a partner I was comfortable working with. It got to the point that I just said fuck it and moved on.

There was a resident on E-Hall who wasn't ready to move on, and his name was Brandon, but everybody called him Swiper because he would steal everything. He was the only resident I knew who stole a laptop from the school floor. He was a skinny Hispanic kid from the Grand Concourse section of the Bronx. He was only fifteen, and he's been in the facility five times for stealing everything from cars to cell phones. I had him on E-Hall when he was twelve.

As much as he liked me, he liked Ms. Bollerio more and would turn it up on supervision every time she wasn't assigned to E-Hall. He was smart because, as much as Okeke tried to move him off E-Hall, he couldn't. Swiper had a court order that was approved by the administration to only be on E-Hall, but it was more about the halls he couldn't go to because of the beefs he had in the building. It was like he had a no-trade clause. He would always give Ebo a hard time, and they would go back and forth until I would put him in his room. He was forever indebted to me because I saved his ass from being jumped on G-Hall. When Steven was in the building he wanted to kill him. He never violated my tour, and we would laugh because when he was twelve, I had to restrain him every day. But I told him to chill because the more shit he does, Okeke takes it out on me. Swiper always thought he was smarter than supervision.

Okeke turned the screws on me the day he transferred this good-for-nothing kid named Raymond to E-Hall. This was a kid who would cut his arm and tag his name in blood on the walls in his room. I was so heated when he said it in roll call. Everybody looked at me laughing, and Carter tapped me on the back and said, "Good luck," because nobody wanted to deal with Raymond. Even though he was a one-to-one resident, Raymond was such a tone raiser.

When Swiper saw the stress on my face, he said, "I got you." He provoked Raymond to the point that he popped on Swiper, and then the next day, Swiper went to the bathroom, peed in a cup, and threw it in Raymond's face. Raymond was a short, stocky kid who had ADHD and was bipolar, but Swiper didn't care. It was so bad one of them had to be moved, so they moved Raymond because he started it. When I got to work that day, Swiper said, "You already know. I told you I got you." I was shocked, it was such a relief, but when you find relief in bad things, it's never good.

CHAPTER TWENTY

It's type hard tryna survive in New York state/
can't stop till I'm eatin' off a platinum plate
Here come the Jake always tries to relocate me/ lock
me up for ever but they can't deflate me 'cause
Havin' cash is highly addictive/ especially when
you're used to havin' money to live with
I thought step back look at my life as a whole/ ain't
no love it seems the devil done stole my soul
I'm out for delfia, selfia, P's not helpin' ya/ I'm
tryna get this Lexus up, plus a cellular

—Mobb Deep
"Give up the Goods"

As TIME PASSED, IT WAS evident that Ms. Perez had no power. Nothing positive came from me writing that statement. When I spoke to Carter about it, he said I was a fool to do it through her. He said that an EEO is done through the union, and whatever she had me do never left the building. He said, "For all you know, it could be sitting in Okeke's office or the ED probably could have ripped it up." Fuck, now I really made them mad. Whenever I saw OM Perez, she would say that she was working on it, which was just lip service; she didn't do anything. I was on the wrong side of the fence, and I hate when people do that. Don't patronize me; this was a common theme in this place.

I started to curve my energy toward the residents on E-Hall. We did our own thing and stayed away from the shadows of supervision. I told the residents that when they're hot, they bring negative attention to the hall, so real bad boys move in silence. Why be on front street when you can be in the cut? They took heed and began to tone down their behavior to where we became almost invisible. There were only seven of them, so we had enough space to not step on each other's toes.

I would let them listen to my iPod on the Xbox, and I would bring in suggestive movies like *City of Gods*, *Shottas*, and *Juice* for them to watch—all stuff that would never get approved to enter the building. But for eight hours, I had to grab their attention by any means necessary. It almost had that college dorm room feel.

It seemed like Okeke had a personal vendetta against me because he would do things to rile up my group. If a resident on E-Hall got into a minor incident, he would take the Xbox and the TV, and he would take their recreation time and give it to another hall, like H-Hall. It was almost like he wanted them to turn it up on me. When we wouldn't react to that, he would raise the ante and have H-Hall use our rec time with the girls. This would infuriate my group on E-Hall, and they would start kicking the door.

Just to help you envision the setting, E-Hall was located in front of the multipurpose area so when a group is there, we were looking right at them. So we were forced to watch them have fun using our time. And guess who was working with the girls? That's right, Ms. Bollerio. She was forced to be there too. He would say to her later, "Now you get to watch E-Hall." It was like a mental torture game Okeke was playing on us.

I would grab them off the door and said to them, "This is what he wants. He wants you to wild out." At this point, I was convinced that he knew about the EEO statement and he was trying to punish me. I guess that's the price I had to pay for reporting him.

This happened around the time Prime was transferred to E-Hall. Prime was a dark-skinned kid from Harlem who came from H-Hall. When he was on H, he was involved in many fights, and he was caught smoking a few times. As soon as he got to the hall, I told him how we do things on E-Hall. I told him they don't smoke or fight and we respect each other's space. I said we play video games, we watch movies, and every now and then, I bring my iPod if we have the Xbox for them to listen to music. I said, "If you bring the heat, this will all end." He said he was glad to get off H-Hall because it was chaotic, and he liked that there were only eight of them on E-Hall. But the real reason he wanted off H-Hall is because he couldn't take over.

Not all the residents were comfortable with Prime being there; he had a dominant personality that draws attention. He was such a hot box. His real name was Preston Mathews, and they called him Prime because he was such a diva and he was always polished from head to toe. He had the freshest waves, and his court clothes looked like they were from a GQ catalog. He was the only resident who would iron his Fairvue uniform every night. He was a fly dude who gave our hall flavor. He was a real Harlem cat with style and charisma.

For a sixteen-year-old, he had a lot of swag for his age. When he talked to Okeke and got us back our rec time, I was impressed; but then when he got Okeke to allow us to rec out with the girls, the whole group was in his fan club. He was a cross between Puffy and Chris Tucker, a fly-ass clown. But he was more a comedian than a soldier.

I could never give him the privileges I gave my old residents. Prime would have taken advantage; he was selfish like that. He couldn't have things in moderation, and he had to have everything and brag about it. If I was trying to avoid front street, Prime was trying to live there and scream, "I rule the world." Sometimes, I wanted to delete his swag instead of sending it. He was so high maintenance and could never lay low. It was always show time for him or maybe the appropriate word would be **Primetime**.

In addition to keeping his clothes crispy, he could dance his ass off. When he heard music, he was like the dancing bear, he would get lite anywhere anytime. It was hard to maneuver with Prime on the hall, supervision stayed making frequent trips to the hall to spy on us. I had to stop bringing in movies and the iPod to avoid being conferenced for contraband. I had a bad habit of conducting showers while the group was in the day area, something Okeke was a stickler about.

Prime didn't help. He wanted to dance in the day area with his towel on like he was at Chippendales. When Okeke saw this, I got conferenced, and I told Prime he was doing too much. He was so apologetic to the point I had to laugh. He would say, "I know you're mad, but you still love me." When I shoved him in his room, he ran to the door and grabbed my leg, begging for forgiveness. He was such a drama queen; everything was a movie.

Prime needed a role in the play *Hamilton* or some other off-Broadway play because he was an actor. His act got played out and his mischievous nature got him sent back to H-Hall where he claimed he was getting picked on. He pleaded with Okeke to send him back to E-Hall, but Okeke wasn't falling for his con game. He knew that Prime was a swindler. When he got nowhere with Okeke, he waited for Okeke to go on vacation then convinced the AM tour commander to move him back. I had a long sit down with him about what I expected from him, and he agreed to tone it down, but I never could tell if he was serious or not.

It was the summer of 2015 and a lot of Harlem kids were getting locked up. You could say they had the building because they all knew each other. Prime's street cred was large—he could dance, he could fight, and he was the best dresser; and all the residents on the hall looked up to him. Without anointing him the mantel, he took the leadership role as that dude on E-Hall, but he could never keep his level up. When he would get to silver, he would fall back to bronze and then get zeroed out. He stopped caring about his level and then relied on his charm to get his way. He was such a badass. I've seen him grab a female JC's ass and another one's tits and both women just laughed. Sounds crazy but it was true.

He treated the building like his playground. There wasn't anything he couldn't get away with. One day, he asked Supervisor Charles for a phone call, but because she was the only supervisor on duty, she said no. He was very persistent and kept begging her. He told her if she didn't give him a phone call, he would pop on somebody. She told him if he did, she had the authority to move him back to H-Hall, but the reality was that only TCs had that power. She just said that to scare him.

He then said that if she didn't give him a call, he would kill himself. She said, "Boy, stop playing. You love yourself too much to do that." He said, "You think I'm playing? Watch this." Then he held his breath, acting like he was going to pass out. Another one of his movies, she told him to stop and then gave in and told him that he can make a call later.

At the time she gave him a call, H-Hall was in the multipurpose watching the NBA Finals. When Prime walked through the multipurpose to go to the TC's office, he attacked a resident on H with a flurry of punches to the face.

Nobody knew that they had beef on the outside, but being the master of jerk and finesse, he caught the kid with a sucker punch. The kid never saw it coming, and it caught everybody off guard. Supervisor Charles almost got written up for allowing him in the area around another group. When Prime got back to the hall, I sent him to his room. I asked why did he do that, and he said, "Because he didn't respect my shit." I said, "But what about your phone call?" He said he never wanted to make a phone call, he just wanted to pop on that kid the whole time.

When he tried to apologize to Supervisor Charles, she wasn't trying to hear it, she was just another victim in Prime's web of bullshit. The longer we were together, the closer we got. He started to call me dad in front of other people. It felt good but I never knew if he meant it. On Father's Day, he wrote me the coolest card that almost brought me to tears. In the card, he said that he only acted up because he didn't like how supervision and Okeke treated me, that he didn't have a father, and that he wished I was his father. It was deep.

He begged me to read it in front of him, but I didn't because I would have gotten emotional. I had a soft spot for him and started to understand him more. To his credit, he never turned it up on my tour, so maybe he did mean what he said. When his behavior improved, he was put on silver. I would use the line from *American Gangster* when Frank said, "The loudest one is the weakest one," to encourage him to behave. I would say, "You're doing way too much, stop wanting so much attention." He would say, "I got you, I got you."

But his personality was too flamboyant he couldn't help himself. He always wanted to shine the brightest. He was always asking to use my phone, but I would dub him. I stopped bringing it in because he could notice it in my pocket and would annoy me to death about it.

During this time, MJ had to get varicocele surgery, which was stressing me out because we never dealt with this before. He got stitches once and he fractured his elbow, but this was something different. I shared my feelings about it with Prime, and he was touched by how much I cared for my son. He said that he wished he had someone care for him like that. He started talking about how he missed his mother and that he wanted to go home. When he started getting hyper and crying, I felt bad for him.

He was nervous about his next court date and didn't know what to expect. I told him to just pray on it and it will be fine. It was after 10 PM and the other residents were asleep at the time, so we got to talk longer than normal. He asked if he could use my phone to talk to his mother, but I told him no because I didn't have it. He said, "Why are you lying? I see it in your pocket." I told him I had it because I was on standby for MJ if he called. He said he wanted to check with his mother to make sure she sent the right court clothes. My head said no but my heart said yes, so I told him to make it fast. I wasn't thinking it was a ruse, I've seen him play before and this time it was different. What I saw was a child who was homesick and needed to speak to his mother.

When supervisor Ebo came to sign the logbook, I closed Prime's door and went to the desk to play it off. As I was rushing Ebo out the door, I was hoping Prime didn't blow me up. When I went to room 202, he was finishing his conversation. To prove to me that he wasn't lying, he said, "If you don't believe it's my mom, speak to her." I didn't want to talk to her but I just did it out of courtesy, I said hi, and she thanked me for holding down her son.

When he hung up, I was relieved it was over and I said, "Don't ask me again." He thanked me more than ten times, and I just said goodnight. His attitude changed and his mood was better, I wanted to help him, but I knew I broke a cardinal rule. In the time he had my jack, he could have emailed the president. I was just glad it was over.

It was coming up on the tenth anniversary of the day my ex-wife bounced, which was kind of symbolic. Man, I've come full circle. Life has shown me its ass and I survived. MJ's surgery was successful, Rosemary was going to camp for the first time, and Jacob and Jordan had a good year of school. Claudia and I were doing swell. We were in the process of moving, and I just sold the condo. It was time for some bigger and better things.

At work, the night TC transferred a resident to E-Hall who was a real pain in the ass, and his name was Nester and everybody hated him. He couldn't go anywhere because everybody wanted his head. The TC thought he would be safest on E-Hall because the count was low due to the fact that one of my residents went home and the kids in E-Hall weren't considered as volatile as the residents were on the other halls. I had Nester on E-Hall six months ago, so I was familiar with him, but at that time, the group was different and Prime didn't know him. Nester was creepy; he used to stare at Ms. Bollerio like he was undressing her with his eyes. I would always put him in his room for fear somebody would pop on him. He was annoying and had a misogynistic disposition. He never got along with anybody, especially the female staff.

I wasn't at work yet, but I was told that Nester spilled some water on the floor playing around and used Prime's sweatshirt to clean it. Next thing I heard was that Prime rocked it off and broke his jaw. When I heard about it in roll call, I knew putting Nester on the hall was a bad decision, but supervision had the luxury to make those mistakes. When I got to the hall, Prime was already rearrested and sent to the Rock. When Nester returned to the building from the hospital, his mouth was wired and he was placed on the SHU. Over there, he started to feel himself and became a terror with the staff there and was labeled the new dickhead of the building.

Later that week, I got word that Prime's mother came to the building to retrieve his clothes in admissions and she was not happy. She flipped on the staff there and said that her son was getting into trouble because of bad counselors. She was heard asking why her son was smoking and how was he on Facebook and that he called her the other night. Everybody looked at me because he was with me at night on E-Hall. I had nothing to do with him smoking or being on Facebook, but I did let him use my phone to call her. When I heard this, I wanted to kick myself in the face for being so naïve. What the fuck was I thinking? Of all the moronic things I've done in my life, this takes the cake.

That same night after I was told his mother was flipping out, the ED came to the hall and took the logbook. She said hello, grabbed the logbook, and left the hall. When she returned it in twenty minutes and left, I felt like I was sitting on the other side of the hall, looking at myself just shaking my head saying, "You dick." It was a matter of time before I knew that shit would come back to me. I couldn't even holla at Prime to get him to check his mother and ask her why was she going so hard. Looking out for him could ruin my career. Now all the things Luke and Platter would tell me was in my head? They tried to tell me instead of worrying about who the Jets were going to sign in free agency, I should have been focused on doing my job which was to avoid being manipulated by one of these little motherfuckers.

On the observation report, there is a section that says check the box to indicate how manipulating the resident is. Prime's observation report should have said always with fifty checks. He had manipulator written on his forehead.

The kid got me, but I got myself. Hopefully, this shit blows over, but once Okeke returned from vacation and got wind of the situation, he put a whole new spin on things.

He called me to the multipurpose a few days later and told me that they were watching me. He said that I was a good counselor but that I was getting sloppy. He said that Prime's mother came to the building and was complaining that he calls her late at night. I acted like I didn't know anything. He said, "Don't play games with me, I'm just trying to look out for you. Stop bringing your phone in the building." But I'm thinking to myself, he brings his phone in the building, everybody brings their phones in the building. I knew what he meant: I couldn't play stupid, he was right. My uncle always said you can't bullshit a bullshitter. I realized then that I was fucked.

CHAPTER TWENTY-ONE

+ + + + + +

It's not about a salary it's all about reality.

—KRS-One of Boogie Down Productions
"My Philosophy"

WITH EVERYBODY TALKING ABOUT PRIME'S mother coming to the building, I got real nervous I began to develop a fear of the unknown. I've always been a control freak, but now I felt like I was in traffic and a giant boulder was going to land on my car and I couldn't unlock the doors. I was completely powerless. I turned to my ace for guidance who was James, my dude from childhood.

As I approached ten years ago to the day that James helped me with my custody dilemma, it was ironic that I needed him to help me out again. He was the only person I could count on to help me without making any judgments on what I did.

Just to give you a little history on James, we go back like Cadillacs. We've been friends since the second grade. When you're friends with somebody for more than forty years, that's real. No matter what the situation is, I could always count on him for support. If someone told him I was dead and buried, James would dig my grave to see if I was breathing. He was always impartial and never judgmental.

He tried to help me by calling Prime's mother and telling her to spare a family man who just made a mistake, but it didn't turn out the way we thought it would. He didn't know this woman, and she was offended that he called her. He said, "Bro, I might have made it worse."

He said when he spoke to her that he told her that I was just looking out for her son and that I don't condone smoking or drinking for minors. He told her that I was a father and that I treated Prime like a son, but she wasn't buying it.

She felt I was just protecting my job which was true, but on this, I displayed bad judgment. The reality is that I looked out for the wrong kid with the wrong mother. I told James to set it up for me to meet her in person to apologize, which he did.

At first she was hesitant, but agreed to meet me in Harlem on 116th Street. It was crazy because this was the same block that I opened the store, everything was coming full circle. When I met her, she was with her youngest son and her sister. Her sister worked for the Board of Ed and was very understanding of my position. She could relate to the politics of the job and has been caught in situation where she tried to help a kid. But Prime's mother had her reservations and wasn't really feeling me.

When she asked me about the smoking and the posting on Facebook, I told her all I did was let him call her, which was wrong. I even showed her the Father's Day card he gave me to prove that he saw me like a father figure, not a homeboy. Nothing about my relationship with Prime was disingenuous.

She loosened up a little and started to see my point. I felt good about our meeting, I even walked with them to the fish market. When she left, I gave her a hug and apologized again. She accepted it and went on her way. After that meeting, I knew I violated all codes of ethics on my job, but I was out to save my own ass. I was treading water and needed to make my own life preserver. I tried to convince myself that what I did wasn't so bad, but the cover up is always worse than the crime. A part of me wanted to come clean and tell the agency what I did, but my mind wasn't willing to admit fault to a bunch of people who covered up everything.

I was one of them. I played the game the way they do. The roller coaster of emotions never ended for me. Just as I got over this, there were rumors that TC Herrera returned to work. The day I saw his car in the parking lot, I got that queasy feeling in my stomach I used to get when he was there before. I was not prepared to deal with his bullshit, but when I went inside, I was told he was only there to do paperwork, but he was scheduled to return the next week. He was the last person I wanted to see, I was tired of Okeke's crap but Herrera was on another level.

The day he returned, I called out. I just wasn't ready, but the next day, I was surprised to see that he wasn't saying anything. Maybe he was feeling things out. It's been over a year, he might be rusty or something. Nevertheless, he was back and I had someone else looking over my shoulder. With so many new JCs, he wasn't fucking with me. I guess my cachet reached a level he found acceptable. He probably figured after ten years, he didn't have to look over my shoulder, but I was still cautious because he could flip the script at any moment.

When Herrera and Okeke worked together, it was like Hitler and Mussolini were running the building. They would do rounds together and both enter the hall, one from the front door and the other from the back door, trying to catch somebody doing dirt. It was totally scripted, and the double-team-tough-guy shit was beyond corny. I would tell the group on E-Hall that both TCs are on the prowl, so be on point. I explained to them that if Okeke is an asshole, Herrera is the whole ass.

It's been so long. None of them were in the building when he was last here and so much has changed. Herrera's hands-on approach was something we all avoided, even Okeke was hip to it. It was a new day with BCW at the helm and Justice Central reviewing incidents.

There was an incident that happened in admissions that had us all shaken up. A few months ago, a resident was being verbally disrespectful toward the staff and started to turn it up in the admissions area. JC Garcia was the only one to address the resident to calm down and to follow the directives that the staff is directing him to do.

Garcia worked for court services, and he was one of the best JCs in Fairvue. Nobody knew that this resident suffered from seizures, so when Garcia restrained him, he had a seizure attack. This goes back to my point that I made that we should know their ailments.

On the camera, it appeared like Garcia was hurting him, but he was just escorting him out the area because of the machinery and furniture in the office could cause him to get hurt. But while backing out of the area, Garcia and the resident bumped into a low file cabinet which caused JC Garcia to sustain a shoulder injury and a cut on his back while they fell to the floor. That's when the resident appeared to suffer from a seizure attack. We were never trained how to manage a resident under those circumstances.

But the agency didn't want to hear that. At this point, all the proper authorities were contacted about the incident. But Justice Central were the only ones who saw different, and they called for JC Garcia's arrest and he was put in jail. This shit was on the news, and we even had protesters in front of the building screaming police brutality. To this day, he is on modified duty, fighting to keep his job and avoid incarceration.

Even the NYPD protects its own better than this, and it's fucking disgraceful. So they want to fire Garcia for child abuse, but if he did nothing, he would be guilty of neglect which is also child abuse. Damned if you do, damned if you don't. It's amazing that 90 percent of the time the JCs are at fault. I saw the same kid walking the streets eight months later, chilling in the town while Justice Central continues to put Garcia and his family through hell. I guess when that kid has another seizure, they will rearrest Garcia and charge him for a telekinetic restraint. Type bullshit.

Where was the ED to defend the credibility of her staff? She was hiding in her office.

This is why I stopped putting my hands on the residents, and I wasn't alone. After Garcia's case, we all fell back; even the supervisors exercised their counseling skills. This was a reality check for all of us.

Herrera didn't get that memo, and after getting bent up by a resident, you would have thought he would have learned his lesson, but it's hard to show an old dog new tricks. Not too long after returning, Herrera came up with the brilliant idea to have all the halls in the main yard at the same time. Prior to his return, every tour avoided mixing the groups because there were too many beefs to take that chance, and it would incite a riot. None of the halls got along. E-Hall had beef with J-Hall, D-Hall had beef with H-Hall, and B-Hall had beef with A-Hall. It was insanity to have them together.

The first day, things went smoothly. I had my reservations, but I kept my opinion to myself. We were all on edge because it was something we weren't used to; it was like Herrera wanted to prove he was still the ringmaster. His unrelenting effort to have all the groups together made me sick to my stomach. I couldn't fathom anybody thinking this was a good idea. But Herrera listened to nobody; the more anybody told him not to do something, the more he wanted to do it just to prove how big his balls were.

That same night, I received two residents whom the whole building wanted a piece of, their names were Rodney and Grip. Rodney was from Harlem and Grip was from Brooklyn, and they were both Blood members. Rodney was a tall slim kid who repped his flag hard and wanted everyone to know he loved his set to death. Grip was transferred to Fairvue from Greenwood, and he looked like Chief Keef with the dreads and was built like Julio Jones the football player. He was a beast, and Rodney felt invincible with Grip in the room.

I supported the transfer of Grip to the hall because he was with me a year ago, and respected my program. He was on C-Hall by himself because in Greenwood he would pop it off on the staff. He was huge, but we communicated well and I felt safe with him. Everybody thought I was crazy, but he had a maturity about him that I wanted on the hall. My group was real silly and needed someone to fear.

The next day when we got the call to go to the main yard, I was praying that Herrera didn't have all the groups out there, but he did. You can catch lightning in a bottle sometimes, but far more often it blows up in your face, such was the case here. When we entered the main yard, I said to myself, *when this shit goes down, I want to know which kid I was going to restrain and where.*

Within twenty minutes of being there, Rodney started mouthing off to Grip that Fairvue residents were pussies, and he was making gang signs to everybody who was watching. He was moving like that dude who played Junior in the movie the *Players Club*, mad staticky. I pulled him aside and said, "What are you doing?" He said, "I'm good."

When Herrera saw him being extra, he removed him from the main yard, and I felt like that was the best decision he made since returning. It was good timing because the other residents were getting restless and were plotting to jump him. But in less than an hour, Herrera brought him back out. Why? I don't know.

Herrera was on his bullshit again, testing the control he had over everyone.

Grip stayed by the pull-up bars and was just peeping the setting through his locks. When Rodney returned, I knew a riot was going to break out. I was posted on the basketball court talking to Trigga, and we were joking, saying who we thought was going to set it off. When Herrera told H-Hall to line up, this kid stepped to Grip and said, "What's cracking?" Grip did just that and cracked him in the face; it was lit.

All the residents started fighting and there was a major melee in the main yard, security came to assist but it was too out of control. It was an all-out rumble in the Bronx. The main yard, which was considered a playground, turned into a danger zone because we were completely outnumbered two to one.

Some residents were fighting until they got tired because all the staff were occupied restraining one resident, some had two. The kid who got the worse was Rodney; for all that mouthing he did, the entire D-Hall pounced on him. They were punching and kicking him in the face while he struggled on the floor to get away. Grip was fucking up everybody and anybody who stepped to him. He was dropping them like flies. It was like the fight scene in the movie *The Wanderers*.

I was restraining this resident I was familiar with on the ground, and out of nowhere, this other resident wanted to kick him. So I attempted to shield him, but I got kicked in the hand trying to protect my face instead.

It was so bad that we were overwhelmed with the responsibility to establish control, and as we were occupied with a restraint, we had to watch as two or three other fights resumed. Women screaming and men yelling as we watch several kids get kicked and punched. It seemed like it would never end. It was beyond crazy seeing these kids beating the shit out of each other with no intervention. I just looked over at Herrera holding on to his one restraint, wanting to say, "Are you happy now?" It was the craziest thing I ever experienced working here.

When things were under control, I escorted a few residents back to their halls and returned to E-Hall. Herrera was in the multipurpose area, explaining his decision to have all the groups in the main yard to a security guard. But at the end of the day, he didn't have to explain his decision to anybody. He had the power to put everybody's life in jeopardy. I told supervision, "When does he get in trouble for shit like this? He puts all our careers on the line just to show he has control."

He liked incidents and encouraged restraints; well, he got his wish. I told supervision I was out. I got somebody to cover my hall, and I bounced. I had a cookie on my eye, a sprained shoulder, and my right hand was swollen. I called Herrera to tell him I was leaving, and he didn't argue. That was the most polite he ever was to me. It meant nothing to him; dude was still a dick.

The impervious manner of Herrera made working under his leadership completely inhuman for all the staff. We weren't people, we were pawns in his game; even the residents were treated like enemies to be defeated. All we needed were horses and lassos and this would be considered a cattle ranch. This incident was the straw of all straws.

After I wrote my incident report, I left and I didn't return for two weeks to heal my wounds. I was thinking how much longer was I going to continue doing this. MJ was preparing for college and we just moved. I wasn't in any position to look for a new job. More than five people were out with injuries, including me, and during that time, nobody in the administration or supervision called to check on me to see if I was okay, which didn't surprise me. I was just a badge number and a body, completely replaceable. Only my coworkers checked on me. We realized we were the field niggas, and if we didn't support each other, nobody would.

When I recovered, I just sucked it up and returned to work. Waiting for workers' comp to pay my bills was an afterthought, so in a desperate haste, I went back. My first day I returned to work, Herrera didn't even say welcome back. He just stood in roll call like nothing happened, maybe I was expecting too much. Was it too hard to have human decency for the people who work for you on the front line? I felt like a paid slave.

What was amazing was the lack of contrition this man had. Sometimes, the more powerful you are, the meaner you are to others. This dude reveled in this. If this dude was a real general or captain, there would have been a mutiny.

The hall was a lot lighter. Rodney was moved to J-Hall and Grip was sent upstate. That week, I had training and there was a coworker who worked at the report center for incidents. She said that she took the report from Herrera about the riot, and he told her that he gave a rap session to every hall before they went to the main yard. That was bullshit; but who was going to question what he said. The agency consigned on all his antics. It was regrettable the number of lives they have ruined from the residents to the staff. We were all victimized by their bullying ways.

During the same week I returned, my world came to a crashing halt because one of my best friends passed away from cancer. My boy Mo, who I use to design with, was very sick; and I wasn't aware just how bad until I went to see him a month earlier. MJ and I went to the movies with him to see the *NWA* movie. I was surprised that his condition was that bad. He looked fine, but for a fit dude, he was moving real slow.

Mo was the fleekiest dude in NYC; his gear stayed type fresh. His swag was on 1000 percent; anybody who knew him would attest to that. When we were roommates back in '92, I used to joke with him that he dressed like Mr. Furley, the landlord from the TV show "Three is Company."

But at the end of the day, he was always crispy and swagadocious. It was hard to see he was fighting for his life because I never saw a fight he didn't win. I will never forget the time before I met my ex-wife. I was dating and living with an exotic dancer who worked at the Golden Lady, a strip club in the Bronx, and our relationship wasn't working out. Mo wasn't feeling her and convinced me to travel with him to Frankfurt, Germany, to get away. He started dating this woman he met at Nell's nightclub who owned her own clothing store in Frankfurt and wanted to sell our clothes in her store. When he got out there, he called me and told me to update my passport, get a round-trip ticket, and they would pick me up from the airport.

Germany was the wave, and after doing our rounds in Frankfurt, we got in his girlfriend's whip and got on the Autobahn highway en route to Amsterdam, the capital of the Netherlands. OMG, Amsterdam was the Mecca, never in my life have I been to a more welcoming place. White, black, brown, or green, it didn't matter what color you were, they showed love to everybody.

We didn't want to leave, but when we returned to Frankfurt, things got crazy. For a skinny flamboyant dude, Mo was a brawler. He never backed down from a fight. We went to a club, and his girlfriend had her purse stolen; and Mo being Mo, he searched everybody and we got kicked out. Before we got the boot, I got acquainted with a smoking Greece airline stewardess who was feeling me, and later that week, I met up with her to hang out.

Mo's crazy ass and his lady went back to that same club, and we agreed to meet up at her place at 2 a.m. When 2 a.m. turned to 3 a.m. and then 4 a.m., I was beyond furious. I ended up sleeping on the street in Frankfurt, and because it was so late, the public transportation system was shut down. No cabs, I don't speak German, and I was sleeping on a fuckin' bench in the streets of Germany.

As much as I loved Mo, it was a rap. As soon as I saw him, I was dropping him. We always argued and fought like real brothers, and on this, there was nothing he could say to me. At about 6:45 a.m. I rested my head on her front step so I couldn't miss them, and as I watch them approach the building, I was thrown off by what I saw. Mo was dressed in a white suit, and his entire suit was filled with blood; and at that point, my anger shifted to concern. They saw the guy who took her purse earlier that week, and Mo being Mo, he beat the shit out of him.

He apologized immensely for leaving me out there, but I respected his gangsta and forgave him. He was just like that. Anybody who knows Mo has a story like that to tell. He was a jack-of-all-trades. He went from designing clothes to promoting parties to becoming an accomplished DJ. He was a modern-day Jean Michel Basquiat.

He hung out with people like Kanye West and Quest Love, he was on the come up. There wasn't anything he couldn't do, it was hard to accept he was gone.

It was then in a private moment that I convinced myself to stop smoking because this was what killed Mo. We both started at the same time, and what saved me was that I left that world. So, to honor him, it was time to clean myself up from the inside. If Mo was looking down on me, he would want me to stop. I could see him say, "Yo, dogs, what's really good with you? You saw what happened to me. What the fuck are you doing?"

When I went to work the day he passed, I couldn't stop crying. I wore my Ray Bans the whole day, but you could see the tears running down the lens. Nobody was more supportive than the residents on the hall. They wanted to give me their snacks, and they did everything to be perfect. Some of them felt so bad for me they cried. I never loved them more than that day.

CHAPTER TWENTY-TWO

'Cause this is the new way, to be proud and brave
And I ain't goin out like a slave

—Big Daddy Kane
"Ain't No Stoppin' Us Now"

T HE RESIDENTS ON E-HALL KEPT asking me if I was okay every five minutes. We shared stories of friends we've lost and how we dealt with the pain. Sometimes being at work can be so cathartic, I felt better from their words of kindness. These kids held no punches; when they got deep, they went deep. Being hurt was 80 percent of their life, and it always amazed me how resilient they were. The camaraderie on the hall was reminiscent of my high school days playing football and the closeness I had with my teammates.

At Mo's funeral, my boy Nitti held no punches and took it to my cranium. He asked me if I was good. I said that I was, but he wasn't buying it. He said, "Don't take offense, fam, then I don't care how you take it. You fell off, son. You stopped going to the gym, you don't take care of yourself, your gear is shabby, and you gaining weight is the result of you settling." At Mo's funeral, I wasn't trying to hear this, but he wasn't done. He said, "The settling nigga and the lazy nigga are brothers; they're the same motherfucka. Bruh, Mo's death is a wake-up call."

I was mute. It was like he threw rocks at my man cave. But I couldn't front, he was right. I fell off from that person who was traveling the world. At the same time, it was hard taking this from a dude with no children. Nitti is MJ's godfather, and we been boys

211

forever, but he had no clue what was involved in managing a family, especially a family of my size. Four kids with me and Claudia; the job was holding us together.

While he was taking vacations in DR and Miami, I was going school shopping. I wasn't a spring chicken, and I wanted to make the best of what this job had to offer. Maybe I was lying to myself, but I was still adamant about moving on.

Not even a week later, I got a call from a friend from college that one of our buddies died from a heart attack the day after homecoming. I just saw him at Mo's funeral a week ago, and he looked fine. My mind was spinning, like something out of the movie *Final Destination*. All these deaths made me want to get a check-up. I wasn't getting any younger, and I'm at that age that we all start dropping like flies.

I set up an appointment with the cardiologist for a check-up, and he said I was healthy. That was great news, and in my usual celebratory fashion, I stopped for a Corona. As I started to drive from the gas station, I got a call from the job. I pulled over to answer it, assuming some bullshit. Maybe they called to tell me I forgot to return a chair to J-Hall.

It was the deputy director at Fairvue telling me that instead of going to work on Wednesday, I had to report on Thursday to the deputy commissioner's office. I had a good relationship with her and asked her if she knew why, but she said she had no clue. I wasn't buying it; they know everything that goes on in that place. I asked her if this was a good thing or bad thing. She said, "It's never good if you have to go to the deputy commissioner's office."

My mind replayed the whole Prime situation like a video tape going in reverse. I knew they were watching me; maybe that's why I had to work on E-Hall alone for five months after that night. It felt like a set up that I had to work by myself; nobody else did. Even on other tours, everybody had a partner. Maybe I was busted for something else or maybe they have me on camera with my iPod or a DVD I brought in from outside the building. It had my mind racing; I just wanted to crawl under a rock.

After I got off the phone with her, I called Platter. He asked me if I knew what it was about, and I told him about the situation with Prime. He immediately put on his TC hat and asked me what was I thinking, I had no answer. It was just a lapse in judgment and I got too comfortable. I could tell in his tone that he was pissed. He had reverence for a restraint or getting caught having your phone in the building, but doing favors for a resident, hell no.

Platter and Luke came from opposite sides of the fence, but they both had the same advice: don't comprise the job for these kids. He put me in touch with the union lawyer, and she told me what to do. Despite how disappointed he was, Platter went with me to see the deputy commissioner three blocks from Wall Street at the BCW headquarters.

On the day I was scheduled to go, I felt jittery. It was a feeling like I wanted to get hit by a bus. On my way downtown, I asked my mother to ride with me to prevent me from doing something stupid.

When I met up with Platter on the elevator, he said, "You're in a lot of trouble." I just stood there dumbfounded, like that feeling you get when you wreck your parent's car but ten times worse. Platter never talked to me like that. I just think he was disgusted that I put myself in this position. I was one of his favorites when he was at Fairvue; we would go to each other's kids' birthday parties. I guess the thought of me doing something asinine embarrassed him.

When we got there, I was thinking I would be shown camera footage of something I did with a bunch of IGs in the room, bombarding me with questions. But when we stepped into the deputy commissioner's office, I was surprised at his demeanor; he was laid back and told me that I was being relocated to his office, pending an investigation for an allegation I was accused of. When Platter asked him, what was the allegation, he said he didn't know. I found that hard to believe. Was this so bad it was top secret? But as discouraging as this was, I was just glad to still be employed. He said it was in the hands of investigation. Platter said that this was good news because a change of scenery could be a blessing in disguise.

As I walked through the office, I realized that I wasn't the only person relocated. Ms. Caroline was down here too. What did she do? Or more appropriately what did she know?

When I spoke to her, she said she was removed from the building because she came in on her day off and had a bag of cookies that she put in the desk for later and was being accused of bringing in contraband. But she knew better. She knew that if she sneezed the wrong way, they were going to remove her. This was funny money; this administration was never short of being spiteful. It was ironic that both our situations were about a phone, the only difference was in her case she was doing her job.

Maybe my situation had something to do with the EEO report I made; I was thinking too hard. I felt like a bull in a china shop. I would ask to go to the bathroom and ask to take lunch. A supervisor down there said, "Relax, you're an adult. We're going to treat you that way." This was culture shock; I was so use to being treated like a resident that I acted like one. I forgot who I was, I became a product of my environment—completely institutionalized.

I camouflaged my situation to make do. Nitti was right, this was never my groove. Everything happening was a sign to get out. Life finds ways of shoving you in the right direction even when you won't listen. What really put things in perspective was when I was given an assignment to help prepare for a ceremony for people who were thirty, twenty, and ten years on the job.

As I'm setting up the tables and chairs, I look at the program and see my name as a ten-year-honorary. If I felt like shit with everything going on, I felt like a piece of shit after seeing that. I wasn't even invited to an event that I was to being honored for.

I wanted to start flipping chairs, but instead, I just kept my cool and asked for my certificate and mug and left early. These people knew how to kick you when you were down, even Ebo told people at Fairvue not to call me because my phone might be tapped. How irresponsible was that? This was BCW, not the CIA. I didn't murder anybody, but you would have thought I did based on how I was treated.

I understand protocol, but damn, I even heard I was banned from the building. When I heard that, I felt ostracized and made out to be a pariah, but in fairness to my coworkers, everyone had to follow the company line or they could be investigated next. They were swift in getting me out the building, you would have thought I groped a resident. I was clueless to why but I wasn't naïve, I was on their radar. It was a matter of time before my cockiness caught up to me, the reality show at Fairvue needed to be canceled.

When I got the call from the investigation's office to meet them, I got real nervous. I didn't know what to expect: was I getting fired, suspended, or arrested? The union lawyer assured me that they just wanted to ask me questions, and then we'll know what this is about. With the meeting with investigations in three weeks, I went into a deep depression. I heard someone say that depression is having to be in the room with the person you hate the most, and that person is you.

I was there, and like I might want to do to my most hated enemy, I wanted to throw myself in front of a train. Literally. I started to fixate on my own mortality, it was hard to avoid. Everywhere I went, I would see ways to hang it up. But do I want to be the guy who emotionally annihilated his whole family? I was better than that. All I kept hearing in my head was Luke telling me, *stop looking out for these kid because it might come back to bite you.* Well, it bit me and bit me good.

When I started this job, I was a proud black man; and now I was reduced to someone afraid of himself or what I might do to myself. I let so many people down with my carelessness, maybe it was complacency or foolishness or just a combination of both.

I felt stupid working in the office with BCW staff, it was demoralizing just sitting at a desk with nothing to do. I had an invisible dunce cap on my head, everybody knew it. There was never any nefarious or malicious intent coming from me; my nature was to give and I gave too much. I always told my children that the cover up was worse than the crime. What was I thinking?

To add insult to injury on top of injury on top of fuckin injury, MJ picked the wrong time to exercise his inner criminal and started smoking weed. Keeping it 100 percent real, we all dabbled with smoking weed, but when it's your child who deviates from their regular routine, weed becomes the op (opposition). I felt like Michael Douglas in the movie *Traffic*. How the hell can I help everybody else's child if I can't help my own? I already knew he was no longer a virgin, courtesy of his mother telling me. Yeah, when she told me, I was thrown back that my son wouldn't want to tell me first. When I asked him about that, he thought I would be mad that he had sex because I always complained about how fast the kids on my job were. I said, "A son should always feel comfortable talking about sex to his father," but maybe as good as I was at communicating to other kids, I wasn't good at doing that with my own. I guess my birds-and-bees talk when he was nine scared him more than anything. Back to the bullshit, again he felt more comfortable telling his mother that he was smoking than me, but on this topic, I was mad. This kid went from Will I Am to Will I Am Not Doing Shit—waking up late, lying, and coming home beyond his curfew like whatever. I had to pull his collar and say, "Homeboy, it ain't that type of party. This isn't Colorado. This is New York Fuckin City. They will lock you up for smelling like weed, how you don't know that?" I only preach that shit everyday with stories from my job of how these kids get napped for the most frivolous shit. But it was hypocritical of me because I indulged at the age of fourteen. How could I come down on him? My argument was that, unlike my mother, I was aware of what he was doing and my mother never saw my dirt. I was on point with mine while he was sloppy and arrogant. When he stopped caring about how he dressed, that's when I knew something was wrong because he was always immaculate. Plus, where was he getting it from? Today, marijuana is synthetic and laced with all kinds of other shit, you don't know who is touching it. It could be the government or some terrorist organization out to zap the minds of his generation. I don't touch nothing that I can't buy at a store, but trying to get that through to my son drew a wedge between us. With everything I was dealing with, MJ had fucked up timing. I flashed back thirteen years ago when he saw me smacked out of my mind and thought maybe this was my fault. Maybe I exposed that to him years ago. But to my credit, it never happened again and it was because of him that I cleaned up my life. I have to help him clean up his. If coping mechanisms are hereditary, I was partially to blame, which would also mean that his motivation gene suffers like mine did when under the influence. The day Claudia caught him smoking outside with his friends, he was so scared he never came home that night, which was probably a good idea because I was going to light his ass up. Even though he was almost eighteen, I just found his behavior disrespectful. He was challenging the head of the household, who was me. The next day, he called to tell me that he wanted to live with his mother, and as mad as I was, I agreed with him because if he lived with me, it was going to be a problem. I never thought that my ex-wife would be my number one ally, but she put the brakes on his decision to live with her, and he came crawling back to apologize. When he came through the door, I punched him so hard in his chest that it lifted him off his feet. I told him, "Don't you ever scare me like that again. You want to do man shit, then I'm gonna treat you like a man, Mr. Grown Ass. You're not gonna slouch on my watch. Never that." He started crying, and said he was sorry. When we got to talking, I realized that he was under a different type of pressure than me. Along with having senioritis, he was dealing with the pressure of getting into a good college and also make it economically feasible for me. MJ was always an honor student and top 10 in his grade, anything less than a scholarship was unacceptable to him. During our sit-down talk, I told him, "Just get accepted into your top choices, and let me do the rest." My mother did that for me, now it's my job to do that for my children. Our relationship got better after that moment, and we communicated better like men. We both had to fix our lives, and it was time to live up to our potential. No more child's play; he had to hold me down and understand the situation we were in as a family. He stepped up his game, and after his wrestling season, he got a job and helped more with his siblings. I couldn't have been prouder. Like all the aces I had in Fairvue, there was nothing like your first-born being that for you.

The day before I met with investigations, I couldn't eat or sleep. It was nauseating not knowing what this was about. I sat in my living room staring at the walls at 4:15 in the morning. A part of me didn't want to go, but that would have implied guilt. I had to be a man and face the music. Being a father of four children, with three being boys, it was important that I stood up and faced my fears like a man. What example would I be otherwise?

The meeting was scheduled at 1:00 p.m., so before that, I met with the lawyer to prepare. When we got to the investigation office, I was befuddled by the moment. I've never had a feeling like this. It felt like my life was in their hands. As I sat there, I was thinking why do these people control me? I might have violated their rules, but I didn't kill anybody, I didn't touch anyone, I didn't steal anything, I didn't physically hurt anybody, and I didn't give anybody any drugs or alcohol. I'm being treated like I was guilty before even knowing what I did. I guess the right to know only applies to chemicals not people.

When the investigator along with her senior adviser sat and asked me her questions, it felt like a game of *Who Wants to Be a Millionaire?* It started out light, then by the eighth question, she went in. She asked me if I knew Preston Mathews, and then if I let him use my phone. She then asked if I ever spoke to Michelle Mathews on my phone, and if I ever met Michelle Mathews in Harlem on 116th Street.

The lawyer advised me on how to answer the questions, but when I was asked if I knew James and his wife, I knew I was cooked. Fuck, this bitch involved James who was trying to help me. The enormity of the situation had me suspended in time. I started counting the number of law books on the wall and reading the titles in my head, my focus was swaying. *Why now, Booker. Why are you pulling a Homer Simpson now?* I just wanted to walk out of there, but I had to keep my composure, now was not the time to have a self-inflicted mindfuck.

As the investigator was asking me questions, I had to swallow (it could have been a ball of nerves), but I held it during the entire interview for fear that whatever I did out of character would have implied guilt. This had to end.

When we left the office, I told the lawyer who James was and that his phone is under his wife's account. Meeting Prime's mother did more damage than helped. As much as I wanted to blame Prime and his mother, this was my fault. I had a responsibility to stay above this cesspool, but I was swimming in it. When I look back at some of the transgressions of my coworkers, I realized that I was as gullible and blatant as they were with my actions. My inability to establish healthy boundaries in an unhealthy environment was my downfall; you can't be a player and a coach at the same time.

When I later spoke to Platter, he said this had everything to do with leniency—giving me up and getting her son less time. Wow, I can see Monty Hall, or now Wayne Brady say, "Let's make a deal with Booker's black ass."

No funny shit, my kids have to eat too. Where's my deal? After ten years of service, this is how you treat me? My times alone were the worst. Depression continued to fester in my subconscious and take over my thoughts. Suicide was on deck with images in my peripheral of love ones who have died. Like where did they really go? It's got to be better than this.

The more pain and shame I felt, the more I wanted to join them. I wanted to be with Mo because wherever he went, there was always a party, but then my thoughts of negative shifted to positive. It was almost like an epiphany or something. Like his soul touched me and said, "Yo, son, finish this journey. The party is where you are. Continue what we started and pick up where I left off."

This was the pick-me-up of my life. Mo's voice became the voice of reason. I stopped feeling scared and felt rejuvenated with thoughts of supremacy. If you knew Mo, he was like a mystic being, and his spirit became my ego. It was time to resurrect my soul from the caverns of despair and doubt; I believe I have a greater purpose. I was done dancing to their music; and after five months and four days of desk duty, I resigned from the job.

I felt the weight on my shoulders disappear. No more living in fear and trepidation, no more restraining, no more shit from Okeke or Herrera, and no more sitting in a cubicle trying to look busy.

After ten years, to walk away in one piece was a blessing; most of my coworkers weren't that lucky. I had coworkers who have suffered broken legs, back injuries, concussions, lost teeth, and severed fingers. Things never got better. But overall, I was much better than the nonsense that went on in there, and it was time to effectuate my true destiny.

Maybe I was put there to bring to light the injustice that most of us endured daily but were too scared to speak on it. I never set out to be a crusader for justice, but when you feel victimized by the system you serve and the injustice is done to you, it means more, which was the case for me. After this, they will probably create a cell phone task force or a policy and name it after me, it's whatever now. I'm completely off this.

But for the countless number of young men who were inspired by my words, I can proudly say I tried to be a positive influence in their lives; so, I served my purpose. I never used my position to put them down; I always built them up and encouraged them to reach a higher level of thinking. In that time, I have never been spat on and I have never been told to SMD which has everything to do with how I communicated with them and nothing to do with how I punished them or what I gave them. Check this out, little man, all thugged out reppin your set, this country only has one use for you and that's to profit off your love for street life. Keep filling those beds and you will be paying for someone else's vacations and luxury home because you will never see that. While you send their kids to college, they're sending you to correctional facilities.

The harsh reality is that it costs $407 a day for one of these kids to be locked up. That's more than it cost to stay one night at the Marriott Manhattan Hotel, which is a five-star hotel. That's almost $150,000.00 a year for one kid, three times the amount of our salaries as juvenile counselors. Mayor Bloombean knew what he was doing when he merged us.

Message to the hood that's real Gansta. Every time you get arrested, the meter starts running. The goal was to maximize profits, and when things go sour, put the JCs heads on the chopping block and cut their losses. Talk about living Gucci, it definitely wasn't the residents or the staff. What else is new in the United States of money.

Sometimes, when I would get a new admit (resident) to the hall, I would have to give him old clothes and sneakers, so where is that money going? It wasn't going to soap or snacks because they were skimpy with that too. It's a primitive system that needs an upgrade from the inside starting at the top.

This building suffers from lack of institutional control and because they control everything, there is no accountability. Their solution to every problem is to cover it up, which is the MO (modus operandi) for most agencies like this one. It can't always be the fault of the counselors repeatedly, that's the easy way out. If the counselors are bad, then the people that do the hiring are bad, and it doesn't stop there.

This is their history and the fall guy is always the JC, never the kids and never the administration. It's just another day in the world of big-city bureaucracy. As Chuck D said, "We are just pieces in one big chess game." Add logic, if there is a child who has more than ten assaults on people in the facility and they get injured during a restraint by a staff member that has never had an allegation in eleven years on the job, why in God's name is that staff in the hot seat?

Most disturbing was this administration's dereliction of duty when it came to monitoring recidivism rates that were through the roof. Analytics say that under this setting, most of these residents are more susceptible to assault others, and the staff has no such pattern. Why incriminate the staff? Why assassinate their character or vilify their names?

Some of these residents need to be in strait jackets, not paper pajamas, real talk. For what it's worth, the mental illness side of this gets lost in this discussion because most of these kids aren't criminal minded, their minds are lost. This is attributed to them being misdiagnosed and overmedicated, which in most cases is the result of their behavior patterns. I never heard the term ADHD so much until I started working for this agency. How is it that almost every resident was diagnosed with ADHD? Who are they being compared to? White and Asian kids? Statistics have shown that 90 percent of juvenile detainees are living with trauma, and black children are three times more likely to suffer from abuse or neglect than white children. So when does it start to matter? It all begins to sound like weird science. But, for this agency, being judge, jury, and executioner is not justice. This is some real *pittura infamante* shit, if you don't know you better ask somebody. It's time to move off the retreads and incorporate fresh ideas, and then maybe there will be hope to change this culture. To successfully engage with these teens, you have to meet them where they're at, but many of us couldn't go there. Society, as we know it, is on the verge of a collapse on the socioeconomic level, and we will only have ourselves to blame. On the flip side of everything, these kids never stood a chance. I was a contributor in perpetuating the stereotype that these children were animals and monsters. I realize now that I was guilty of that. In the prologue, when I said that BCW saw these kids as victims, they were right, these kids are victims. Victims of a racist society that sees black and brown men as a threat, so they get them while they're young and label them criminals before they reach high school. This system was never made to benefit these children. It's almost like if they fall through the cracks and end up in this system, they will be used for the profitability of the system, which is not cool. The state of the black youth is reminiscent of the old school rapper Grandmaster Melle Mel's lyrics in the song "The Message." He said, "But now your eyes sing the sad, sad song of how you lived so fast and died so young." That song was released in 1982, and nothing has changed since. Nor will it until we stand up for these children.

I can't count the number of times a child between the age of twelve and fifteen has asked me if they should take five years' probation or finish their time, which was usually more than six months. I would just tell them I'm not the one to ask, but in the back of my mind, I was thinking ain't this some slave-of-the-state shit. That's like asking a child to choose between candy or vegetables. Come on, man, nobody wants to be locked up. Once they accept the probation deal, they were back in the facility in less than a month for shit like waking up late for school. The system is a beast that fucks these kids over before some reach puberty. Now, you can say they did this to themselves. But five years? That's beasting. They're kids, they're gonna fuck up. We all did, but none of us had five years' probation hanging over us. That's not justice, that's insanity. The true crime is the ratchet job these appointed lawyers do defending these children. They're the real stick-up kids, they're just stealing money. If it was up to me, they would be disbarred if any of them lost more than five cases, and sadly, some of them lost five cases a day. They all need to be exiled for misrepresentation. They juggle cases the way a waiter juggles trays. How the hell can you successfully represent somebody you just met five minutes ago? Like I said, these kids never stood a chance.

Today's young people need direction because they don't listen to their teachers, they don't listen to their parents, and they damn sure weren't listening to us in secure detention because we never had the right tools. We were asked to work with our hands tied behind our backs, and in essence, we were failing them. Programs that deal with coping skills and life skills is the answer and then facilities like this wouldn't be needed. Most of the nonsecure placement centers should incorporate these ideas and stop being extension of places like Fairvue. Having correctional youth camps is not the answer, it's a revolving door that prepares young black and Hispanic men for a life of incarceration. Their methods and policies might not be the Willie Lynch letter, but it damn near felt like it. Once you walk through those doors, don't get it twisted, you're an inmate. This building doesn't need a Band-Aid, it needs a wrecking ball.

In 2018, they plan on changing the law to keep youth offenders from going to Rikers Island. The death of Kalief Browder sparked this new "Raise the Age" law; which is great, but this is kind of ass backwards. Like, you can't take people from prison and put them in detention. That's like saying, "You're an adult. No, my bad, you're a child again." Those young men aren't having that. Good luck with that. A viable solution would be to grandfather the law, meaning send the sixteen- and seventeen-year-olds on Rikers Island to an alternate location off the Island and send the ones from juvie that age out to the Raise the Age Law facility. This way, you get them acclimated to the new environment. But knowing the Administration for Children's Services (now we can call them ACS), they will fuck this up. #NoCages4Kids, that's the hashtag I'm jackin. Let's invest in students not criminals. Did you know that youth are 39 percentage points less likely to finish public school than their peers after experiencing incarceration or detention? That's bananas, and type unlawful, ineffective and wasteful. It's time for New York City to end the school-to-prison pipeline, not now right now.

I flashback a lot to my days in high school because that should be the best time in a young person's life. I use lots of football analogies because playing organized football as a youth, I realized just how pivotal it was in contributing to the man that I am today. People want to get rid of football on the high school level, but it's the best sport to teach young men teamwork and discipline.

Working together to achieve a common goal, where does that happen today? If this city invested more in team sports, less kids would be joining gangs, I'm just saying. When I was fifteen, it meant everything to walk the streets with my jersey on and have people I didn't know say good game and show me love. It's a great feeling that never leaves you, and thirty years later, I still have that mentality. I played cornerback in high school and my job was to keep the other team from scoring on me.

How ironic, I still try to keep people from scoring on me especially when they referee the games too. They play dirty pole, but homie don't play that. I met up with Garcia for some drinks so we could show support for each other, and he said, "God takes care of good people like us."

I agreed. I am a good dude. Sometimes, when you go against your true nature, the universe finds ways to bring you back. The moral of this story is, have control of your life or somebody else will. I heard Steve Harvey once say, "The road to success is always under construction."

This might have been a roadblock in my life, but the road can't be blocked forever. With the support of my family, I will be okay. I don't know what I will do next, maybe I will start a young men's mentoring service and call it Meccatropolis. With Mo's spirit and my physical presence, it will feel like Amsterdam all over again. Or maybe I will make a shirt that says… "Let me shut up before somebody steals my idea." But whatever I do, I know I won't feel locked up anymore. It's just good to be free—*mind, body,* and *soul.*

> *You caught an attitude, you need food to eat up*
> *I'm scheming like I'm dreaming on*
> *a couch with my feet up*
> *You scream I'm lazy, you must be crazy*
> *Thought I was a donut, you tried to glaze me*

—Rakim
"Eric B For President"

BIBLIOGRAPHY

Sneed, Tierney. 2014. "What Youth Incarceration Costs Taxpayers." U.S.News.com. https://www.usnews.com/news/blogs/data-mine/2014/12/09/what-youth-incarceration-costs-taxpayers

Love, David. 2016. "There Are Too Few School Counselors for Traumatized Black Children – But Plenty of Punishment." AtlanticBlackStar.com. https://atlantablackstar.com/2016/09/27/report-there-are-too-few-school-counselors-for-traumatized-black-children-but-plenty-of-punishment/

QUOTES

*Never stepped foot on the field and understand
how you can get a personal foul.*

—Sherman, Richard (2016)
Interview with ESPN's Jim Trotter, p.147

Pieces in one big chess game.

Chuck D of Public Enemy
"Rebel without a Pause", *It Takes a Nation of
Millions to Hold Us Back*, verse 3, p.221

The road to success is always under construction.

Harvey, Steve (2015)
Interview with Oprah Winfrey on
"Oprah's Lifeclass", p.224

*"But now your eyes sing the sad, sad song of
how lived so fast and died so young."*

Grandmaster Melle Mel and the Furious Five
"The Message" 1982/ Sugar Hill
Label, verse 76, p.222

Youth are 39 percentage points less likely to finish public school than their peers after incarceration or detention.

Maria Brenes of Inner City Struggle(2018)
Interview with Jeremy Loudenback on
The Chronicle of Social Change, p.223

CPSIA information can be obtained
at www.ICGtesting.com
Printed in the USA
FFHW011712030319
50772836-56203FF